Decisive Years in Fran[ce]
1840-1847
DAVID H. PINKNEY

"Pinkney's book is, without question, a major contribution to the field."
—*W. W. Rostow, University of Texas*

David Pinkney challenges accepted views of the timing of France's Industrial Revolution and the accompanying transformation of French society. Arguing convincingly that the early and middle 1840s mark the watershed of modern French history, he shows that these years were filled with innovations more significant than those of 1789-1799, 1799-1814, 1848, or the 1880s and 1890s. This work is a history of the developments that occurred during this critical period and a complete reassessment of their place in the course of French history.

In the 1830s France was agrarian, rural, decentralized, divided by language and transportation difficulties, populated largely by peasants, and dominated by landed notables. Between 1840 and 1847 the nation turned irrevocably onto the road to the industrial, urban, centralized, bourgeois, and imperial France of the twentieth century. Professor Pinkney's work describes changes in the economy, in concentration of power and population in Paris, and in the professions and labor, public education, social ideology, the arts, diplomacy, and colonial expansion.

David H. Pinkney is Professor of History Emeritus at the University of Washington. He is the author of *Napoleon III and the Rebuilding of Paris* and *The French Revolution of 1830* (Princeton, 1958 and 1972) and coauthor, with G. de Bertier de Sauvigny, of *History of France* (Forum).

Decisive Years in France

DECISIVE YEARS
IN FRANCE
1840–1847

by

David H. Pinkney

PRINCETON UNIVERSITY
PRESS

ALBERTUS MAGNUS
LIBRARY

Copyright © 1986 by Princeton University Press
Published by Princeton University Press, 41 William Street,
Princeton, New Jersey 08540
In the United Kingdom: Princeton University Press, Guildford, Surrey

All Rights Reserved

Library of Congress Cataloging in Publication Data will be
found on the last printed page of this book

ISBN 0-691-05467-3

This book has been composed in Linotron Sabon

Clothbound editions of Princeton University Press books
are printed on acid-free paper, and binding materials are
chosen for strength and durability
Printed in the United States of America by Princeton University Press
Princeton, New Jersey

944.063
P 655

TO

HELEN

· CONTENTS ·

· LIST OF ILLUSTRATIONS ·

· PREFACE ·

THE SUBJECT of this book—France in the 1840s *before* the Revolution of 1848—first occurred to me when, having completed my book on the French Revolution of 1830, I considered writing a general history of the July Monarchy. I then read widely on the subject, and the more I read the more I became convinced that the most exciting and most significant years of the regime were the neglected years of the Soult-Guizot ministry, 1840–1848. Contrary to the common perception of them as dull and reactionary, characterized by Louis-Philippe's and Guizot's unyielding resistance to change, they were filled with change—change that in almost all areas of national life turned France in new directions and shaped its long future. The book is in essence a history of those changes and of their influence on France and the French; and it is principally a reassessment of their place in the long course of French history, a reassessment that suggests a historical pattern in which the years 1840–1847—not 1789–1799 or 1848 or the early decades of the Third Republic—form the crucial watershed of modern French history.

I am grateful to friends and colleagues who have helped me in many ways to bring the book to completion, from the definition of the subject and applications for research grants to the critical reading of final drafts. I thank especially G. de Bertier de Sauvigny, Meredith Clausen, William B. Cohen, Douglas Collins, Robert Forster, Wilton Fowler, Constance Hungerford, Lloyd Kramer, Stanley Mellon, Morris David Morris, Dwight Robinson, Eugen Weber, James Winchell, and Gordon Wright. There are many others, and, though I cannot name them all here, I am warmly grateful to them, too.

I would also record my thanks to the National Endowment for the Humanities for a fellowship that made possible a year of uninterrupted research for the book and to the Rockefeller Foundation for the gift of a month for writing in the ideal conditions of the Villa Serbelloni at Bellagio.

This book is the last book on French history—and my third—that R. Miriam Brokaw sponsored for the Princeton University Press before her retirement in 1984. Her services to me, as to many other American historians of France, and her contribution to the profession, though beyond adequate thanks, I here gratefully acknowledge.

DAVID H. PINKNEY
April 1985

Decisive Years in France

· I ·

The 1830s: The Old Regime Lives On

IN 1889 FRANCE CELEBRATED the centenary of the French
Revolution with a lavishness and éclat recalled to us today,
after the passage of almost another century, by the Eiffel
Tower. It was the centerpiece of the great international exposition that marked the anniversary and proclaimed to the
world the strength and the accomplishments of the Third Republic, itself a product of the Revolution. Fifty years earlier,
in 1839, the semicentennial of the Revolution passed un-
marked by official celebration or even notice.[1]

The omission in 1839 was surely deliberate. Since 1830
militant workers and republicans had adopted 14 July as an
annual occasion for protest marches, and the government
wished to offer them no encouragement.[2] Moreover, although
the leaders of the Orleanist monarchy viewed the regime as
the ideal and ultimate outcome of the revolution begun in
1789, they were not disposed to sponsor celebrations that
might suggest to an impressionable and volatile citizenry that
disorder and violent revolution might be beneficial and glo-
rious. In that very year, 1839, the government had removed
from public display all paintings celebrating the Revolution
of 1830.

The neglect of the Revolution's anniversary in 1839 was
appropriate in another way, which its authors certainly did
not intend. In France of the middle and later 1830s, one can
now see, the *ancien régime* lived on. The Revolution of 1789
had not produced a new world or even a new France. Institutions of government and administration and the persons in
positions of power were different, but the storms of revolution, however much they had agitated the surface of events
in the 1790s and the succeeding decade, had left largely un-
changed the fundamental aspects of French life—economic

activity, social structure, distribution of population, language, and communication. France in the 1830s was, as it had been in the 1780s, agrarian, rural, far from centralized, divided by language and distance, populated largely by peasants, and dominated by an aristocracy of landowners. Those democratic institutions that survived from the Revolution remained, as in the 1790s, alien grafts on a hierarchical society.

In the final years of the decade, however, a new age was on the horizon, and in the 1840s it clearly dawned. In the early and middle years of the latter decade decisions were made, laws passed, innovations launched, careers begun, ideas formed and disseminated, and the effects of a few events of the 1830s emerged that turned agrarian, rural, divided, peasant France definitively toward the industrial, urban, culturally unifed, bourgeois France of the twentieth century. Simultaneously there emerged the ideology of the principal challenge to that older society, the positivism of August Comte, and the ideology of what would prove to be the most widely appealing substitute for it—socialism, both utopian and scientific. In the arts a few seminal figures—Henri Labrouste, Gustave Courbet, Gustave Flaubert, and Charles Baudelaire—during that same critical decade turned French architecture, painting, fiction, and poetry into new paths that would be followed for half a century and more. France's role in the larger world of diplomacy and empire took new directions. After coming close to renewed war in 1840 France and Britain began the rapprochement that ended their centuries-long enmity and led to what was probably the most important bilateral alliance of the twentieth century. The French decision in 1840 to remain in Algeria and to subjugate and colonize that territory marked the beginning of the second French colonial empire, which in fifty years far exceeded in extent the great empire of the Bourbon monarchy two centuries earlier.

The principal thesis of this book is that the years 1840–1847, long regarded as a backwater in French history, were uniquely decisive and seminal years in the century and a half between the Revolution of 1789 and the fall of the Third Republic in 1940.

In the 1830s France was an agrarian and rural society. Land was the principal form of wealth, the primary source of revenue for most individuals and for the country as a whole, and the determinant of a citizen's position in society. Fifty-five to 60 percent of the population lived directly from agriculture. Seventy-five to 80 percent were nominally rural, and they and, indeed, many of the minority formally classified as urban—those living in communes with a town of 2,000 or more population—were enmeshed in the agrarian economy and in rural society.[3] Paris, with a population of 899,000 in 1836 (about half the population of London), was the only city with more than 200,000 inhabitants; and less than 3 percent of the French population lived there in that year.[4] Today 19 percent of the French lives in Paris and 56 percent in urban zones with a population of 100,000 or more.[5]

Paris was, of course, the seat of government, but distance and the still-primitive technology of transportation and communication restricted its practical influence on day-to-day life in the provinces. Provincial economy and culture still enjoyed considerable autonomy. Regional capitals such as Lyon, Marseille, Bordeaux, Toulouse, Nantes, Rouen, and Lille continued to play important roles in economic decision making and as cultural centers.

At the top of the social hierarchy were the *grands notables*—the titled aristocracy, the wealthy though nonnoble landed proprietors, and a few wealthy bankers, wholesale merchants, and industrialists. Neither precise enumeration nor categorization by source of wealth is possible, but save for the relatively few businessmen in the group, the *grands notables* owed their wealth and position in society and polity to their ownership of land. The right to vote and the right to hold elective office were conditional on the payment of prescribed levels of taxation, and the principal taxes were on land. Possession of substantial holdings assured them of the vote in all elections, national and local, and the right to stand for any electoral office. They sat in departmental general councils, in electoral colleges, in the Chamber of Deputies, and in the Chamber of Peers, and they filled top posts in ministries and on the bench and held the higher commands in the army and navy.[6] The Revolution of 1789 and the Reign of Terror had been deadly for many of the aristocracy, but it had survived as a class and during the Empire had been reinvigorated by the injection of the new Napoleonic nobility. After the Revolution of 1830 many of the old nobility, loyal to the deposed Bourbons, had renounced any political role under the usurping Louis-Philippe and dramatically withdrew to their estates, but by the latter thirties most had returned from their self-imposed exile. They sat in large numbers in both chambers of Parliament and on general councils, and, as under the *ancien régime*, they again served in high positions in ministries, in the Church, in the diplomatic corps, and in the armed forces. Some with disposable capital from their lands invested in commerce and industry. Among the two hundred members of the General Assembly of the Bank of France, in 1840 fifty-five were nobles.[7] But the vast majority of aristocrats were exclusively landowners, and in their positions in Parliament and administration they represented the agricultural interests and gave an agrarian bias to the decisions and legislation they influenced.

At the local and provincial levels the *grands notables*—nobles and others—were not only the most influential leaders in politics; they also played a directing role in intellectual life as members of local academies and learned societies. They and their families shaped values and social standards and, as the arbiters of taste, set the fashions in their districts.[8] Their local, rurally biased influence in these matters retained a potency now lost, because at that time the barriers of distance, expense, and inconvenience of travel and the costs of printing and post still narrowly confined the influence of Paris.

The opposite end of the social hierarchy in France of the 1830s was even more distinctly agrarian and rural. Three-fifths of the population were peasants, ranging from agricultural laborers through sharecroppers, renters, and part-time artisans to substantial peasant proprietors.[9] Most of them lived on farms or in small farming villages. No generalization on lives, concerns, and roles is applicable to all 25 million of them, but it is certain that most led hard and confined lives dominated by an unending struggle for existence that left little time or energy for interests separated from the land and its cultivation. Between the beginning of the century and 1836 rural population had increased by at least 1.7 million, perhaps as much as 5.3 million,[10] but agricultural productivity, after an upward spurt in the 1750s and 1760s, had yet to experience its revolution. In more than half the departments in 1840 the yields of wheat were at levels now associated with underdeveloped countries and with primitive methods of cultivation. Harvesting was still done largely with sickles rather than with the more efficient scythes and hooks already in use in England. Only two departments had achieved yields comparable to those of contemporary England and the Low Countries.[11] Since the dramatic improvements of the 1770s individual productivity of male agricultural workers had by the early 1830s increased at a rate of less than 0.3 percent annually.[12] In the existing state of technology in French agriculture too many people were trying to live off the land. Peasants, nonetheless, saw land as the only source of economic security, and in the thirties they were in fierce competition to acquire it and to increase their holdings. So committed were they to the cult of land ownership that they borrowed money at usurious rates, ordinarily from local lawyers, and were becoming heavily indebted while forcing up the price of land. Even in those regions in which barren soil precluded higher yields and the lack of raw materials, capital, or adequate transportation precluded development of petty industry, so that peasants were forced to migrate in search of additional income, they chose seasonal migration to jobs in more flourishing regions, hoping to earn enough while away to purchase more land on their return.[13]

Another reaction to the threat of dearth and impoverishment was the development of the domestic craft industry. In search of supplementary income peasant families turned to crafts as secondary occupations for men and women, the latter engaging especially in lace making, spinning, and weaving. A recent regional monograph reported the example early in the century of a single canton in the Department of the Rhône, where in the winter months ten thousand persons worked at spinning and weaving cotton as a supplementary employment. In the 1830s the situation was little changed. In the Department of the Haute-Loire a single merchant house contracted with 3,500 women scattered over twenty communes to make lace. In one *arrondissement* of that department the weaving of silk ribbons, largely in rural households, provided more employment than any other industry. In Lower Alsace the absence of almost all migratory movements until after 1840, despite an increasing population, attests to the expansion of rural industry in the province, the only way for surplus workers to survive without migration. The development of such industry is sometimes referred to as "protoindustrialization," but it was, in fact, more a revival of old economic practices than a precursor of modern industrialization. Its effect was to permit the survival of both backward agriculture and backward industry.[14]

Peasants had little time or inclination and few resources to engage in activities not related directly to the onerous task of earning a living. Few paid sufficient taxes to qualify as voters even in local elections, where requirements were lower, or to hold public office. They saw little value in education and resisted sending their children to schools that the Guizot School Law of 1833 required every commune to maintain. Conscription records indicate that in 1838 less than half the conscript class knew how to read and write.[15] Popular speech was in the local patois or even in foreign languages—Provençal in the south, Breton in the far west, Flemish on the northeast frontier—and these linguistic differences, combined with high levels of illiteracy, cut the peasantry off from the influences of high culture. Stendhal, writing in 1835–1836, declared that the people living in the large triangular area in the south of France bounded by Bordeaux and Bayonne in the west and Valence on the middle Rhône "believe in witches, can't read, and do not speak French"; on the southeast, he said, Grenoble was the last outpost of "civilization."[16]

Most French lived their lives in the isolation of villages or farms. Travel was difficult, time consuming, and expensive.

In 1839 fewer than three hundred miles of railways existed in all France, and for most citizens a steam train was still only a curiosity. The vaunted system of royal highways, well drained and hard-surfaced for travel in all seasons, served only major cities and towns and the few hamlets that happened to be on their undeviating routes between one center and the next. Local roads were usually no more than wagon tracks across fields, passable only in dry seasons. The traditional method of road maintenance by the royal corvée, compulsory road work by neighboring peasants, had been discontinued in 1787 on the eve of the Revolution, and not until 1836 did the state make adequate provision for regular maintenance, repair, and improvement of local roads.[17] A primary school inspector of the Ministry of Public Instruction, describing a rural department of central France, the Indre, in 1843 sketched a picture applicable to many parts of France in the preceding decade before local road maintenance was organized: "Vast stretches of land lying waste, lack of highways, almost impassable secondary roads, houses separated by long distances, the rural population in extreme poverty, the working class in deep ignorance and inertia."[18]

Some few departments had long-established connections with Paris, such as those in the Limousin that supplied seasonal construction workers to the capital, but for most of the provincial population Paris was as far away as the moon. Even the prefect, the personification of the central power of Paris in each department, was a remote and shadowy figure for most peasants. For them the central state existed as the tax collector, who imposed a resented levy on their meager livings, the conscription officer, who spirited away their sons just when they became productive adult hands, and the school inspector of the Ministry of Public Instruction, who tried to coerce them into more public spending on the luxury of a local school. Aside from these intrusions of Paris most peasants lived their lives unmindful of and unconcerned with the great issues of the day that occupied the politicians in the Palais Bourbon, in the Luxembourg, and in the ministries, the intellectuals in the academies and salons, the press, and the angry insurrectionaries dreaming and plotting in the narrow streets and passageways of the workers' quarters in Paris and Lyon.

The new age of heavy industry, world trade, investment banking, and the business bourgeoisie, epitomized in the nineteenth century by Great Britain, had not yet dawned in France. G. de Bertier de Sauvigny has observed that, "From the point of view of the economists . . . the France of the Restoration was nearer to that of Louis XV than that of Napoleon III," and the same contrast is applicable to France of the early July Monarchy.[19]

Total industrial production in France had increased steadily though slowly since the beginning of the nineteenth century. Crouzet's index of industrial production, including artisanal industry as well as more advanced forms, based on 100 in 1913, rose from 19.2 in 1815 to 23 in 1835.[20] The typical industrial establishment was small, composed of the proprietor and one or two workers, all working side by side and dependent on manual power. The few big enterprises in existence were confined largely to coal mining and the metallurgical and cotton textile industries. The narrow limits of mechanization are suggested by the fact that in 1839 only 2,450 steam engines, with a combined horsepower of 33,000, were used in all of France, contrasting with more than 4,900 a decade later. In the thirties annual applications for authorization to install steam engines never exceeded seven except in one year, 1833, when they rose to eleven.[21]

The iron industry may be used as bellweather of industrial development in the nineteenth century, for it was the industry on which others depended for the essential material of machinery, rails, and much building. In 1839 a French observer wrote, "The iron industry in France is still exercised in many places in France with all the ancestral naiveté of the Druids and the Gauls."[22] He was thinking of the hundreds of charcoal-fired forges then in operation in the country. In the 1820s many ironmasters had installed new coke-fired smelting furnaces, but the depression of the latter years of the decade struck just as they were ready to operate, and many failed. In

1835, 83 percent of all French iron came from some four hundred charcoal forges, the remaining fraction from twenty-eight coke furnaces. The typical production unit was a small forge in a rural area that could supply wood for charcoal and had a river or stream to generate the small amount of mechanical power required. Many were owned by local seigneurs, who installed them on their properties. The workers were usually part-time agricultural workers; the technics of iron making were simple and required no precise skills. Sales were largely to local markets. In dry seasons or when demand fell, the forges could be left inactive without difficulty; fixed costs were low, and workers could return to agricultural employment. The Tariff Law of 1822 sheltered the industry from foreign competition, and while demand for iron remained stable and the price of charcoal low relative to the cost of mineral fuels, there was little incentive to make the large investment and commitment to the high fixed costs required by coke-fired furnaces. Moreover, in the thirties improvements in the technics of charcoal smelting permitted reduction of fuel costs in the tradtional smelting process even when the price of charcoal was rising by more than 50 percent. Nonetheless, a handful of enterprising ironmasters were exceptions to the rule of inertia. They invested in new plants and technology, and a few companies in the latter thirties—Schneider, De Wendel, Boigues Frères at Fourchambault, the Fonderies de l'Aveyron at Decazeville, for example—were not technically backward. They were to become a critical element in the great spurt of industrial activity in the next decade.[23]

The high cost of coal handicapped the development of other heavy industry in France. The most economical and dependable source of mechanical power, it was, as the experience of England and Belgium had demonstrated, the key to industrialization. Two-thirds of French coal came from just two fields—the Loire Valley around Saint-Etienne and the Department of the Nord near the Belgian frontier. Both were less than ideally located to fuel industrialization in a prerailway age, being on the edges of the nation's principal concentration of population and markets in the Paris basin. The mines of the Loire Valley, then the larger of the two fields, were exploited by old and inefficient technics, and productivity was low. The Nord field was a conspicuous exception to the rule of small enterprises in France. The Anzin Coal Company dominated the field, produced more than one-fifth of all the coal mined in the country in the latter thirties, and with five thousand employees was a symbolic, though rare, precursor of new large-scale capitalist enterprise.[24]

The textile industry was still dominated in the thirties by its traditional elements. In 1830 almost two-thirds of the cotton spinners still worked in their homes and only one-third in factories (a decade and a half later the proportion was approximately reversed), but even in the latter forties more than 80 percent of the production of cloth, measured by value—including the traditional woolens, linens, and hemps—came from domestic industry, and it was still enmeshed in the agrarian economy. Most spinners and weavers were peasants who tilled the soil when agricultural employment was available. Especially characteristic of the production of linen and hemp, this combination of employments was also common in the woolen textile industry, where mechanization was little advanced. Philippe de Girard's linen-spinning machine, invented in France in 1810 and widely adopted in England after 1815, was not reintroduced into France until 1832–1835. In the industrial exposition of 1839 it was still exhibited as a recent novelty. Machine weaving of linen lay a decade or more in the future.[25]

The relatively new cotton textile industry, unhampered by the inertias and vested interests of an old industry, was in the 1830s developing into a mechanized industry of factories and comparatively large-scale enterprises. In the mid-thirties the number of factory workers in the cotton industry for the first time exceeded the number of workers producing in their homes. Dolfuss Mieg in Mulhouse employed 4,200 spinners in 1839, and Schlumberger at Guebweiller operated fifty thousand spindles, Charles Naegely at Mulhouse eighty thousand. Nevertheless, in the mid-thirties the traditional textiles still dominated the market, and in 1835–1836 the cotton industry was hurt by the sudden inflation of the price of raw cotton. Only in the early forties, with the dramatic drop in the price of raw cotton, did cotton move decisively toward the domination of the whole industry and market.[26]

The industrial development that transformed England in the late eighteenth century and much of western Europe in the nineteenth required low-cost and dependable transportation for movement of raw materials and finished products. Since the seventeenth century France had been famed for its highways and canals, but in the 1830s the nation's transportation system, though extended and improved since 1789, was still that of the eighteenth century. The royal roads had been built primarily for political and strategic reasons—to facilitate the central government's control of the provinces and the defense of borders—not for the mass movement of freight or persons. They linked Paris and the provincial cities, but lesser cities and towns were dependent on the departmental roads, a lesser category of public highways. The government of the Restoration built some three thousand miles of these secondary roads, increasing the length of the departmental network from fewer than twelve thousand miles in 1814 to nearly fifteen thousand in 1830. They provided connections among scores of communities and served as feeders into the royal roads, but their use was seriously restricted by rapidly deteriorating surfaces resulting from poor construction, excessive grades, and inadequate maintenance. The primitive local roads were impassable in bad weather and always costly to use because only small loads could be moved on them. The Law of 21 May 1836, for the first time since the abolition of the royal corvée on the eve of the Revolution, assured continuing resources for the construction and maintenance of local roads, and in the next four years large sums were spent on these roads. But the government's efforts encountered many obstacles—shortage of qualified engineers and supervisors, reluctance of local authorities to impose taxes or labor service, and inadequate funds for the immense task at hand—and at the end of the decade most rural communities were still poorly served.[27]

Average speeds of movement even on the royal highways, though increased in the first decades of the nineteenth century, were still strikingly low. At the end of the eighteenth century stage coaches moved at an average rate of 2.1 miles per hour, in 1830 at 4 miles per hour. An investigation of freight transportation made during the empire reported that freight wagons then took ten to twenty days for the trip from Paris to Orléans, eighteen to twenty-two days to Nantes, and thirty-six to forty days to Lyon. Since freight wagons achieved little improvement in speed in the first half of the nineteenth century, these times may be assumed to characterize approximately the best service available to shippers in the 1830s. Average shipping costs, though down from the high levels of the first decade of the century, were in the mid-thirties as high as the 1780s, still expensive.[28]

The availability, the quality, and the costs of road transportation in the 1830s varied considerably from region to region. The Paris basin, the flat north, and the river valleys, where construction of roads was relatively simple and less costly, were best served. Mountainous areas were still scarcely incorporated into the national road system.[29]

Ships and barges on inland waterways and coastal waters provided low-cost transportation for bulk materials, such as coal, wood, and other building materials, that required neither special handling nor speedy delivery. In 1814 the inland waterways included about 4,000 miles of nominally navigable rivers and 750 miles of canals, more than half of them built in the seventeenth century. Between 1820 and 1840 the restored Bourbons and then the Orléans monarchy added more than 1,600 miles to the canal network, more than tripling its total length. Completion of canals in the north, where essential resources were conveniently located, facilitated the development of the iron industry in Anzin, Denain, and Maubeuge in the later thirties, and the Canal du Berry, begun in 1822 and completed in 1839, permitted the development of the iron manufactories at Montluçon and Commentry in the Department of the Allier. But such influence was not general throughout the economy. Canals did little to cut freight charges generally. Not all resources or all markets were located in regions served by waterways, both because natural obstacles of terrain and insufficient water supply could preclude building and operation of canals and because decisions to build particular canals were often based on considerations of local or regional prestige or political influence rather than on demonstrable requirements of traffic. The area that a canal could serve was narrowly limited by the deficiencies of local roads that served as feeders. Moreover, canals constructed with various widths and depths restricted the system's general use to barges that could be accommodated by the narrowest and most shallow canals. Frequent transshipments added to costs and delays. All waterways were subject to interruption by freezing in winter and by water shortages in summer and autumn, and rivers by high waters in the spring—serious limitations on their utility, especially to highly capitalized industries, such as coke-fired smelting, with high shutdown and start-up costs.[30]

Steamships were introduced on the Saône and Rhône rivers in the late 1820s, and in the 1830s both passenger and freight steamships operated on these and a number of other rivers. In 1839 six shipping companies provided two or three daily departures between Lyon and Arles. The downstream trip required only fourteen hours, considerably faster than the stage coaches, but the upstream journey took three to four days. These speeds were possible, moreover, only under favorable conditions that prevailed for less than half the year. Any change in water levels disturbed schedules. High waters on the Rhône forced complete suspension of operations for about six weeks in the summer, when the demand for passenger service was highest. High waters in the spring were at least equally disruptive. Ice closed the river five or six days each year. Operations on the Saône were sometimes also closed by fog. On the average shippers had to count on the Rhône's being closed three months of the year, and the Saône only slightly less. The Loire River between Tours and Orléans lacked sufficient water for about half the year, and the Seine above Paris was closed about two months yearly.[31]

Coastal shipping carried as much freight as did the inland

waterways in the latter 1830s, three-fourths of it along the Atlantic and Channel coasts, but it, too, was slow and unreliable. The run from Le Havre to Bordeaux required about three weeks in summer and longer in winter; service was frequently interrupted by unfavorable winds or stormy seas, and it was handicapped by lack of adequate port facilities.[32]

The roads and waterways of France as they existed in the 1830s met the needs of artisanal industry and of agriculture oriented around local markets. They were not capable of sustaining either a modern industrial economy or a national agricultural market. It was the railroads that made possible France's move into the modern economic world. At the end of the thirties, however, the nation had only 300 miles of steam railways in operation. Britain was then operating more than 900 miles, serving a much smaller area, and even the still-divided German states had more than 350 miles.[33] Beginning in the early thirties the French directing classes came to the conclusion that railroads were an indispensable part of the future of any great power and that the location of rail routes, the methods of financing the immense investment required, and operational policies would have profound economic and social consequences for the entire country. Through that decade and into the next they engaged in a great public debate in which all the issues of transportation policy in an emerging industrial society were explored and discussed. A few authorizations for short lines were approved, but in the absence of any general policy, while the debate went on, extensive construction of rail lines was postponed. The most significant among the short lines authorized was the Paris–Saint-Germain line, approved in 1835 and opened in August 1837. It was only twelve miles long and no great undertaking, but it was the first railway in France built specifically to use mechanical power, the first built as a passenger carrier, and from the beginning an unqualified financial success. The Rothschild Bank had provided a fourth of the capital, and its good fortune on that enterprise moved it to invest more heavily in the company forming in 1837 to build the line from the Right Bank in Paris to Versailles. The bank took 7,000 of the

22,000 shares, making it the holder of the largest single bloc of stock. The participation of this prestigious banking house was a signal to investors that railroads were a promising investment.[34] In 1838 the government took advantage of rising investor interest to grant concessions to private companies for building and operating railroads from Paris to Orléans, from Paris to Rouen, Le Havre, and Dieppe, between Lille and Dunkerque, and between Strasbourg and Bâle. These undertakings were scarcely started, however, when the financial crisis and depression that began in 1838 and unexpectedly high costs of materials and of land of the right-of-way plunged them into financial difficulties. Investors lost interest, many of them refusing to pay installments on their stock subscriptions enthusiastically agreed to only a few months earlier. The Paris–Le Havre and the Lille–Dunkerque companies were unable to carry on, and the government canceled their concessions in 1839. The improvised, piecemeal policy of railroad construction by private entrepreneurs under government license, it now became clear, would not provide the country with the railroads essential to its economic health and growth.[35]

The French banking system of the 1830s was well attuned to serving the requirements of the state, local commerce, and wealthy individuals. At the top of the structure stood the Bank of France. Though privately owned and under only minimal government control, it was the bank of issue (a privilege that it shared in the provinces with a handful of regional banks after 1835), the government's fiscal agent, and lender of last resort to other banks. Both in Paris and, through its branches, in the provinces it provided commercial banking services in competition with other banks. It did not make long-term investments in industry or commerce or act as intermediary for such investment by its clients. The exclusively private banking system was composed of commercial banks (whose services were supplemented by scores of discount agents) and the merchant bank, the so-called *Haute Banque*, and many small private houses that combined banking with other lines of business. The *Haute Banque* included the great banking houses of Rothschild, Mallet Frères, Laffitte et Blount, and twenty or so others in Paris. The provincial capitals had their private banks, but none was of comparable size or importance. The Parisian *Haute Banque* served a clientele of rich families and individuals and invested their own and their clients' money chiefly in government bonds. They also provided financial services for clients—buying and selling securities, commodities, and foreign currencies and granting short-term credits. Three or four decades earlier, under the Directory and Napoleon, the unusual circumstances of the time had moved enterprising Parisian bankers to offer financial services for wholesale merchants and to invest in commerce, both foreign and domestic. Some also provided credits for industry and even invested their own capital in industrial enterprises. Such opportunities diminished with the decline and fall of the empire, and banks pulled back to more restricted roles; but in the 1830s there were among the private banking houses of Paris those capable once again of catering to the long-term needs of industry and trade.[36]

Mechanization of the textile industry starting in the 1820s required relatively little capital. The enterprises were small, and financing could be handled by individual entrepreneurs. The sale of a farm, Paul Bairoch holds, could in the twenties and thirties provide the capital for a small plant. A converted barn or *hangar* could house it. Local banks could supply the necessary commercial credit for operations, and, if the firm prospered, expansion could be self-financed. Charcoal-fueled iron furnaces had similarly low capital requirements, but the new coal-based iron industry and especially the railroads required immense capital investment, unprecedented in French experience. In 1837 the Parisian banker, M.-F. Pillet-Will, citing the experience with the early rail lines, placed the cost of construction of a national railway network at 2 billion francs, as much as was then invested in the entire road and waterway networks combined. In addition to sheer size of capital requirements, railroads had the further complication of immobilizing investment longer than did early industry. The first railroads—the short freight-carriers of the twenties

and early thirties—were underwritten largely by local firms outside the banking community, commonly coal, iron, and textile companies. After the success of the Paris–Saint-Germain Railroad the Parisian *Haute Banque* began placing funds in railways, and railroad shares were traded publicly on the Paris Bourse. But the French banking community still had no banks that specialized in long-term investment in industry or acted as underwriters of securities issued to finance industry.[37]

The banking system of the 1830s also lacked any institutions that offered low-cost agricultural credit to small borrowers. Peasants, eager to achieve the security that they associated with the ownership of land, turned to local moneylenders, ordinarily the town *notaires*, and borrowed at extortionate rates; these loans put such a high levy on their earnings that they had little left for personal expenditure beyond necessities or for investment in improved tools and equipment. The existing banks proved able to adapt more readily to the needs of industry and the railroads than to the needs of peasant agriculture. The underdevelopment of credit institutions was a significant force in holding French agriculture back in the economic world of the *ancien régime*.[38]

In the 1830s France had already entered the time of the "Bourgeois Monarchy," but the bourgeoisie of that regime remained predominantly the bourgeoisie of the *ancien régime*. At the top levels it was composed of professional men—lawyers, doctors, professors, scientists, publishers, higher civil servants, bankers, wholesale merchants, and only a few manufacturers. French scholars also include the nonnoble landed proprietors. The values and aspirations of the bourgeoisie were still predominantly those associated with landowners and not those of businessmen or the English captains of industry, fully committed to the pursuit of profit and to a regimen of work that left little time for independent intellectual or cultural interests.[39]

The industrial working class was in the thirties but a small part of the total population, only a fraction of the size of the peasant population. Even fewer were the factory workers. Outside Paris and a few industrial centers such as Lille or

Lyon the distinction between industrial worker and agricultural worker or peasant was not firmly established. Many persons were both industrial workers and peasants, moving back and forth from one employment to the other with changes in the seasons or with the demands of the market. In the cities the working class was made up of artisans who worked in their own shops, and hence this class merged into the lower levels of the petty bourgeoisie, artisans who worked as wage-earning journeymen, pieceworkers such as seamstresses or artificial-flower makers working in their own rooms, and unskilled and casual laborers who worked as porters, longshoremen, and servants. Labor unions intended to influence the level of wages or conditions of work were forbidden by law. The principal labor organizations that did exist were the illegal but officially tolerated *compagnonnages*, secret fraternities of bachelor journeymen in particular crafts. They provided hospitality and aid to itinerant members, but at the time they were probably most conspicuous in their frequent street brawls with *compagnonnages* of other crafts, an activity that emphasized how far removed they were from being instruments of class solidarity and interests. They did not engage in collective action against employers.[40]

Although Paris is not all of France, it does represent France to the world, and across the centuries it has been on the cutting edge of the development of French society. Here the revolutions occurred, most of the influential ideas were formulated and published, the critical decisions were made, the experiments in government were launched. The Paris of the 1830s in its appearance and in its public service and amenities was more like the Paris of Louis XV or even Louis XIV than like the Paris of 1870 or of our own time. Its 900,000 inhabitants lived within the present second ring of boulevards, where the octroi wall cut off the city from the countryside, and almost half the population was crowded into the area of the Right Bank between the inner ring of boulevards, the so-called *Grands boulevards*, and the Seine, on the islands in the river (three of them then), and an even smaller area just south of the river. Except for the Champs Elysées, the Tuileries Garden, the Gardens of the Palais Royal (all on the western edges of the heavily settled quarters), the Place des Vosges, and, on the opposite bank, the Luxembourg Garden and the Jardin des Plantes, this area was almost completely covered with buildings. Until the seventeenth century successive governments, concerned with the military security of the capital, had forbidden construction of houses outside the city walls, and, as population increased, parks and gardens were built over, courtyards filled, and story added upon story. The density of population in the central quarters in the 1830s exceeded even that of New York's Lower East Side before the days of public housing and urban renewal.[41]

Except for the *Grands boulevards* on the Right Bank, built in the reign of Louis XIV on the site of a demolished ring of fortifications, and the unfinished rue de Rivoli started by Napoleon, the central city was served almost entirely by streets dating from the Middle Ages. They formed a maze of narrow passages, many too narrow to permit the passage of two carriages or wagons side by side. Gutters in the middle of their concave surfaces served as open sewers. Sidewalks were rare, and sunlight only briefly penetrated the narrow canyons formed by five- or six-story houses. The only throughways available to carry north-south traffic across the built-up area of the Right Bank were the rue Saint-Denis, rue Saint-Martin, and rue du Temple. On the opposite bank the rue Saint-Jacques alone cut across the built-up area. These, too, were medieval streets built for horsemen, sedan chairs, and pedestrians. Between the Right Bank boulevards and the quais no streets whatever led across the city from east to west. The rue Saint-Honoré came into the old city from the west but ended on the western fringes of the central maze. The new rue Rambuteau, the thirties' contribution to the Parisian street system, ran boldly and quite spaciously from the Marais district on the east for a thousand yards into the Montorguiel Quarter only to end abruptly in the impasse of old streets and houses east of the Palais Royal. The Left Bank was no better served than the Right with east-west streets; no street existed to carry traffic across its built-up area.[42]

Streets were not alone in marking Paris of the thirties as a city of the ancien régime. The lack of public parks, the open sewers—which included the Seine and its tributary, the Bièvre, the water supply pumped from the river, the Canal de l'Ourcq, and a few wells were other urban characteristics surviving from an earlier age.[43]

Functionally Paris of the thirties might be described as a prodigal capital of an agrarian state, prodigal in the sense that it was a center of consumption, living off the production of the rest of the nation. Its governmental and administrative functions and its financial, intellectual, and artistic roles were sustained economically by the nation, and its own economic products—chiefly clothing and accessories, food products, house furnishings, and buildings—were consumed almost entirely by the Parisian market itself. The modern industrial and commercial metropolis, producing for and serving the national market and even world markets, had scarcely begun to emerge.[44]

The essential preparations for the new turnings of the 1840s were being made long in advance, especially from 1789 onward. The consequences of these turnings, moreover, were half a century and longer in coming full fruition, and their effects were felt differently in the various parts of France. Nonetheless, hundreds of thousands of French men and women living in the 1850s who could remember the 1830s must have thought themselves to be living in a world turned upside down. Imagine the astonishment of a peasant seeing a railroad train for the first time or a worker not long off the land encountering the great steam hammer at the Schneider ironworks. Or think of the amazement of a servant girl gazing at a dazzling display of brightly printed cotton dresses in a Parisian department store, or of an infantryman who remembered days-long marches to new billets being whisked overnight from one end of the country to another. Heinrich Heine, living in France in the 1840s, wrote in a letter of May 1843, when railway construction had scarcely begun in earnest, "The railways are again such a providential event as gives mankind a new start . . . so that a new era begins in universal history."[45]

Industrial Takeoff

USE OF SUCH TERMS as "Industrial Revolution," "takeoff," or "great spurt" in the writing of economic history changes with evolving concerns, methods, and fashions among historians. W. W. Rostow's "takeoff," though now out of favor, is a concept useful in describing and illuminating what happened to the French economy and more especially to French industry in the 1840s. Rostow defined the takeoff as a period when long-established barriers to steady growth of national output are finally overcome, and forces making for economic growth, which have previously set off limited spurts, expand and come to dominate, and growth becomes normal.[1]

In the past three or four decades French economic historians have painstakingly identified and collected a mass of relevant data, and from it they carefully constructed indices of industrial production from the early eighteenth century to the first decade of the twentieth.[2] Four indices, those of Maurice Lévy-Leboyer and T.-J. Markovitch and two by François Crouzet, reveal an extraordinary phase of acceleration in industrial production in the period 1835/1840 to 1860. Crouzet computed a measure of the annual change in the level of industrial production expressed as a percentage, positive or negative, of variation from the average annual increase over the years 1815–1913. This measure, presented visually in Graph 1, shows a modest but clear upward movement between 1835 and 1838 followed by two years of retreat, then an upsurge in 1841 more than 50 percent greater than that of any preceding year. Production continued to rise to a high in 1846, fell back in the recession year of 1847 (but remained well above the average), and dropped slightly below in the tumultuous year of revolution, 1848. It recovered quickly, however, soared to a new high in 1853, and continued at high

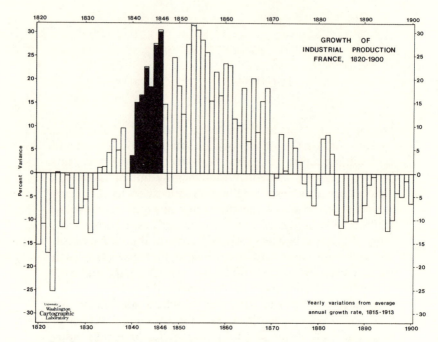

Graph 1. Based on data from François Crouzet, "Essai de construction d'un indice de la production industrielle au XIXᵉ siècle," *Annales: E.S.C.*, 25ᵉ Année (1970), Table 11b, p. 99

levels throughout the fifties and sixties. Here, then, is a thirty-year period of industrial growth broken only by the exceptional circumstances of 1848 and then but for a single year.[3] Crouzet concludes, "If one wants to identify a phase of takeoff or of Industrial Revolution in French economic history it has to be located during this period [1840–1860]."[4]

The takeoff in Rostow's model requires coincidence of three conditions—the existence of political, social, and institutional frameworks congenial to expansion and capable of mobilizing capital in quantity, the development of at least one manufacturing sector with a high rate of growth—a "leading sector," in Rostow's terminology—and a rise in the rate of investment from 5 percent or less of national income to 10 percent or more.[5] The first of these conditions was certainly met in the

1840s. The revolutionary governments of the 1790s and Napoleon had given France institutions and laws that secured property and profit, safeguarded inventors against infringement, protected employers against organized labor, and provided a flow of trained engineers and technicians. Merchant banks and the government, the latter following long-established practices of state promotion of industry, were capable of mobilizing the capital essential to accelerate economic growth. The second condition was met by the heavy-metals industry, including the production of machinery as well as metallurgy. Fed by the swelling demand for rails, locomotives, and wheels, axles, and other car parts, and for steam engines, iron ships, and textile machinery, it achieved a high rate of growth in the forties. François Crouzet's index of production of the metallurgical industries, hovering around 6.4 in the latter thirties, rose steadily from 1840 through 1847 to 10.9 in the latter year, achieving an average annual growth rate in excess of 8.5 percent in those eight years. His parallel index for industries engaged in "the transformation of metals" rose at a lesser but still impressive annual rate of 6.3 percent between 1840 and 1845.[6]

Demonstration of Rostow's third condition presents some difficulties. Despite the diligence and ingenuity of French economic historians in accumulating and analyzing relevant sources on investment, income, and productivity it is not now possible to compute the rate of annual investment in France in the first half of the nineteenth century. The most that can be affirmed with any confidence is that investment rose sharply after 1835. François Perroux estimated the total industrial and commercial capital investment in France at 2 billion francs in 1815, 3.3 billion in 1835, and 6 billion in 1853.[7] The total capital investment in 1815 amounted to 26 percent of the estimated annual gross national product, in 1835 to 29 percent. By 1853 it had soared to 53 percent.[8] The volume of investment year by year is not known. One need not, however, accept Rostow's view that the increase in investment in the modern sectors represented a *net* increase in total investment as a proportion of income. Much of it could have come in the form of reallocation of fixed and working capital from traditional economic activities.

The takeoff as seen by Rostow involves revolutionary changes in agricultural production arising from adoption of new technics. J.-C. Toutain's data on total French agricultural production, organized—unfortunately for my chronology— by ten-year periods beginning and ending in mid-decade, show that production in the decade 1834–1844 grew at an annual rate never previously reached in France and never exceeded until 1925–1934. Marczewski's similar data show growth in that earlier decade unsurpassed until the "Agricultural Revolution" of the 1950s. Yet another piece of evidence contributing to the confirmation of takeoff at this time is Paul Bairoch's recent calculation that the French gross national product per capita rose 45 percent in the thirty years after 1838–1842, an upsurge comparable to that of Germany in the thirty years after 1858–1862, and close to that of England between 1770 and 1798.[9]

To fix the beginning of takeoff in a particular year or even in a particular cluster of years involves subjective judgments on which universal agreement is impossible. Rostow places the beginning in France in the 1830s.[10] Crouzet's data, presented in Graph 1, may reasonably be taken as a confirmation of that judgment. The upward movement in industrial production was unmistakably beginning in 1835, and it contrasts with the negative results in the preceding years. However, the change beginning then does not meet the requirements of sustained growth. It did not survive the cyclical crisis of 1838–1839, virtually a normal episode in the nineteenth-century economy. By contrast, the growth that began in 1840 and more strikingly in 1841 reached much greater heights and was reversed only in 1848, a year of events beyond ordinary expectations. For three decades after 1840 growth was normal.

The latter 1830s can be understood as a period of preparation, such as Gerschenkron finds preceding his "great spurts" in industrial growth, a period marked by the "limited bursts" of growth that Rostow places before the takeoff. These years provided the technological base for the rapid expansion

of the 1840s. The initiation of the first railway building projects in the period developed essential knowledge of costs and
of methods of financing, and the intensifying debate on railway policy prepared the way for adoption of the Railway Law
of 1842, a critical element in sustaining the takeoff. The completion of new canals—more than 550 miles between 1835
and 1840—and the law of 1837 providing for the maintenance
and improvement of local roads were probably necessary preliminaries to continuing economic growth. The accelerated
opening of primary schools required by the Guizot School
Law of 1833 gave assurance that a minimally literate population could be trained as the evolving economy required it.
Moreover, the latter thirties brought resolution of some political and security problems born of the Revolution of 1830.
France entered the 1840s with the Orleanist regime more stable and society somewhat less threatened by revolutionary
disorder. Men of property, presumably, felt more secure than
in the preceding decade and consequently more inclined to
invest in novel enterprises.[11]

The development of the iron industry offers an illustration
of technological preparation in the latter thirties. As reported
in the preceding chapter, that industry in 1840 was still artisanal. Eighty percent of the iron produced in France came
from small charcoal furnaces widely scattered over the country
in locations where wood and water were readily available.
Under the stimulus of a growing demand for iron the industry
had begun to modernize in the thirties. The average annual
production of *fontes* and *fers* in the years 1835–1839 was 40
percent higher than in 1830–1834, but while the production
using charcoal as fuel rose only 23 percent, production using
coke rose 100 percent. Thirteen coke-fired blast furnaces were
added to the nation's industrial plant between 1835 and 1840,
increasing the total of such furnaces by nearly 50 percent. In
1840, although only one furnace in ten was coke- or coal-
fueled, they produced one-third of the nation's iron.[12]

To supply iron to a market now clearly changing both quan-
titatively and qualitatively, new companies were formed and
old companies reorganized and reequipped. The Société de

Creusot, a long-established ironworks and coal operation in the Loire coal basin, had failed in the early thirties. In 1836 a company organized and managed by Adolphe and Eugène Schneider, sons of a landowner and notary in Lorraine and themselves at the time employed by the Sellière Bank of Paris, purchased the defunct enterprise. Capital for the venture came from the Sellière Bank, from Adolphe Schneider's father-in-law Louis Boigues, an ironmaster at Fourchambault in the Loire basin, and from the Schneider family. Together they invested 3.4 million francs in improvements in the enterprise over the next three years, and in 1838 it produced its first rails and its first locomotives—six for the Paris–Saint-Germain railway, and in 1839 five more. It opened a shipbuilding yard at Châlons-sur-Marne and in 1839 won a contract for six river vessels from the Compagnie Bonnardel Frères et Four of Lyon. The next year it received an order from the Ministry of the Navy for two steam engines to be installed in French naval vessels. The company's annual report of 1840 noted that its machinery-construction shops had produced very good profits. In that year it began to build an unprecedentedly powerful steam hammer, which it subsequently patented, a machine that enabled it to profit from the burgeoning market for finished iron products such as boiler plates, ships' plates, and structural iron.[13]

Other Parisian entrepreneurs acquired and reorganized ironworks at Rosée in Burgundy and at Champagney and Ronchamp in the Department of the Haute-Saône. A company newly formed in 1836 leased the ironworks at Alais in the Department of the Gard, unprofitable since its establishment seven years earlier; the company added two blast furnaces, and in 1839 made a profit for the first time. In 1839, when the Paris–Orléans railway entered the market for rails, eight French companies, including Schneider and Alais, bid for its business. Six years earlier iron rails could not have been purchased in France.[14]

The demand for coal, real and expected, stimulated the creation of many new companies and a feverish search for untapped coal deposits in the Department of the Nord. Sixty-eight companies, capitalized at 140 million francs, were formed in three years—1836, 1837, and 1838—and attracted investors not only there but in Paris and in Belgium.[15]

The incentives for modernizing the iron industry in the thirties were the perceived opportunities for profit in supplying iron for textile machinery, steam engines, ships, and railroads. Bairoch would add agricultural tools and machinery to this list. Demand mounted, as French agriculture began to improve its technics in the 1830s, for metal plows, scythes, harrows, ditch-diggers, clod-breakers, and threshing machines; the latter two required more than a ton of iron each. Iron had replaced wood in the construction of textile machinery by the early thirties, and the expansion of the cotton industry consequently produced a considerable new demand for iron. Imports of raw cotton, which may be used as a measure of activity in the cotton textile industry, amounted to 28,200 tons in 1831, jumped to 44,300 tons in 1836, and exceeded 51,000 tons in 1838. A mechanical loom required at least 2,600 pounds of iron and a modestly-sized spinning machine of 200 spindles, more than six tons.[16]

Mechanization—in whatever industry—required power, and steam engines were its most commercially feasible source. The dramatic upsurge in their use came after 1840, but the number of steam engines in use in industry rose from 150 or 200 in 1816 to 1,447 in 1835 and to 2,591 in 1840, an increase that generated a considerable additional demand for iron. The iron industry itself was using only six steam engines in 1824. A decade later it had more than fifty in use and in 1840 well over a hundred. The increasing use of steam to move ships—France had 227 steam ships in 1840, two-thirds of them equipped with French-built engines—added to that demand. Schneider, Cache et Guibert, Cavé, Antoine Pauwels in Paris, and Alexandre Hallette in Arras were the principal beneficiaries. The first iron-hulled vessels were coming into use on French waterways in the 1830s, and each vessel required a considerable amount of iron—twelve tons for a vessel of two hundred tons displacement, a common size at the time—but the very large demands of ocean-going vessels and of armored naval vessels still lay in the future.[17]

The demands of the railroads for iron products were just beginning to be felt in the latter thirties. The first concessions for lines of more than suburban length—the Paris–Orléans, the Paris–Rouen–Dieppe, and the Strasbourg–Bâle lines—were granted in 1838, and the Paris–Orléans placed its first orders in that year. The volume of iron products required by the early railroads was less than might be assumed from perusal of lists of equipment ordered, because iron rails were then relatively light, carriages and wagons were constructed largely of wood, and the first locomotives were only about one-fourth the weight of those introduced in the 1840s. Expansion of the iron industry in the thirties attributable to the railroads would have been more in expectation of demands than in response to specific orders.[18]

As the first year of the new decade drew to its close, the stage was set for a period of accelerated industrial growth that before its end would set France on the path toward a modern, urban, industrial society. The threat of imminent war with Britain and the old anti-French coalition of 1813–1815 had been averted in the summer and autumn of 1840, and a new ministry, whose composition gave promise of a cautious foreign policy and the avoidance of war, was in office. The latest incipient revolution in Paris—the Society of Seasons Revolt of 1839—had been quickly and reassuringly ended by the application of the army's new plan for containing "serious troubles" in the capital. The Army and the National Guard, which executed the plans jointly, had at last, it seemed, learned how to preserve order in Paris.[19] Even more important, the new industrial technology, which included coke-smelting of iron, puddling, mechanical-powered rolling, mechanized textile spinning and weaving, and steam marine engines, had been tried and adopted by enterprising firms, and vigorous and venturesome captains of industry were ready to exploit their potentialities.

In 1841 the growth of industrial production jumped to 16 percent above the average annual rate for the century and in the next year to 20 percent above. Crouzet's index of production of the newer and more dynamic branches of industry, namely mining, metals, chemistry, and cotton and silk textiles, rose 61 percent from 1839 to 1846. In the first two or three years of the takeoff the expansion was fueled by renewed demand for agricultural tools, for textile machinery, for steam engines, for iron ships, and for rails and railroad equipment. Increases in the productivity of agricultural workers indicates the growing use of tools, even machinery. The use of scythes continued to spread in the 1840s, and French scythe makers had so improved their technology that they could compete with foreign producers. By 1845 they were reported to hold a near monopoly on the French market. Bairoch estimates that cotton spinning machines mounting 2 million spindles were installed between 1837 and 1847, and since 1838 and 1839 were recession years, most of them must have been added in the forties. Thirty thousand mechanical looms, a machine little used in the thirties, were installed in the same period. These two instances of reequipment alone, Bairoch maintains, created a demand for more than 126,000 tons of iron, about one-fourth of all the increase in finished iron products (measured in tons) between 1837 and 1847. Mill owners increasingly turned to steam engines for power, unwilling to tie the operation of their expensive machinery to the uncertainties of water power. The number of applications for authorization to install steam engines rose from six in 1840 to fifty-eight in 1846; the number of engines in operation rose from 2,591 in 1840 to 5,212 in 1848. The navy added more than fifty steam-powered vessels to the fleet between 1840 and 1845.[20]

In reaction to the war scare of 1840, when the French government realized that it lacked the ships and the trained crew to sustain a naval war in the eastern Mediterranean, and because advancing technology indicated that wooden, sailing warships might soon be obsolete, the French navy in the 1840s began the construction of a new, technologically advanced fleet. Ocean shipping was revolutionized after about 1820 by the introduction of iron hulls, which were stronger, lighter, and more economical to maintain and operate than wooden hulls; by the adoption of steam power; and by the use of propellers. The first iron ship was built in 1828 and the first iron *paquebot* in 1838, both of them in England. The first commercially practical steamships, also British, began crossing the North Atlantic in 1838, and the propeller, which made possible the use of steam power for large ships, was successfully adapted to commercial use in 1836. The French navy in 1840 had two steam-powered vessels—a corvette of seven guns and a fifteen-gun frigate, 235 feet in length. Both were moved by paddle wheels. The navy then had no iron-hulled ships, but since the 1820s French engineers and naval officers had been studying the possibilities of iron-armored ships, and in 1842 the Minister of the Navy sent a young officer and *polytechnicien*, Henri Dupuy de Lôme, to England to study the newest methods of shipbuilding. Before his return and the publication in 1844 of his report, which had profound influence on naval construction in all maritime countries, the ministry granted contracts for three iron-hulled steamships and three iron-hulled corvettes and dispatch boats. In his report Dupuy de Lôme insisted on the advantages of iron over wood in ship construction and described the most recent and effective building methods. The next year in a supplementary report he advocated vessels powered by steam engines, retaining sails only as an auxiliary source of power and with iron hulls protected by a belt of armor six and a half inches thick and extending from six feet below the waterline to three feet above it. He held that existing technology made such revolutionary vessels practical in the 1840s. Construction of a fleet of such armored ships would generate an enormous demand for iron, and for a time its impact seemed close at hand. In 1846 the Ministry of the Navy won from the chambers an appropriation of 93 million francs to build and equip some twenty steam-powered, armored vessels over the next seven years. Reconsiderations by the naval staff, the recession of 1847, and the Revolution of 1848 ended the building program for the forties. Nonetheless, orders for iron naval vessels and the high level of interest in them in the top command of the navy

surely had an impact on the iron industry and on planning to
expand productive capacity in anticipation of orders. Napoleon III in the mid-fifties revived the proposals of the forties
and did begin the rebuilding of the French navy, creating a
demand for iron that must have contributed to sustaining the
takeoff in the fifties and sixties.[21]

Within a few months of its passage on 11 June 1842 the
Railway Law began to generate an unprecedented demand for
finished iron products—rails, spikes, rail chairs, wheels, axles,
locomotives, and structural iron—a demand that from about
1844 or 1845 onward accelerated the takeoff and sustained
it through the next two and a half decades with interruptions
only in 1848. Railroads became a leading sector of the economic growth of those years. They stimulated development
of the iron and engineering industries, the coal industry, and,
through the great demand for ties, the timber industry. By
reducing transportation costs—once appropriate operating
procedures were devised, employees trained, and the reluctance of shippers to abandon established practices and connections was overcome—railroads expanded the market, creating demand for many other products as well. The Railway
Law of 1842, particularly its timing and the distinctive railway
policy that it fixed, therefore, held a key place in the causal
pattern of the first great upsurge of French industrialization.[22]

Serious public discussion of railway construction and finance began in France about 1832. For ten years it produced
no national policy, and the country fell far behind Britain and
some German states in railway building; but the delay assured
that when the huge demands of railroad companies for rails
and rolling stock burst upon the market, the leading suppliers,
who had been responding to the modest requirements of the
few short lines that had before 1842 been conceded to private
builders, had the technology and the skilled workers to handle
most of the demand. At first they lacked the capacity to fill
all orders, and some were placed in Britain; but, being technically prepared, they were able to expand when the demand
justified the required capital investment.[23]

The particular provisions of the Railway Law of 1842 had

a critically important effect on the development of France's heavy industry. In Britain the national railway system evolved from the construction of many short local lines, such as the Stockton and Darlington, thirty-eight miles in length (inaugurated in 1825), and the Liverpool and Manchester, thirty miles (opened in 1830), promoted by local entrepreneurs and financed by local capital. Each was authorized by a separate act of Parliament. In the spring of 1842, as the *Journal des chemins de fer* reported, seventy-two separate railways were in operation or authorized in Britain. Population and economic activity there were sufficiently dense and distances sufficiently short to make many railroads commercially feasible, and the promise of profits attracted the requisite private capital. By the time the French passed their general railway law in 1842 a decade and a half of railway building had already given Britain nineteen hundred miles of operating railroads—five times the French mileage at the time. A new burst of construction activity in Britain beginning in 1845 raised the mileage to five thousand miles in 1848. Big promoters were involved in the second stage, the amalgamation of short, established lines began, and a national system emerged. The working of private initiative produced a national railway network.[24]

In France distances were greater, and the commercially significant resources were more widely separated. Economic activity and population were insufficiently concentrated to make many rail lines certainly profitable. Had the building of railways been left to private initiative and profitability been made the determinant of what was built, France would not have quickly acquired a national network, nor would the railroads have become a leading sector in the industrial takeoff of the 1840s. Even those routes beyond the Parisian suburbs that did early attract private capital—the Paris–Rouen–Le Havre, the Paris–Orléans, the Lille–Dunkerque, and the Strasbourg–Bâle—proved to be beyond the capabilities of the private companies that undertook to build them. Only with the financial assistance of the state did these projects (though not in all cases the original companies) survive and come to completion.

In the spring of 1842, when the Paris–Belgian frontier, the Rouen–Le Havre, the Versailles–Chartres, and the Orléans–Tours lines were being considered for government authorization, no banker or other entrepreneur came forward to finance any of them.[25]

Equally important with the constraints imposed by geography and demography in shaping railway policy in France was the widely held conviction, dating back to the seventeenth century, that transportation was properly a public service provided and directed by the state. In the eighteenth century the excellence of the French royal highways and canals was well known throughout Europe. Arthur Young praised the roads and canals he saw on his journeys in the 1780s. In contrast with the situation in Britain, where private entrepreneurs built and operated turnpikes and canals, in France the state built and maintained them. The conception of highways and waterways as part of the national patrimony, essential to national security and to a prospering economy and as a public monopoly, had a body of powerful and influential advocates in the Corps des ponts et chaussées, the state's corps of civil engineers founded in 1716, which after 1834 had a particularly able and articulate director-general, B. A. LeGrand. To LeGrand and his fellow engineers railways were simply a new element to be added to the nation's transportation system. They believed that the railroads should be integrated into the system and that they must be planned and built by the state—and planned and built to serve all France, not only the regions where they might at the moment promise to be financially profitable.[26]

Between 1832 and 1842 Parliament, departmental councils, the press, and provincial societies publicly debated transportation policy. In the record of that debate can be found the arguments of free enterprise versus government monopoly, of railroads as a private industry versus railroads as a public service. Here, too, are the ambitious projections of the entrepreneurs and the advocates of industrialization such as the Pereire brothers and the Talabot brothers, the romantic visions of the "great technician poets"—Michel Chevalier, Prosper

Enfantin, and Henri Fournel, the misgivings of notaries responsible for family savings and investments, the hostilities and apprehensions of those vested interests clustered around roads and waterways—the stagecoach and haulage companies, the wagon drivers, the posthouse owners, and the canal and river-boat operators. The possible contribution of railways to national defense and their impact on foreign policy were duly considered. Involved in the debate were the government's pending proposals for the construction of particular lines and for certain methods of financing them. Until 1842 none of these, except some limited concessions to a few private companies, got beyond the state of discussion. Although decision was long in coming, the record of the debate makes clear that by its end the French of the directing classes did understand that railroads would have shattering economic, social, and strategic consequences. On a practical level they understood, too, that high costs precluded the building of many railroads without financial participation by the state.[27]

Out of this long debate came the Railway Law of 1842. It was marked by the powerful influence of the Corps des ponts et chaussées. The law prescribed the building of a national network of railroads—about two thousand miles, in all, including the few fragments already completed. The main lines were to radiate from Paris—to the English Channel, to the Belgian border, to the German border near Strasbourg, to the Mediterranean via Lyon and Marseille, to the Spanish border via Bordeaux, to the Atlantic via Nantes, and to the center of France via Bourges. Two transverse lines would connect Bordeaux and Marseille in the south and Lyon and Mulhouse in the east. This pattern was essentially the work of the Corps des ponts et chaussées. All parts of the country would be served, not only those with the population and economic activity to assure immediate profitability. Profit was subordinated to the national interest. The state, using public funds, would acquire the land for the right of way, prepare the roadbed, and build the bridges, tunnels, and embankments. The lines would be conceded—in the whole or in separate but connecting parts—for a limited number of years to private companies by individual laws passed by the chambers. The companies would lay the rails, provide the rolling stock, and operate the railroads. By this arrangement the state assumed the more unpredictable costs. The companies' responsibilities were made palatable to private investors; their costs were predictable, and the duration of each concession was fixed to permit recovery of the initial investment within that time. The Corps des ponts et chaussées supervised construction of the roadbed and tracks and imposed rigorous standards on, for example, the radii of curves, the weight of rails, and the quality of ties.[28]

The decision to build a national network and the state's commitment of its resources to financing it assured that railroads would be built throughout the country. The state's assumption of the greatest initial risks and the assurances to private investors made investment in railroads seem safe even to cautious French bankers and notaries, who in the past had been dubious of any long-term investment save in land or government bonds. Moreover, high protective tariffs on rails and rolling stock gave to French industrialists assurance of the lion's share of the domestic market and encouraged investment in new plants to supply that market. The passage of the general railway law was consequently like the opening of a dam. It released a flood of public and private capital, more than three-quarters of a billion francs in the next five years, and a flood of orders for rails, structural iron, locomotives, wagons and carriages, ties, and ballast. Accumulated expenditures "de premier établissement," which stood at 188 million francs at the close of 1841, passed the 500 million franc mark in 1845, approached 700 million in 1846, and fell just short of 1 billion francs in 1847.[29]

In the spring of 1843 the government's orders for rails and rail chairs for use in preparing railway roadbeds began to come to the market. In April the Ministry of Public Works invited bids on 11,600 rails and 46,400 rail chairs for the section of the Paris–Mediterranean line between Dijon and Châlons. Schneider won the contract for rails. In August the ministry called for bids on 33,443 rails and 135,772 rail chairs for parts of the lines from Paris to the eastern and northern borders. This order—then very large—was divided among Schneider, De Wendel, the Société des Forges de Denain, the Fonderies de l'Aveyron at Decazeville, and the ironworks at Anzin, all large, technologically advanced companies. Announcements of impending purchases by the ministry continued to appear in the *Journal des chemins de fer* through 1843 and 1844.[30]

Meanwhile the government and the chambers were occupied with concessions to operating companies, and in 1844 and 1845 the authorizing acts began to issue from the Palais Bourbon and the Luxembourg. In 1845 eleven companies with a combined capitalization of 563 million francs were formed, including the Nord Railway, the Paris–Strasbourg, and the Orléans–Bordeaux. Early in 1846 came the Paris–Lyon, the Lyon–Avignon, the Bordeaux–Cette, and the Creil–Saint-Quentin companies. Their combined capitalization exceeded half a billion francs. Orders from these enterprises soon began to reach the ironmakers and the engineering works. The Nord Railway, financed by the Rothschilds in association with a number of other leading Parisian banking houses, placed its first orders in the summer of 1845, and at the beginning of the new year the management reported to stockholders that in the preceding six months it had ordered 130 locomotives (all from French companies), 100,000 tons of rails, 1,200 pairs of wheels, 2,400 freight and coal wagons, 420 passenger carriages, and 120 luggage and mail vans. By April 1846 the accumulated orders amounted to a commitment of 25.8 million francs. They were distributed among thirty-four companies, and the railroad itself already employed forty thousand workers.[31]

The Paris–Strasbourg railway placed its first orders in February 1846, when it contracted with De Wendel in Lorraine for 32,000 tons of rails (and took an option on an additional 28,000 tons); with Meyer of Mulhouse for thirty-five locomotives; with Cavé and with Derosne et Cail, both in Paris, for twenty-five locomotives each; and with A. Motteau et Cie of Angoulême for three. In May of that year it ordered another

26,000 tons of rails from De Wendel and in July 25,000 tons from Talabot Frères at Denain. In 1847 the Talabots received an additional order for 12,000 tons of rails. Beginning in April 1846 and at intervals throughout the spring, summer, and autumn the company placed orders for 785,000 railway ties, 26,000 tons of rail chairs, 2 million spikes, and 200 pairs of wheels and axles for carriages. In October 1846 the company contracted with the Compagnie des messageries générales for the delivery of 300 passenger carriages, 300 wheels and axles, 2,700 tons of rail chairs, 60,000 ties, and several hundred turntables, switches, and crossovers. Early in 1848 it ordered 365 freight wagons. By the end of 1847 the company had spent or committed expenditures of 50 million francs. The other railway companies, as they were authorized, came into the market with similar demands. The impact of these massive orders could have been no less than a powerful source for sustaining and accelerating the industrial takeoff.[32]

The iron and engineering industries were confronted with a demand for which they were technologically prepared—within the limits of the current technology—but which they could not fill with existing productive capacities. Railroad companies' directors, mindful of the expectations of investors, were anxious to get into profitable operations as quickly as possible. High French tariffs discouraged the purchase of rails and rolling stock in England. To assure deliveries of essential equipment from their French suppliers some railway companies furnished capital—or other tangible support—for expansion of plants. In July 1846 the Strasbourg Railway lent 2 million francs to Talabot Frères on favorable terms to finance the construction of a new rail mill. A quarter of the principal was to be repaid in rails. Its second contract with De Wendel for rails, concluded in May 1846, was tied to an agreement that De Wendel would build a new plant at Forbach, and in return the Strasbourg Railway would haul the company's iron ore requirements at reduced rates for fifteen years after the opening of the new plant. The Nord provided capital to at least two of its suppliers, Gouin et Cie. and Farcot of Paris, from whom it ordered locomotives and tenders, and on one occasion, to induce a rail mill to accept an order, the Nord agreed to supply the necessary iron.[33]

The huge orders issuing from the railroads forced expansion of the iron and engineering industries' productive capacities tied to improved technology. The nation's production of pig iron rose from 403,000 tons in 1840 to 592,000 tons in 1847, an increase of 47 percent in just seven years. One-third of the increase was attributable to rail production alone. The demand from the railroads, once started, was sustained at a high level for the next quarter century except for a brief reversal in 1848–1851. New orders continued to come on the market as additional lines were conceded to operating companies, and the new orders were soon supplemented by unending replacement requirements. François Caron estimated that between 1845 and 1854 13 percent of the production of the French iron industry, measured in volume, went to fill railroad orders, from 1855 to 1864 18 percent, and from 1865 to 1874 12 percent. The demand was met both by expansion of established firms and by the creation of new ones. Schneider, which made six thousand tons of iron in 1837, produced twenty thousand in 1847; its work force expanded in approximately the same period from 1850 persons to 2,250, and this force continued to expand in the fifties and sixties, reaching 12,000 in 1870. In 1846 Schneider built its sixth blast furnace and in 1847 added three more. The Fonderies de l'Aveyron at Decazeville thrived on orders for rails and in 1846 added two blast furnaces. De Wendel added two in 1847, bringing its total to six, and planned to build four more. Brouillard Benoist et Cie. at Alais added its fourth blast furnace in 1844 and another in 1847; it more than doubled its production of iron from its furnaces between 1844 and 1847. Derosne et Cail, manufacturers of machinery for the sugar industry, in November 1845 and January 1846 obtained orders from the Nord Railway for forty locomotives, and J. F. Cail, the managing partner and soon the sole owner of the company, successfully transferred his firm's expertise and his workers' skills to locomotive production. He recruited additional employees as needed from among the skilled metal and mechanical workers of Paris. The number of his employees jumped from 570 in 1845 to 1,500 in 1848. In the mid-fifties it was around 2,500, and the company was producing ninety-five to one hundred locomotives each year. Another machinery manufacturer in the Paris area, François Cavé, moved into locomotive production with orders obtained in 1845, 1846, and 1848. This company also shared in the concurrent demand for iron-hulled and steam-powered ships. With Schneider and Hallette of Arras it filled the French navy's order of 1844 for steam frigates and later concentrated its business on shipbuilding and the production of marine engines.[34]

Many entirely new companies were formed to profit from the mounting and seemingly endless demand for iron and iron products. The Ateliers Gouin, established in 1846 especially to supply railroads and with capital advanced by railway companies, had orders for thirty-six locomotives before its plant opened. In the same year the Parisian banking house Laffitte et Blount formed the Hauts Fourneaux de Maubeuge in the Department of the Nord. A large iron-producing center was developed at Commentry and Montluçon in the Department of the Allier. New companies were established at Bessèges in the Gard coal basin in the south, at L'Horme in the Loire Valley, at Aubun and Fumel in the Ardèche, and at Stiring-Wendel in Lorraine. The capital for these new enterprises and for expansion of established companies was in part self-generated, but it also came, as noted earlier, from railway companies anxious to insure timely deliveries and from banks and individual investors. In the forties banks, including the Rothschild bank, invested some 30 million francs in the iron industry.[35]

Railroads and steamships required iron of higher quality than that sufficient for most earlier uses, and this, combined with the much larger quantitative requirements of the forties, stimulated adoption of the advanced technology of the time—notably coke smelting and refining in reverberatory furnaces. The technique of coke smelting had been introduced into France in the 1820s, but its adoption by the industry generally had been hampered by the high cost of coke and the relatively low cost of charcoal. In the thirties, however, diminishing production of charcoal forced the price up by about one-half, while improvements in coal-mining methods and in transportation reduced the price of coke in the principal coal field—the Loire Valley. The initial cost advantage of charcoal smelting was overcome. Moreover, the huge demand, largely for standardized products, created and sustained by the railroads could support the continuous operations that coke-fired furnaces required to achieve maximum economies in operation and the lowest unit costs. By the early 1850s the market price of coke-smelted iron at the Fourchambault forges had dropped to 29 percent below the price of charcoal-smelted iron. The rising demand for iron and improvements in charcoal smelting enabled charcoal furnaces to survive, and they continued to turn out more than half of the iron produced in the 1840s; but the large-volume orders in the forties went to the technically advanced companies who alone could fill them, and these companies continued to expand and modernize. The number of coke-fired furnaces rose from 41 in 1840 to 106 in 1846, and their production tripled, from 77,000 tons to 240,000.[36]

The reverberatory furnace for refining iron into steel had been brought to France from England in the teens of the nineteenth century, but the initial costs of construction and the shortages of suitable coal and of skilled workers restricted its adoption. In the 1840s, however, the rising demand for high-quality metal began clearly to overcome these handicaps, and between 1840 and 1847 some two hundred reverberatory furnaces were installed in France. The production of steel rose from 245,000 tons in 1840 to 390,000 tons in 1847.[37]

The combined influence of improved technology and surging demand favored concentration of production in large enterprises. On the one hand, initial capital costs of adopting new methods were often so high that only a large concern could afford them. Management at Fourchambault in 1845 estimated the costs of building and equipping a new rail mill at close to 300,000 francs. The installation of a reverberatory furnace with the capacity to process the output of three blast furnaces cost half a million francs; only the needs of a large concern could keep three coke-fired furnaces in the continuous operation necessary to achieve minimal production costs. On the other hand, large-scale purchasers such as railway companies or the government favored the big producers who could fill large orders and do so within prescribed and relatively short time spans. In 1842, the year of the passage of the general railway law, the government drew up a list of companies that had the capacity to supply rails in the required volume then foreseen. Eleven companies appeared on the list, and they were the big operators—Schneider, De Wendel, the Fonderies de l'Aveyron, and Boigues Frères at Fourchambault among others—companies with more than a thousand employees each. Not even all of the select eleven were able to compete with the giants, however, and most of the companies newly established to supply the railroads had little success. The big companies got the orders and expanded. Production of iron by the entire industry increased by 59 percent between 1840 and 1848, but in the same period De Wendel's production rose 278 percent, Schneider's 200 percent, and Fourchambault's 109 percent. In 1848 four-fifths of France's iron production came from just five companies.[38]

The new technology also contributed to the concentration of employment. A charcoal-fired furnace required only four to six workers, a coke-fired furnace twenty. An old-style hearth for steel making needed one or two workers, a reverberatory furnace ten. The more advanced enterprises also required more administrative personnel and more engineers and supervisors. The total employment in the iron industry rose by about one-sixth between 1835 and 1846, but employment in coal-fueled enterprises rose by one-third. By the end of the 1840s the once modest work force of Decazeville iron works had risen to more than three thousand. Employment in the Schneiders' plant at Le Creusot then reached about the same level.[39]

The spreading adoption of coal and coke in the iron industry contributed also to the geographic concentration of industry. Coal, measured in terms of weight, was a very large part of the production process, but being entirely consumed in that process it did not enter into the weight of the finished iron. Consequently, location of manufacture at the source of coal could achieve significant economies in transportation. Under the old technology of charcoal the industry had been widely dispersed, but by 1847 the three leading coal-producing departments—the Nord, the Loire, and the Seine-et-Loire—also produced 28 percent of the nation's iron measured in monetary value.[40]

About the same time bankers in Paris, Lyon, and Geneva with interests in the Loire coal basin combined their operations into two large companies—the Compagnie générale des mines de la Loire and the Société des mines réunies de Saint-Etienne. In 1845 the two companies controlled about one-half of the mines in the Loire basin. The former, the more important of the two, employed more than three thousand miners and produced 1.2 million tons of coal annually. Its formation represented the extension into the Loire coal field of the kind of large-scale, capitalist enterprise that had earlier existed only in the Compagnie d'Anzin in the Nord coal field.[41]

French industry was not, of course, in five or ten years suddenly and completely taken over by advanced-technology, large-scale enterprises. As pointed out earlier in this chapter, a number of iron and textile firms were in the twenties and thirties adopting new technologies, developments that helped to make possible the great spurt of the forties. But throughout the forties and beyond traditional technologies and traditional forms of industrial organization survived and even flourished. In the iron industry, for example, the old and the new existed side by side. Isolated charcoal forges, protected by still-high transportation costs in areas not yet served by railways against both imported coal and the products of the new advanced iron producers, continued to serve local markets and in some cases limited demands for special-quality metals. As late as 1864 three hundred charcoal forges still produced 20 percent of France's pig iron. But the small, artisanal operations, even those that improved their methods, were hurt by the evolution of the market, which was demanding more sophisticated products, large quantities, and uniform quality. They were also hurt by the railroads, which soon enabled the new sector of the industry to reach markets everywhere in France and, after the conclusion of the Anglo-French Treaty of Commerce of 1860, by English competition. When, in addition, demand began to shift from iron to steel in the latter sixties, the small artisanal forges, unable to adopt costly steel-making processes, could not long survive.[42]

The beginning of a revolution in banking coincided with the upsurge in industrial growth. It might be dated from the founding of Jacques Laffitte's Caisse générale du Commerce et de l'Industrie in 1837. The Caisse and similar banks that followed its lead reversed the established rule of prudent banking—borrowing at long term and lending at short term. They sold to the public both limited-liability shares and five-, fifteen-, and thirty-day interest-bearing notes, which meant that in effect they accepted deposits, then placed the capital thus raised in long-term loans to industry and railroads, prefiguring the practices of the Pereire brothers with the Crédit mobilier after 1852. The *caisses*, of course, could fill only a small part of the growing capital requirements of the times. The earliest railroads were financed largely from outside the French banking community by industrialists and wholesale merchants who foresaw direct benefits to themselves in railroad services and by foreign investors, especially English and Swiss. The Parisian merchant banks in the early years of railroad building invested only in the Parisian suburban lines and in the Paris–Orléans. The railroad building of the forties and the industrial expansion necessary to supply it required a much larger volume of long-term investment than could be raised by traditional methods and from usual sources. The problem was resolved in part by the state's participation in the construction of the railroads, that is, by using the state's fiscal powers to raise capital; but additional resources were required, and the merchant banks moved in to fill the gap, changing both their practices and their personnel in the process. The *Haute Banque* alone had the experience and the contacts required to make large accumulations of capital. They had experience in floating public loans and in forming syndicates of underwriters, and they had the contacts with investors in France and abroad. Some had actually engaged in financing commercial and industrial enterprises during the Empire. They had financial specialists expert in analyzing investment proposals as well as in arranging the mechanics of capital transfers, and they added engineers to their staffs. Their reputations for judicious investment gave to their approvals of then-novel placements the cachet of the most reassuring endorsement conceivable. The latter circumstance enabled them to draw money from a public not hitherto involved in industrial investment or in joint-stock ventures. Beginning in the late forties inventories of family fortunes in Paris showed for the first time a significant increase in the percentage of holdings of industrial stocks and bonds and a decline in the percentage of traditional holdings of real property.[43]

The demands of railroad and industrial financing began to blur the lines of distinction between the direction of banking and the management of industry. With financial participation bankers took on new entrepreneurial and management roles. Bankers effected the consolidation of the mines of the Loire coal basin into two giant companies. Both the Rothschild Bank and Laffitte et Blount took control of iron works in the Nord in 1846–1847. Those same banks held seats on the boards of directors of seven railroad companies in the latter forties. The Rothschilds, their representatives, and banking associates took nine of the eighteen seats on the board of the Nord Railway. James Rothschild himself was the chairman of the *comité directeur*, which actually managed the company, and three of the other five members of that committee were from the Rothschild Bank. Three of the seven managing directors of the Paris–Lyon railway in 1846 were Rothschild representatives. At the same time, railroad men and industrialists came onto the boards of banks. The number of bankers on the board of the Bank of France, more than 50 percent in 1840, began to decline about that time, and the percentage of industrialists began to rise sharply—from about 15 percent to near 40 percent thirty years later.[44]

TABLE 1
Freight Rates, 1825–1913
(in centimes per ton-kilometer)

Years	Railways	Highways	Canals	Sea
1825–1834	—	33	5.8	6.0
1841–1844	14.5	25	5.4	6.0
1845–1854	10.6	25	5.3	5.6
1855–1864	8.7	25	4.6	3.3
1865–1874	7.5	25	3.5	2.8
1875–1884	7.4	25	2.9	2.8
1885–1894	6.8	25	2.6	2.6
1895–1904	6.0	25	2.3	2.5
1905–1913	5.4	25	2.2	2.4

SOURCE: J.-C. Toutain, *Les Transports en France de 1830 à 1965.*
Cahiers de l'Institut de science économique appliquée, Series AF, 9
(1967), p. 279

The railroads would in time have revolutionary effects on
the size and on the supply of markets and on consumers'
habits. The cost of moving a ton of freight by rail was one-
half or less of the cost of movement by road and for some
commodities even less than movement by inland waterways.
At first the ability of railroads to attract shippers was handicapped by the force of habit and by inferior service offered
by inexperienced railroad personnel. Nonetheless, the increase
of freight traffic on the railroads soon became spectacular. In
1845 the railroads carried 102 million ton-kilometers, in 1850
423 million, 1855 1.53 billion, and in 1860 3.14 billion.
Traffic continued to rise through the remainder of the century,
and the increase represented largely new business, for the
volume of freight moved by water remained at about the level
of 1847 until the 1880s, then began to increase, and freight
traffic on highways continued to increase.[45]

The emergence of a national market, which improved transportation would in time achieve, and the bringing of millions of new consumers into the market (a consequence of waxing industrial production and diminishing production costs as well as of improved transportation), did not come until after the 1840s—in 1847 only about nine hundred miles of railways were in operation. Nonetheless, the critical initiatives and decisions on the railway system were made in the forties. Even then one might discern the shape of things to come. Jules Michelet wrote in *Le Peuple*, published in 1846, that in 1843—when the price of raw cotton, which had dropped just short of 40 percent since 1820, again fell sharply and the new, mechanized cotton industry was ready to move this saving on to consumers—France changed from a producers' economy to a consumers' economy. Formerly, he said, every Frenchwoman owned a single dress, either black or blue, and she wore it for ten years. Now, he said, her husband with a single day's wages could buy for her a flowered, cotton dress. For the first time in history, he went on, the poor could afford changes of clothing, underclothes, bed linen, curtains, and many other goods now being machine produced.[46] "It was," he declared, "a revolution little noticed but great."[47] The first Parisian *magasin de nouveautés*, harbinger of the large department stores, those emporia of consumerism which in the Second Empire would become symbols of affluence and instruments of fostering bourgeois tastes among the masses, was opened in 1843 on the Rue Montmartre. The Paris Chamber of Commerce's report on its industrial census of 1847–1848 commented on the rapidly growing production in recent years of ready-made—and less costly—clothing for men. Per capita consumption of meat, which had scarcely changed over half a century after 1780, began to increase in the ten-year period 1835 to 1844, when it rose 8 percent. In the next decade it rose another 15 percent, and in the years 1855 to 1864 17 percent. In 1830 Paris drew its fresh fruits and vegetables from an area within a radius of about thirty miles of the city, products from greater distances incurring transportation costs that made most of them too costly for the market. By 1855, when all the main railroad lines out of Paris were completed, the commercially feasible limit had been extended to 150 miles, and the composition of Parisian diets was beginning to change.[48]

Improvements in transportation and the growth of cities, together with changes in agricultural technics, began in the 1840s to accelerate the shift of French agriculture from production primarily for subsistence to production for sale. This in turn was to have a profound influence on peasant grievances and on rural politics. Rural well-being henceforth depended less on abundance or dearth of the local harvest than on food prices in often distant urban markets. The depression of 1847–1848 had been in part started by a poor harvest in 1846, but it was exacerbated and prolonged by industrial dislocation as well as by political revolution, and the continuing agrarian crisis in 1848–1851 was attributable to the inability of urban markets to consume agriculture's increasing production. The old forms of peasant protest—bread riots to protest the high cost of bread and grain riots to block the movement of cereal away from local markets—had become irrelevant. Instead, peasants seeking ways to influence the government to provide relief in the form of lower taxes or cheap credit turned to interest-group politics, beginning a new age in rural politics in France.[49]

· III ·

Centralization Made Real

ALEXIS DE TOCQUEVILLE, in his *L'Ancien régime et la revolution* of 1856, firmly planted in historical writing the belief that even before the Revolution France was a highly centralized state and that republican governments and Napoleon continued the centralizing trends of their predecessors. Certainly in 1814 the institutions of the modern centralized state—the prefectoral system, the Université de France, the network of law courts, for example—were in place. Yet, under the restored monarchy France was still in practice essentially decentralized. The government in Paris managed foreign policy, provided for defense of the borders and the maintenance of public order, and administered justice; but day-to-day, routine, grass-roots government and administration remained in large part in the hands of local notables. Distance and the still-crude technology of transportation put provincial cities, towns, and hamlets temporally far from Paris. Communications, slow at best and, in bad weather, uncertain, narrowly limited the capital's sustained and practical influence beyond a narrow radius around the city. The economy, being overwhelmingly agrarian, was necessarily dispersed, and the deficiencies of transportation assured the fragmentation of the country into many small, almost autonomous economic units. Most markets were local or, at their largest, regional. Prices varied significantly across the country, and local food shortages were still a threat to public order. Regional banking and commercial centers such as Marseille, Lyon, Lille, and Bordeaux played important roles of service to the economy. The widespread use of patois demonstrated the limited effects of cultural centralization and unity.[1]

The great barriers to the achievement of centralization in practice, "to the conquest of the national space," in the words of a French economic historian,[2] were the existing states of transportation and communication. As mentioned in Chapter I, the restored Bourbons and the Orléans were canal builders. In 1840 France had more than 2,300 miles of waterways, triple the mileage of 1820. The years 1820–1840 were indeed the great age of canal building in France, but they had little influence on the structure of the economy or on mobility of persons. The canals and rivers were poorly maintained and frequently closed by ice, fog, flooding, or shortages of water; and, of course, movement on them was slow at best. Stendhal reported that the river steamer that took him from Bordeaux to Agen in 1834 averaged a bit more than one mile per hour. Under the most favorable conditions horse-drawn barges, which in 1840 still carried three-fourths of the upstream tonnage on the Rhône, required about twenty days for the 150-mile trip from Arles to Lyon. Passenger steamers could make the run from Lyon to Marseille in twelve to fourteen hours but required three or four days for the return journey. In the two decades during which accessible mileage of waterways tripled, freight traffic on them increased less than 50 percent.[3]

The pre-Revolutionary monarchy, as mentioned in Chapter I, had built a system of royal roads radiating from Paris to the provincial cities and to the borders, which Napoleon restored after years of neglect during the Revolution. These highways were built to serve the requirements of mail, administration, and the movement of persons (in the small numbers who could afford to pay the fares) among principal cities. In the provinces departmental roads were few and ill maintained, and wagon tracks, impassable in bad weather, served as local roads. One could move fairly expeditiously from Paris to Lyon or to other provincial centers, but travel between provincial towns and villages was slow and difficult. In 1832 the young Georges-Eugène Haussmann, moving from Poitiers to his new post in Yssingeaux, Department of the Haute-Loire—only about 220 miles distant—found that he had to travel nearly 350 miles and to use two stagecoaches, two primitive mail carriers, and a hired carriage. He spent six days traveling.[4]

After 1830 the new Orleanist monarchy launched a program of road construction and improvement that by mid-century had accomplished a *révolution routière*. By 1840 more than three thousand miles of new royal roads had been completed and another thirteen hundred miles before 1848. The percentage of the royal roads maintained in good condition was raised from 53 in 1830 to 96 in 1847. The length of the departmental road network, about 15,000 miles in 1830, exceeded 26,000 in 1847, 92 percent of them in good condition. Once the Law of 12 May 1836 had made provision for revenues, and labor and initial difficulties of application had been overcome (see Chapter I), the construction and improvement of local roads went forward at an unprecedented pace. By 1848 France, almost without serviceable, all-weather local roads in the thirties, had 36,000 miles of year-round local roads and by 1870 nearly 200,000 miles.[5] With good reason did an observer write in 1860, "The law of 1836 on local roads transformed France."[6]

At the same time old roads were improved or entirely rebuilt. On both the old and the new the state's engineers, drawing on the techniques developed in Britain by John MacAdam and Thomas Telford as well as those devised by some of their French predecessors, applied the latest technology of road construction. The roads now had solid foundations, hard surfaces, effective drainage, and more gentle curves and inclines than had been usual in the past. Hundreds of new bridges replaced fords and ferries. These improvements made the roads usable through most periods of bad weather, and the hard surfaces and gentle inclines permitted substitution of wagons for pack horses and enabled horses to pull heavier loads at greater speeds, with savings in both time and money.[7]

The *révolution routière* had immense economic and social consequences. The extended and improved roads together with the railroads created new bonds between provinces and the now less distant capital, and by breaking down geographic isolation facilitated the integration of once-remote areas into a national market and the ultimate transformation of their residents from Bretons and Limousins and Gascons into Frenchmen.

Alain Corbin, in his study of the Limousin region (embracing the departments of the Creuse, the Corrèze, and the Haute-Vienne) in the nineteenth century, offers a vivid illustration of what this *révolution routière* meant to a particular provincial area. A report on the Department of the Corrèze in 1830 complained, "Our communications with the neighboring departments are almost nonexistent."[8] In the whole region movement of stagecoaches and freight wagons was possible on only four royal roads and two departmental roads. The high country in the southeast remained almost totally isolated. By the end of the July Monarchy nine royal roads crossing the region could carry heavy vehicles, and nearly four hundred miles of departmental roads were open and in good condition. Limoges was an important center for a growing market area. Each day twenty-two stagecoaches left the city for cities and towns outside Limousin, including Paris, and fifteen for other towns in the region.[9]

More and better roads opened horizons of new mobility, expanding market areas, and cultural unity, but movement of both goods and persons remained slow and costly. Even with the improved roads and lighter carriages introduced in the 1840s the maximum average speed of stagecoaches was only about six miles per hour, and the speed of freight wagons was lower. The trip from Paris to Bordeaux by stagecoach required forty to forty-eight hours in 1847 and from Paris to Strasbourg forty-nine hours. Individual passenger fares ran about 0.14 francs per kilometer, prohibitively high for all but the well-to-do. Freight rates varied from 0.20 to 0.23 francs per ton-kilometer for ordinary service and from 0.43 to 0.45 francs for accelerated service, not much changed since the latter eighteenth century.[10]

It was the railroads that breached the barriers of time and cost. The early locomotives in use on the French railways could move trains at thirty miles per hour, five times the speed of stagecoaches and three times the speed of the fastest mail coaches. After the main lines of the national rail network were put into service in the late forties and the fifties, the Parisian traveler could reach Calais in four and a half hours, instead of the twenty-eight required by stagecoach, and Lyon or Strasbourg in about ten hours instead of two days. By the early sixties the Nord Railway was moving freight from Paris to Lille in three days; horse-drawn wagons on the highway required eight days for the same journey. Passenger fares on the early railroads varied from about 0.06 francs per kilometer in third class to about 0.10 in first class, approximately one-half to two-thirds the rates on stagecoaches. In the succeeding decades they dropped even lower, in third class to about one-fourth of the old coach fares. For freight the early railroads charged 0.12 francs per ton-kilometer for regular service. By 1851 the rate had fallen to 0.077 francs, about one-third the charge for ordinary highway transport and one-sixth that for fast service.[11]

Railroads made possible the first revolutionary conquest of the national space, and the rapid acceptance of the railroads by travelers and shippers alike made that conquest a reality. When the general railway law was passed in the spring of 1842, the nation had about 350 miles of operating railways, and Paris was connected by rail with no major provincial cities except Rouen and Orléans. In the next five years operating mileage almost tripled; by 1860 it exceeded five thousand miles, and in 1870 fifteen thousand miles, joining Paris with every city in the country. In 1846 the new steam trains—though they as yet served only a few cities and towns, most of them in the Paris basin—carried more than 10 million passengers. In 1860 the expanding network carried 56 million and in 1867 more than 100 million. By the end of the century annual passenger traffic exceeded 400 million. These swelling numbers represented new movement of Frenchmen, for passenger traffic on roads held steady from mid-century to the latter 1880s and then receded only to the level of the 1840s. The volume of freight moved by the few operating railways just before the passage of the general railway law barely exceeded 1 million metric tons, necessarily on short runs averaging about twenty-five miles per ton. In 1847 freight carried by the railways exceeded 3.5 million tons, in 1860 27 million, and in 1869 44 million. The average distance each ton was moved had quintupled by the latest date. Some of this traffic was taken away from highways and waterways, but much of it was new, generated by the railways themselves.[12]

Because the national railway network radiated from Paris it produced a dramatic contraction of the national space around the capital. With unmatched connections to an expanding hinterland it attracted new economic activities and new population. The Paris Chamber of Commerce estimated the value of its industrial production in 1847 at 1.464 billion and at 3.369 billion in 1860. The city's population almost doubled in the two decades after the opening of the principal trunk lines that converged on it.[13]

Other cities favorably located in the system grew similarly. Lyon, for example, had 177,000 inhabitants in 1851, 342,000 in 1876. Bordeaux grew from 131,000 to 215,000 inhabitants. Industrial cities expanded even more rapidly. The population of Lille and of Tourcoing doubled in the twenty years after 1846, and in Le Creusot, the principal seat of the Schneider family's metallurgical business, the population tripled. The cases of Le Mans and Alençon, neighboring towns in western France, illustrate the powerful influence of the railways on established towns not associated with any growth industry. The citizens of Alençon, population 14,000 in 1851, opposed the passage of the Paris–Rennes railway through their town, and it was built through Le Mans, population 27,000, thirty miles to the south. Twenty-five years later Le Mans had 50,000 inhabitants; Alençon's 14,000 had increased by scarcely a thousand.[14]

These instances of rapid urban growth were part of a nationwide redistribution of population. Indeed, in the 1840s began the most important demographic reversal of the nineteenth century. For almost half a century before 1846, since the first systematic census in 1801, France's population had increased steadily, and the increase had been distributed fairly evenly over the country. In 1846 all save one of the eighty-six departments were more populous than they had been in 1800. Both urban and rural population increased during these years, and rural population (officially defined then as the num-

ALBERTUS MAGNUS
LIBRARY

ber of people living in communes of two thousand or fewer inhabitants) reached its peak both relatively to the total population and in absolute numbers. Then came the great reversal. Between 1846 and the next census year, 1851, twenty-five departments, almost a third of the total, lost population, and for the first time since census taking began rural population declined. The principal gainers were the industrialized and industrializing regions and commercial centers—Paris, Lyon, Saint-Etienne, the north, Alsace, and similar places favored by resources and transportation.[15] "It was," writes the demographic historian André Armengaud, "the announcement of a new age."[16] The decline of rural population that then began has continued in absolute numbers with one interruption (in 1872–1876) and in relation to the total population without interruption into the second half of the twentieth century.[17]

In the three decades after 1815 rural France had the highest density of population it ever achieved. The countryside was overpopulated in relation to its agricultural productivity, and the burgeoning population sustained itself only by combining cultivation of the soil with domestic industry. The industrial base of the rural economy was undermined and eventually destroyed by the new factory industry. The first great crisis came in the depression of the latter 1840s, when the cotton industry, its capacity expanded in the "great spurt" of early and middle forties, its low-cost distribution to a national market assured—or at least promised—by the proliferating network of railways and local roads, overwhelmed its rural competitors. The small, dispersed, charcoal-fired iron forges could not in the long run compete with more efficient, coke-fueled blast furnaces of the big iron companies. Rural industry was a casualty of forces, clearly emerging in the early and middle forties, that were brought to bear on it by the economic depression of 1847–1850. With it went the means of support of a considerable part of the rural population, and these people, forced to seek new sources of livelihood, found them increasingly in towns and cities.[18]

Migrations had been common in the early decades of the

nineteenth century, both within the rural milieu and between village and city, but the latter were temporary migrations, not an exodus from the rural areas of France. Modern industry, beginning to grow rapidly in the 1840s, demanded a stable work force, and workers absorbed into factories became permanent residents of industrial centers.[19] Marcel Blanchard, a historian of the Second Empire, writing in the 1930s declared that "between 1850 and 1880 our grandfathers saw before their eyes the end of the old rural, agrarian, and unchanging France of ancient, sleepy, discreet, little towns."[20] Had he known what we know, the first date could have been 1846 or 1847.

Railroads contributed to this movement not only indirectly, by providing the low-cost transportation on which both industrial and commercial concentration depended, but also directly. Their hastily recruited construction crews attracted laborers off the land in areas where rail lines were built, often occasioning the first break with village ties. Their low fares made travel, even relatively distant travel, in search of employment a possibility for thousands of the rural poor and, by affirming the prospect of occasional return visits, made initial uprooting more acceptable.[21]

Another technical innovation of the 1840s contributed to the shrinking of the national space and to the concentration of both economic and political power. In 1844 Parliament voted funds to establish the first electrical telegraph line, a line joining Paris and Rouen. Twenty-nine French cities were then served by semaphore aerial telegraph, which under ideal conditions could transmit messages at amazing speed—from Paris to Lille in two minutes, Paris to Strasbourg in six and a half minutes, Paris to Toulon in twenty minutes. But it was frequently interrupted by mist, fog, rain, or snow, and it was useless at night. Moreover, since it required transmittal stations at intervals of about seven miles (fifty stations between Paris and Strasbourg, one hundred between Paris and Toulon), each manned by a crew of two, it was costly, and it was restricted to official use. The electrical telegraph assured almost instantaneous communication in all weathers and at all times, with minimal labor costs. By 1851 six thousand miles of line connected Paris with the capital of every department of France.[22]

Together with the railroads, which by 1860 had brought every major provincial city within sixteen hours of the capital, the electrical telegraph multiplied the central government's powers of coercion both in the provinces and in Paris. At least as early as 1842 Adolph Thiers foresaw the utility of railroads in maintaining civil order, and Louis Auguste Blanqui saw the electrical telegraph as a "formidable weapon" for repressive governments, comparable to the rifled cannon and the rapid-firing rifle. Responsible military commanders and civil officials anywhere in the country could now be promptly directed and troops and police quickly moved to trouble spots. A battalion of infantry in seven hours of marching could cover about seventeen miles, which had to be followed by twenty-four hours of recuperation before the battalion was ready for action. Traveling by rail a battalion could cover 125 miles in seven hours without disabling fatigue. In November 1846 the minister of war assured an apprehensive deputy of the Department of the Loiret that the army, using railways, could now move troops from Paris to Orléans, capital of the Loiret, in four hours and from Blois in two hours; and when, the next day, serious disorders threatened in nearby Department of Indre-et-Loire, he illustrated his point by moving four hundred troops from Paris to Tours in the course of a single afternoon. In the June Days of 1848 two infantry regiments with their supporting artillery and cavalry arrived in Paris by rail on the second day of fighting, 24 June, and by the close of the fourth day more than 100,000 provincial national guardsmen had flooded into the city, many of them arriving by train from Rouen, Pontoise, Senlis, Compiègne, Amiens, Boulogne, and a number of other cities and towns already served by railroads. On this occasion the government prevailed over the insurrectionaries. Eighteen years earlier in the Revolution of 1830, when armies still moved on foot, the government was able to bring only a handful of additional troops into the capital before the insurrectionaries won control of the city on the third day of fighting. Feeding the suddenly-arrived mass of armed men in 1848 presented a logistical problem that in 1830 would have been well-nigh insoluble. In 1848 it was readily solved by using the railroads to carry quickly to the capital bread produced in the bakeries of nearby towns and villages. Railroads and the electrical telegraph were by 1848 clearly giving to administrative centralization a meaning and an effectiveness that it had never had under the Bourbons, the Committee of Public Safety, or Napoleon.[23]

The combination of railroads and the electrical telegraph, which was opened to public use in 1850, also had the effect of concentrating and centralizing wholesale commerce. Until the 1840s producers with their goods met buyers and made their deals in markets like the Halle aux Toiles in Rouen or at seasonal fairs scattered about the country. In the forties large manufacturing concerns, seeking more efficient and speedier procedures, made increasing use of specialized wholesale merchants (*commissionaires*). These marketing specialists had first appeared in France in the eighteenth century, but their role had been small until in the forties mechanization multiplied industrial production and improved communications began to revolutionize the market. Then, operating especially out of Paris but cultivating close relations with the large manufacturing centers throughout the country, they used samples to display their clients' products; after the electrical telegraph network became available to them in 1850, they could place their orders quickly, and railroads increasingly assured expeditious delivery anywhere in the country. Regional cotton markets, characteristic of the old fragmented economy of the early nineteenth century, were quickly displaced by Le Havre, the port of entry for American raw cotton, once that city was linked into the rail and telegraph networks. Already in the forties some manufacturers were establishing their own permanent sales offices in Paris, attracted there by the unmatched communications and transport connections with all of France and by the ready access to credit at the hub of the increasingly concentrated banking system. The surging volume of business of the electrical telegraph suggests the growing dependence on this new instrument of commerce. In 1858 it moved 350,000 messages, in 1869 more than 4 million, in 1880 15 million, and by 1900 140 million.[24]

Fast and dependable mail service was another boon that the railroads brought to business and to individuals, and in both cases the mails contributed to increasing coherence within the shrinking national space. The first railroad postal cars, on which mail was sorted en route, were introduced on the Paris–Rouen line in 1844, and they were placed on other lines as the lines were opened to traffic. The number of letters posted annually rose from 94 million in 1840 (about four letters per adult inhabitant) to 127 million in 1847. In 1849, the year in which postage stamps were introduced, it jumped to 159 million. Before the end of the Second Empire in 1870 it reached 357 million and in 1901 exceeded 1 billion. The last figure represented about forty letters for each adult Frenchman. This exploding use of the mails reflected, of course, spreading literacy as well as inexpensive, readily accessible, and dependable postal service.[25]

For many businesses the new rapid and reliable delivery of mail had far-reaching consequences. To urban newspapers it opened the possibility of acquiring large regional and even national circulation. The first two low-cost dailies, *La Presse* and *Le Siècle*, had been established in Paris in 1836, and within a decade their circulations had soared to 22,000 and 33,000 respectively. Together with the electrical telegraph, efficient mails also made possible the development of branch banking in the 1860s.[26]

At no other point in the country were the revolutionary influences of the railroads and the electrical telegraph as evident as in Paris. In the 1840s it was losing its traditional character as a prodigal, parasitic center of consumption, living on the productivity of the rest of the nation, its own industry producing largely for the local market. It began to emerge as an industrial as well as a commercial metropolis. The Etablissements Cavé in Paris with eight hundred workers and the Etablissements Pauwels at La Chapelle with four hundred were building steam engines for railroads, transatlantic steamers, and the navy, and rolling stock for the railroads, while a number of other companies were producing heavy machinery for the national market.[27] The construction of the national railway system, once the general railway law had been passed in 1842, required the mobilization of a massive capital investment, and in France Parisian banks alone had the organization and contacts to effect such a mobilization and the technical expertise to put the capital quickly and profitably to work. For the Nord Railway the Parisian banking houses of Rothschild and Laffitte and their English connections took 270,300 of the 400,000 original shares of stock. All of the French directors of the railroad were Parisians, and all of the six members of the executive committee were Parisian bankers. The largest stockholders of the Paris–Strasbourg railway were Parisian bankers, and all members of the board of directors lived in Paris save for one member from Saint-Quentin. Four of the seven members of the executive committee of the Paris-Lyon railway were Parisian bankers.[28]

In the first four decades of the nineteenth century France had been ruled at the local level by the *grands notables*, landed proprietors whose wealth, family connections, and long presence in their districts gave them standing as "natural" leaders, well positioned to serve as intermediaries between the state and the local population. But as the railroads and the electrical telegraph concentrated power, especially on Paris, and as new forms of negotiable wealth—stocks and bonds—began to rival wealth in land, the notables' economic power and political influence diminished. The power of Paris was moving ever closer, and the minister or department head in the capital, able to communicate with the prefect or other subordinate in the provinces in minutes and himself able to be on the scene in an expanding area of the country in a matter of hours, had less need of unofficial intermediaries in the provinces. Already in the latter forties electoral districts in the provinces could not find local candidates to run in parliamentary elections and had to settle for Parisians, who might or might not be residents of the departments they were called upon to represent. Of the

459 deputies elected in 1846, 188 were Parisians. Increasingly the fate of the provinces was determined and local issues decided in Paris. Moreover, as the notables invested in stocks and bonds, as many of them were doing in the forties and after, they moved, consciously or not, closer to Parisian bankers and away from local peasant interests, subtly altering their relationships with traditional clients in the provinces. At the same time the emergence of more and more industrialists and other businessmen into the electorate further eroded the political power of the landed notables.[29]

Several parliamentary decisions moved the central government into a more activist role in the forties, making its presence and its power felt throughout the country as never before. The Railway Law of 1842 and two supplementary statutes in 1845 and 1846 gave Paris immense new powers—for the expropriation of property, the regulation of fares and rates, the control of investment and returns, and the enforcement of construction and safety standards.[30] The metric system of weights and measures had been introduced into France in the 1790s, but only beginning on 1 January 1840 did the government undertake to enforce its use. From that date forward the use, public or private, of any weights or measures other than the metric was forbidden. Henceforth, all the local and occupational varieties of measurements, ruggedly surviving for centuries, had to give way to nationally uniform measures.[31] In 1841 the government took its first hesitant steps toward telling its citizens how long they and their children might work and under what conditions. The Law of 21 March 1841, passed by overwhelming majorities in both parliamentary houses, limited the rights of factory owners to employ children and limited the equally cherished right of parents to compel their children to work at an early age. In practice the law had little immediate effect, for it lacked provision for effective enforcement, but as the first break at the national level with the theory and practice of nonintervention in labor-employer relations, it was a landmark in the history of labor legislation. In the debate on the bill in the Chamber of Deputies in December 1840 a Legitimist deputy, the Vicomte Al-ban de Villeneuve-Bargemont, posed to a French Parliament for the first time in history the whole vast problem of the protection of industrial workers, opening an immense new field of official concern and government regulation.[32] "His speech," wrote J. B. Duroselle a century later, "began a new epoch."[33]

In another area—the care of the mentally ill—the central government was in the 1840s moving into a more active role throughout the country. The Law of 30 June 1838 required every department to maintain a public asylum or to contract with a private institution for the care of the mentally ill and forbade the establishment of private asylums without express authorization of the government. An enabling ordinance issued on 18 December 1839 laid down requirements for the staffing and administration of public asylums and specified the conditions of authorization of private institutions. The effect of the law and the ordinance was to impose the methods and procedures of Parisian asylums and the theoretical and practical psychiatry developed in Paris in the 1830s on the provinces.[34]

Even popular protest was becoming more centralized. As Paris, making use of the railroads and the electrical telegraph, and of more deadly weapons as well, completed the establishment of its control over the provinces, the traditional, "reactionary" forms of collective protest, as Charles Tilly designates them—local food riots, tax revolts, and machine breaking—disappeared. The last great wave of food riots came in 1847, the last tax revolts in 1841 and 1847. Within about two decades after 1845 these spontaneous, local responses to local grievances gave way to strikes, demonstrations, even revolution directed against national authority, and to some kind of association with organizations operating on a national scale.[35] As Tilly explains, "Men found it much harder to ignore the national scene, and much harder to accomplish anything requiring collective effort or common resources without working through men working on a national scale. . . . The national state won a durable victory over local power-holders and traditional particularisms. Louis-Napoleon simply captured and consolidated."[36]

In mid-century, then, one can discern the beginnings of a political maturation, as collective popular concerns ceased to be predominantly local and economic and became predominantly national and political. Ted Margadant, in his study of the peasant revolt of 1851, argues that even so early a significant part of the peasantry was already integrated into the national political scene. Eugen Weber maintains that the process was more gradual, and well into the second half of the century village politics remained a preserve of the local notables; but he does agree that railways, better roads, growing opportunities for alternative employments, public education, and universal suffrage were undermining the political monopoly of the notables and making the populace more politically aware and more active.[37]

The institutions and procedures of the government in Paris in the forties were changing to accommodate the expanding functions of the central government. It was during the July Monarchy that the role of the parliamentary deputy was defined for a century to come as a man with the ability to speak well in the chamber and to represent effectively the interests of his constituents to increasingly powerful ministries in Paris. An elector of Troyes in 1846 asked the candidates in the forthcoming general elections, "Our roads, our railways, the taxes, the upkeep of [public] buildings—what have you done for them?" By the eighties and nineties the increasingly politically-minded popular electorate was coming to understand that the central government had the ability to grant local favors, so that the criteria of political support established by the bourgeois electors of the forties (illustrated by the preceding quotation) became theirs, too.[38]

The ministerial *chef de cabinet* was another creation of the July Monarchy. The increasing contacts between the central administration and local interests required that the first minister especially have an assistant to handle relations with deputies, with other ministers, and with the press. Guizot's *chef de cabinet*, Alphonse Génie, a product of the Conseil d'état and the Cour des comptes, performed this role for eight years, 1840 to 1848, and became the prototype of this still-important French official. The Ecole nationale d'administration, the archetypal institution of the omnipresent Gaullist state of the twentieth century, was foreshadowed in 1843 by a proposal that the government establish a school, comparable to the Ecole polytechnique, to train civil servants for their growing and increasingly complex responsibilities.[39] (This proposal is discussed further in Chapter IV.)

In the 1840s the requirements of the Guizot School Law of 1833, combined with the demands of an emerging national market and expanding industry, were perceptibly moving France toward linguistic unity. The Guizot law, giving institutional form to a cherished aspiration of eighteenth-century French revolutionaries for education for all and for a truly national language, required each of France's 37,000 communes to maintain, either alone or jointly with a neighboring commune, a boys' primary school, either public or Church, open to all boys and free to those whose parents could not afford to pay the tuition fee. If a commune should fail to provide adequate financial support for a school, the state could, on its own authority, impose additional taxes on the commune, and, if necessary, the department and state would supplement the communal contribution. For the first time in French history primary education was to be available, under compulsion of the state, to all male children whose parents sought it. A comprehensive system of primary schools did not quickly spring into existence. Many peasants saw education as a luxury that offered no material benefit to them or to their sons (save perhaps teaching the latter how to sign their names, a useful skill in a litigious society) and deprived them of their children's labor. In many areas hostility to education or to taxes required for its support, or simple indifference, delayed the establishment of schools. Nonetheless, between 1833 and 1840 8,500 communes opened schools, and in 1840 only about 6,000 still lacked them. Enrollments rose from about 1.6 million in 1833 to 2.9 million in 1840 and continued to rise in the forties, though not as rapidly as in the preceding decade.[40]

Enrollment figures can be misleading, suggesting a higher level of actual attendance in class than actually occurred. Attendance of individual students was sporadic, tending to be higher in inclement winter months and minimal during planting and harvesting seasons. Data for the nation as a whole, moreover, obscures striking differences among regions in both the availability of schooling and in attendance. Best served was the Department of the Seine (the Parisian department), which in 1837 had 870 primary schools, double the number a decade earlier, and 55,000 students, probably about 60 percent of the children between the ages of six and fourteen. In the Department of the Puy-de-Dôme in the Massif Central 233 among the 400 communes in 1840 were still without schools in compliance with the Guizot law, and in the Department of the Vaucluse in the lower Rhône valley in 1836–1837 summer attendance in predominantly agricultural communes was only about 20 percent of the eligible age group. The Department of the Seine-Inférieure (now Seine-Maritime), an economically advanced department that included the cities of Rouen and Le Havre, by 1840 had primary schools in almost all of its 759 communes, but in the Nièvre, a rural department about 150 miles southeast of Paris, a third of the communes still lacked schools in 1840.[41]

Nonetheless, in France as a whole children were going to school in increasing numbers and with some effect. The proportion of illiterates in each year's conscript class (the best available quantitative measure of literacy) was still in excess of 50 percent in the 1830s and 47 percent in 1840. By the 1850s, when the first generation to benefit from the new schools was coming of age, it had fallen below 40 percent. By the end of the Second Empire it was approaching 20 percent. Marriage registers show a similar increase in at least minimal literacy in these years. In 1816–1820 only 54 percent of the bridegrooms and 43 percent of the brides nationwide could sign their acts of marriage. In 1872–1876 77 percent of the men and 76 percent of the women signed. These figures, too, obscure large regional variations. In some remote departments more than 50 percent of the men and 70 percent of the women in 1872–1876 still lacked even the ability to sign their names. In 1886 the literacy of conscripts varied from 99.1 percent in the Department of the Jura to 64.9 in the Breton Department of the Morbihan.[42]

The substantial increase in literacy on the national level reflected not only the availability of schools but also changing popular attitudes toward education, changes being forced from the 1840s onward by industrialization, the increase in geographical mobility, and the emergence of a national market. Knowledge of a standard language was becoming imperative for those obliged—or aspiring—to find work far beyond the traditional limits of their isolated village lives. A worker on a railroad construction crew or in a rail mill outside this little world had to be able to understand his foreman's orders and instructions; he had to be able to communicate with fellow workers. Employers valued the discipline and good work habits that they believed schools instilled in their pupils. The ironworks at Fourchambault, one of the technologically advanced enterprises thriving on the soaring demand for iron in the 1840s, would not hire a young worker who had not attended school. Moreover, the growing impingement of the central state on the lives of more and more citizens was imposing a written culture on society. In a world of official notices, declarations, and forms the ability to read and write French was becoming imperative.[43] "With French you can go anywhere," a Breton peasant told his grandson, "With only Breton, you're tied to a short rope, like a cow to a post."[44] Primary school enrollments reflect the spread of this understanding. Voluntary enrollments rose steadily, and by the time attendance became compulsory in 1882 almost all school-age children were at least formally enrolled in school.[45]

Adults, too, were going to school, attending evening classes in growing numbers. Guizot, when minister of Public Instruction in the early 1830s, had encouraged the establishment of adult courses; and they thrived, especially in towns and cities, offering training in reading, writing, and arithmetic. In 1841,

3,400 courses attracted more than 68,000 students; by 1847 their numbers had grown to 6,900 courses and 117,000 students, and by 1868 to more than 33,000 courses and 793,000 students.[46]

The spread of education, both of children and of adults, meant that a growing number of Frenchmen, especially the young, were learning to read and speak a standardized French. The Guizot Law of 1833 prescribed only three areas of instruction for students in the primary schools—moral and religious training; arithmetic; and reading, writing, and "the elements of the French language." One consequence of the linguistic emphasis in the curriculum was growing use in the country of standard French. In the Department of the Var on the Mediterranean coast, "Just before 1848," writes the department's most eminent historian, "the linguistic situation was in rapid evolution."[47] The language of ordinary speech there had been Provençal; in the 1840s it was giving way to French. A local poet, Victor Gelu, who cherished the old language, in 1855 lamented, "In the past fifteen years the discredit of the Provençal idiom has taken a giant step."[48] Some years earlier he had predicted that within a few decades that language would be as incomprehensible as hieroglyphics to 99 percent of the population of the region's largest city, Marseille. In some areas—Brittany, Corsica, the Basque country, for example—the native languages tenaciously survived despite the best efforts of the French schoolmasters. In 1865, nonetheless, a careful screening of the 322,000 army conscripts of that year, initiated by the Ministry of Public Instruction, showed that 68.5 percent habitually spoke French and another 20.5 percent could speak French, though imperfectly. The conversion to French as the common language varied greatly from department to department and even within single departments, but the combined influences of the schools, a modernizing economy, and growing presence of the state assured, from the 1840s forward, that by the century's end French would be in fact, as well as in name, the national language.[49]

The Guizot law, in providing for the establishment and support of public primary schools, ended the preceding regimes' practice of leaving primary education to the Church, and this, coming simultaneously with the Catholic revival of the July Monarchy, contributed to the reopening of the festering dispute over the state's control of schools and the Church's role in the education of French children. Events in the 1840s foreshadowed the bitter and acrimonious shape that this dispute would take decades later under the Third Republic. In 1843 the Ultramontane Louis Veuillot began his long career as editor of the Parisian Catholic newspaper, *L'Univers*, and began filling it with his polemics against the forces of irreligion, which for him included not only Voltairians and Protestants but Liberal Catholics as well. From then until his death four decades later Veuillot contributed powerfully to the polarization of the Church-State conflict. In 1843 also Charles de Montalembert published his pamphlet, *Du Devoir des Catholiques dans la question de la liberté de l'enseignment*, in which he proposed the formation of a Catholic party to campaign for "free" schools—that is, Church schools free of state controls. Several newspapers were established to publicize and support the cause. In 1845 a parish priest, Emmanuel d'Alzon, founded the Order of the Assumptionist Fathers with the avowed purpose of combating the secular doctrines of the French Revolution, especially by freeing Catholic schools from the state monopoly. In the early decades of the Third Republic the Assumptionists became the Church's militant fanatics in "France's last religious war." These men of the forties and their followers and associates, who included Jean-Baptiste Lacordaire, Frédéric Ozanan, and Félix Dupanloup, were moved to take their position by their fear of the pernicious influence of "Godless" schools, but it is reasonable to conclude that they were also motivated by a perception that the retreat of the old, stable, agrarian society before the advance of a new urban, mobile, materialist, state-centered society was itself a threat to religion and to the Church.[50]

· IV ·

Search for New Identities

IN 1843 Pierre-Joseph Proudhon wrote in his *Carnet* No. 1, "One can sum up all the causes of the malaise that troubles France in a single sentence—France does not know herself."[1] The country, he regretted, lacked knowledge of its own government, of its industry and commerce, and of its beliefs, goals, and inclinations. For individual Frenchmen, too, the years of the forties brought a crisis of identity, most clearly among professional men but also among others.

Professionals were finding that the old bases of individual identification—personal reputation or family ties in small town or neighborhood—no longer served in rapidly growing Paris, or in other large cities of the 1840s, overcrowded with doctors, lawyers, writers, architects. Like their counterparts in England and in the United States they sought to establish their status in society on their possession of expert knowledge. Joining with others in their fields they formed professional organizations that defined the respective professions in terms of training and competence required to join and sought to limit access to them.[2] In 1838 authors and journalists, on the initiative of Honoré de Balzac, had formed the Société des gens de lettres, originally both a mutual aid society, providing sickness benefits and pensions to members, and a professional organization dedicated to defending its members' literary property against copyright violations.[3] As such it enhanced the status of writers in a society that above all respected property. School teachers, occupying a lower rung in the social hierarchy, sought to raise themselves to professional status. In new capitalist industry, where the old man-to-man relationship between *patron* and skilled worker could not survive, both workers and employers formed organizations that reenforced the effects of economic change that was already setting them off as distinct and separate elements of the new society.

On 1 November 1845 some thousand doctors, pharmacists, and a few veterinarians met in Paris for a two-week-long congress, the first such professional medical meeting held in France. In the preceding decades some doctors had been anxious to induce the government to regulate the practice of medicine and to fix standards of medical education. In 1825 a few Parisian doctors had met to discuss the problem, but nothing further had come of their initiative. Under the Restoration and the July Monarchy medicine and law were the most popular professions among the young, and in cities medical practice was overcrowded. Except for a few at the top, doctors' earnings were less than those of other professional men. The competition for patients and fees was compounded by the existence of a lower order of medical practitioners, the *officiers de santé*, a type that achieved literary immortality in Gustave Flaubert's Charles Bovary. The doctorate of medicine required completion of the baccalaureate of letters, a baccalaureate of sciences, four years of medical study, a thesis, and the passage of five examinations. An *officier de santé* could qualify for certification by completing six years of study with a doctor or five years in a hospital or three years in a faculty of medicine or fourteen *trimestres* in a preparatory school of medicine and pharmacy and by passing an examination before an itinerant examining board. An *officier*'s certificate authorized practice only in the department where it was granted, and an *officier* might perform major surgery only under supervision of a doctor. These restrictions were not enforced, however, and the public often confused the *officiers* and *docteurs en médecine*, calling all "doctor" indiscriminately—like "Dr. Bovary." Napoleon had created the lesser office in 1803 as an expedient to provide medical care when there was a temporary shortage of physicians as a result of the disruption of medical education during the Revolution. The office was intended to be temporary, but nearly half a century later—in 1847—7,500 *officiers de santé* still shared the practice of medicine in France with some 11,000 doctors, and they were still being trained and licensed.[4]

The doctors also suffered the competition, especially in rural areas, of local pharmacists and midwives, of army doctors in garrison towns, and of charlatans. The *Journal de médecine* estimated in 1845 that eight hundred persons practiced medicine illegally in France. At the meeting of the medical congress in Paris in 1845 a doctor from the Department of the Vosges protested that priests were providing medical services in his department and that magistrates failed to enforce laws on illegal practice. Both illegal practice and *officiers de santé* were more commonly encountered in rural areas, which deterred doctors from settling there, with the doubly unfortunate consequence of perpetuating inferior health care in rural France and concentrating an excess of doctors in cities. Everywhere men who had completed the arduous doctorate of medicine felt that they were accorded inappropriate status in society and inadequate financial rewards.[5]

Seeking relief of their grievances from the government, a group of Parisian doctors met in June 1845 to discuss the convening of a national congress that would speak for the profession, which at that time lacked any national organization. Six weeks later delegates from local medical and pharmacy societies in Paris and the Department of the Seine, with the blessing of the minister of Public Instruction, N. A. Salvandy, approved the calling of the congress. They defined its purposes as, first, to encourage "a spirit of association" in the medical profession and, second, to inform the government of the profession's needs and wishes and to lobby for their satisfaction. In the latter part of August invitations went out to doctors, *officiers de santé*, pharmacists, and graduate veterinarians across the country to assemble in Paris on 1 November to discuss problems of medical education and the regulation of the practice of medicine, pharmacy, and veterinary medicine. In the succeeding two months registrations, membership dues (a nominal 5 francs), and *cahiers* of grievances flowed into the headquarters in the capital. At the opening session on 1 November, held in the Salle Saint-Jean of the Hôtel de

Ville, the secretary announced that 3,400 men—no women, for women were not admitted to medical or pharmaceutical training—had joined the congress. An additional 1,400 registered before the final roster appeared in December. Doctors dominated the membership, outnumbering the pharmacists and veterinarians two to one. Fewer than a dozen *officiers de santé* joined. About a thousand persons attended the meeting in Paris, and it, too, was dominated by doctors.[6]

The congress met in daily sessions between 1 and 15 November. The delegates earnestly and sometimes stormily discussed the questions and recommendations prepared by twelve committees. Their reports dealt with faculties and schools, admissions to schools, curricula and examinations, illegal practice, foreign-trained doctors and pharmacists, hospitals and dispensaries, professional organizations, and a few other concerns. The doctors, as the record of the debates makes clear, were first of all anxious to find ways to restrict the practice of medicine to those who had completed the doctorate of medicine, and this meant especially the elimination of the *officiers de santé*. No delegate spoke for the *officiers*, though a case could be made that they provided indispensable health care in remote areas where doctors declined to practice. Nonetheless, the congress voted with but two dissenting voices to recommend to the government that there be a single order of medical practitioners in France, the doctors of medicine who had completed the officially prescribed curriculum and passed examinations in a faculty of medicine—that is, in Paris, Montpellier, or Strasbourg. *Officiers de santé* with five or more years experience, the congress noted, might obtain the degree of doctor and the right to practice by passing examinations given by one of the faculties of medicine in both medicine and surgery. The congress unanimously urged severe punishment of *officiers de santé* and others who engaged in illegal practice. However, the effort by one delegate, who seemed to have considerable support from the floor of the congress, to charge the committee on illegal practice to investigate illegal practice by priests was not acted upon.[7]

The delegates did adopt a number of other recommendations intended to improve and to maintain standards of training and performance, to raise public confidence in the profession, and to enhance respect for it. Among its proposals, for example, was a ban on advertising by doctors in the press or on handbills or hoardings and the creation of councils to maintain what they called "professional dignity."[8]

The pharmacists were exercised over the existence of inferiorly trained men practicing pharmacy. In addition to the full-fledged pharmacists trained and examined in schools of pharmacy were those authorized to practice by juries of medical doctors, presumably after some experience as apprentices. Like the *officiers de santé* the latter were restricted to practice in the departments in which they had originally been certified. The congress recommended to the government that there be a single order of pharmacists—those formally trained in schools of pharmacy.[9]

Salvandy, the minister of Public Instruction, spoke at the final session of the congress and declared his sympathy with its objectives. Three days after the congress adjourned he appointed a committee of eminent doctors to study reform of the profession, and in February 1847 he presented to the chambers a bill that would enact into law most of the recommendations of the congress. Under its provisions the practice of medicine would be restricted to doctors of medicine. The *officiers de santé* would be gradually phased out and illegal practice severely punished. All medical education would be brought under control of the state, and the years of medical training would be extended by two additional years. The bill won approval in the Chamber of Peers in July 1847. Salvandy brought it to the lower house in January 1848, but it had not been acted upon before revolution ended the Orleanist monarchy in February. Its essential provisions were eventually adopted but not until many years later.[10]

The organizers of the medical congress had declared that its first purpose was to encourage "the spirit of association in the medical profession." When they assembled in Paris, the behavior of some of their number reminded them that they were less than a fraternal group. The first meeting of the

Section of Medicine on 3 November was disturbed by "noise," "disorder," "effervesence," and "explosion!" Two days later the secretary-general of the congress proposed adoption of new rules of order and admonished that the majority deserved "order and dignity in our sessions," a statement suggesting that sessions had been less than orderly and dignified. Nonetheless, before the congress adjourned it instructed its permanent committee, which had been set up in Paris, to organize a national medical association composed of local and district societies. By the next summer societies in most departments had been brought into the national federation. The committee subsequently defined the purpose of the association to be the advancement of science and of the professional dignity and welfare of its members. In the spring of 1846 and again in the autumn, pursuing the latter purpose, it urged its members to seek commitments to support of doctors' interests from candidates in the forthcoming parliamentary elections and to organize petitions to both chambers in support of Salvandy's bill on medical education and practice.[11]

In 1846 thirty doctors, pharmacists, and veterinarians in Paris raised 100,000 francs among themselves to start a medical journal, L'Union médicale, which marked a new departure in medical journalism. Its editors proposed not simply to provide its readers with scientific and practical information and instruction, as existing medical journals did, but also to represent the professional interests of doctors, pharmacists, and veterinarians. The first number declared that the journal would support the newly organized medical association, and in the coming months it would be keeping its readers informed of the progress of the ministry's bill on the organization of the medical profession and representing the profession's wishes to deputies—perhaps, the editors declared, by distributing copies of L'Union médicale to all of them. The journal was edited by a board of doctors and one pharmacist, and to underscore its professional standing it accepted no advertising.[12]

In 1843 a group of architects who had been meeting informally over the preceding three years to discuss professional interests formed the Société centrale des architectes. Their principal concern, revealed by a report of a preparatory committee in 1840, was similar to that of the doctors—the lack of a strict definition of the qualifications required to practice architecture and the consequent invasion of the field by the untrained. The profession was at the time totally unregulated. The distinction between architects and builders had never been clearly fixed, nor had the distinction between architects and engineers, who, with the introduction of industrial building materials, were beginning to impinge on the architects' traditional field. Moreover, the profession, being freely open to all, had attracted many incompetents, who not only took business away from qualified architects but also discredited the profession in the public eye. The new society appointed three committees to study the problems, and on their recommendation the society in 1846 petitioned the government to establish a diploma of architecture, which would be a certificate of capacity that alone would give the holder the legal right to the title of architect and the right to practice architecture in either private or public employment. The society suggested a "grandfather clause," which would guarantee the diploma to all "honorable" practicing architects without examination; but in the future, it recommended, the diploma would be granted only to those aspirants who had satisfactorily completed a prescribed course of study that included not only drawing and construction methods but also the history and theory of architecture, mathematics, mechanics, applied physics and chemistry, accounting, and law. The examinations to determine candidates' competence in these fields should be conducted, the society proposed, by a jury "composed largely of architects." The diploma of architecture was not established until 1867, but the professional concern, the sensed need for a new and firm identity, emerged clearly in the 1840s.[13]

An "engineer" in the 1830s, as in the eighteenth century, was a man trained at the Ecole polytechnique and working for one of the great *corps d'état*—the Ponts et chaussées, the Mines, the Army, or the Navy. But developing private industry also required men expert in mathematics, mechanics, and applied science, and in 1829 a group of private citizens founded the Ecole centrale des arts et manufactures to train "civil" engineers. Early graduates of the school lacked the clear identity and prestige of the state engineers from the Ecole polytechnique, and they were often treated by their employers as little more than skilled artisans. In 1840 graduates and students of the Ecole centrale, seeking to acquire "an official identity," asked permission of the faculty to form an association. The faculty, fearing that the association might become an instrument of radical political activity, refused permission, and they continued to deny it in succeeding years when the request was renewed. After the February Revolution of 1848, however, they acceded, and on 4 March 1848 forty engineers met at the Ecole centrale to organize the Société centrale des ingénieurs, later the Société des ingénieurs civils de France. Its stated purpose was to represent engineers to the public and the government and to advance their own professional identity and worth at a time when they were playing an increasingly active role in the expanding economy. At the end of its first year the society had 130 members, and by 1872 more than 1,000. Although it accepted nongraduates of the Ecole centrale as members, the *centraux* dominated the society, and their upper bourgeois backgrounds and values shaped the identity and status they sought to establish for civil engineers in France. So prestigious did the society become under their leadership that its fiftieth anniversary celebration in 1898 was attended by the president of the Republic and by delegates from around the world. The dress of members appearing in photographs taken at the celebration suggests that they had indeed found a place in the French upper bourgeoisie.[14]

In the 1840s, too, came stirrings among the civil servants who toiled obscurely in the myriad offices of the state's bureaucracy. Government employment had the appeal of conferring a measure of security, and many from the middle class sought it as a refuge against the threat of proletarianization. But the mass of civil servants—the "employees," distinct from the elite *fonctionnaires*—were ill paid, bound to long hours and tedious work, unsustained by hopes for advancement, and they lacked the prestige of office that their forebears had enjoyed under the *ancien régime*, when no elected officials stood between them and the monarch himself. The first independent journal for government employees, *La France administrative: Gazette des bureaux, boussole des administrés*, was founded in 1840, and the editor announced that he would expose these abuses and grievances and show how they could be remedied. The journal's formally stated purpose was the promotion of unity among all public employees, the defense of their rights and interests, and the encouragement of measures to increase their pay and improve their standing. It called specifically for a charter of civil servants defining the rights and duties of public employees and establishing firm rules of appointment and advancement. Legislative efforts, in response to these and other pressures, to fix standard personnel practices failed, but there is evidence of growing professionalism in the civil service in the late 1830s and the 1840s. One ministry introduced competitive examinations for applicants for positions. Another established a formal procedure for internal promotions. Recent graduates of universities and the *Grandes écoles* were choosing to make careers in the civil service, and the duration of periods of service increased.[15]

In 1843 a minor civil servant and political writer, Charles Duveyrier, published a proposal for the creation of a national school of administration, modeled on the Ecole polytechnique, to develop the science of administration and to train civil servants for the principal ministries. Two hundred seventy-five students in each annual class, selected by competitive examination, would spend two years studying a uniform curriculum of law, geography, political economy, industrial relations and processes, administration, history, art, and the rudiments of science. This training would provide the sole track into ministries other than those with their own schools (Public Instruction, Public Works, Navy, and War). All prospective civil servants would thus be required to complete professional training and meet clearly defined standards of mastery of professional knowledge and methods. Duveyrier was proposing essentially the same kind of professionalization and identification based on possession of expert knowledge that the architects were seeking at the same time and the doctors and pharmacists two years later.[16]

He was not alone in his advocacy of such reforms. Salvandy, the minister of Public Instruction who sympathetically received the doctors' recommendations, publicly expressed his support of Duveyrier's proposals, and one of the earliest acts of the Second Republic was the establishment of a national school of public administration. It opened its doors to its first class in July 1848. The school immediately encountered intense opposition—not only from other schools and high governmental officials but also from ordinary civil servants, who saw in it a threat to their job security. It was abolished in August 1849. Nonetheless, the idea of the systematic training of professional administrators had been planted. It revived occasionally over the next century and finally in 1945 blossomed into the Ecole nationale d'administration, now one of the nation's most prestigious schools.[17]

The clerical attack on the state's monopoly of secondary education beginning in 1840 forced *lycée* and college teachers to recognition of their common interests. It moved them to associate in order to protect their interests as well as to press for redress of grievances, especially their low pay and ill-defined rules of advancement. In 1840 some graduates of the Ecole normale supérieure teaching in Paris began to meet annually, and in 1846, the year that the clerical attack on the state's schools reached its height, they formed the Association amicale des anciens élèves de l'Ecole normale de Paris. Though nominally only a mutual aid society, it filled a professional purpose in contributing to a sense of solidarity and identity among its members. By 1847 it had more than 450 adherents in Paris and a number of correspondents in the provinces. In 1840 journals devoted to public education began to publish articles that contributed to a sharper definition of the Napoleonic Université de France, that is, the national corps of school teachers. The *Journal général de l'instruction publique*, for example, traced the histories of long-established colleges in Paris and sought to demonstrate their continuation in the

Napoleonic *lycées*. In 1845 the *maîtres d'études* in the Parisian *lycées*, perhaps following the lead of the *normaliens*, formed an association. Its first purpose was to represent their interests to the Ministry of Public Instruction, and in 1846 it asked for statutory definition of the position of the *maîtres d'études* in the educational system, a kind of formal establishment of professional identity.[18]

As the 1840s moved on, primary school teachers—the *instituteurs*—were beginning to see themselves as a group distinguished from the crowd by expert knowledge and skills that were valuable to French society. In demanding appropriate financial rewards and respect they were, in effect, seeking public recognition of a professional identity. The Guizot School Law of 1833 created the conditions that made such aspirations possible. By requiring every commune in France to have—or to have jointly with another commune—a boys' primary school and by requiring every commune to pay its schoolmaster a minimum annual salary from tax revenues, to collect student fees and remit them to the teacher, and to provide him with housing, it gave the schoolmaster the status of a civil servant. At the same time the government raised the standards of training and performance required of teachers, essential preliminaries to greater self-esteem and public recognition.[19]

Before the effects of the Guizot law were felt, schoolmasters had been near the bottom of village and town hierarchies of prestige and rewards. They were paid at about the rate of manual laborers. They were held in low esteem by villagers, who had little respect for education and thought of teachers as lazy, failures in other occupations, draft dodgers, and excessive drinkers. A primary inspector in a rural department of central France characterized village teachers, excepting some sons of *instituteurs*, as ex-soldiers, ex-seminarians, young men anxious to avoid army service but too poor to pay for release from an unlucky conscription number, and physically handicapped men unable to engage in manual labor. Many were itinerants even as teachers, remaining only a year or two in any one post before moving on. The occupation clearly had not attracted able persons, and the villagers' low opinion of them was probably justified. In the latter thirties and even later school inspectors in their annual reports frequently complained of the incompetence of the older teachers whom the Guizot law had allowed to continue in their positions.[20]

Teachers' pay before the Guizot law and in small communes even after its promulgation—and most communes were small—was usually so low that married men could not support their families on their earnings as teachers, so they had to take supplementary income from whatever casual employment they could find. They commonly worked as harvest hands, clerks in mayors' offices or courts, and, especially in rural communes, as assistants to the local priest. In the thirties they were perhaps as much lay clerics as teachers, and their association with the Church might give them more status in the village than did their positions as teachers. However, the teacher's role as lay cleric was a lowly one. He might assist the priest in the celebration of the Mass—some communes would not hire a teacher who did not have a good voice— but he also rang the church bells, swept out the church, cared for the cemetery, and might even be the gravedigger. The ringing of the church bells could be a time-consuming responsibility requiring the *instituteur's* presence at the church at least four times a day, more frequently on Sundays, and for frequent special occasions such as a marriage, a burial, or the visit of the bishop. One inspector reported that he often found classes unsupervised during school hours while the teacher attended to duties in the church. Priests insisted that teachers' clerical duties took precedence over their teaching responsibilities and ordinarily treated them as inferiors, even as servants, requiring that they wear their hair short and dress in cassock, surplice, and square hat when performing clerical duties and that they stay away from cafés and dances.[21]

By 1840, seven years after passage of the Guizot law, school inspectors were beginning to complain of a new breed of *instituteurs* who thought of themselves as virtually professional teachers and protested against being obliged to work at other jobs and to being subjected to the control of priests and ignorant villagers. The government itself had created this new type. The Guizot law not only provided for financial support of teachers in every commune but also required every department to maintain at least one normal school for the training of primary school teachers. The new teachers coming into the primary schools were consequently better educated than their typical predecessors. The Ministry of Public Instruction increased the difficulty of the examinations for certification to teach and made them more comprehensive, including both substance and teaching methods. The ministry also organized, at public expense, summer refresher courses and short courses during term time for incumbent teachers on teaching methods, reading, grammar, and arithmetic. In 1845 one-fifth of the teaching corps attended summer courses. In 1835 the ministry had created the office of primary school inspector in every department and charged the holders with making periodic visits to every school in the department to assure that the schools were receiving adequate financial support and to enforce higher standards of performance by teachers. Two years later it supplemented them with assistant inspectors in most of the departments. These measures tended to frighten away the indolent, the incompetent, and the misfits who had previously drifted into teaching and to attract abler and interested candidates. At the state normal schools they received academic and professional training, and the government's examinations and the requirements of the inspectors placed new value on academic training and knowledge—that is, on the kind of expertise that nurtures professional identity and pride.[22]

Annual reports of inspectors in 1839 and after include frequent complaints that graduates of the normal schools took excessive pride in being *normaliens*, that they had inordinate ambitions and wanted to be treated as town and village notables along with mayor and priest. The graduates refused to take jobs in small and impoverished rural communes where they would be poorly paid, obliged to find demeaning supplementary jobs and to serve as the priest's handyman. Many who did take such rural positions left them at the first opportunity for more lucrative employment. This practice became so frequent that the ministry resorted to the intimidating practice of reporting names of defectors to the Ministry of War—that is, in effect, withdrawing draft deferment—and to instituting court proceedings to recover the costs of normal school training from those teachers who taught less than their contracted time. Teachers protested against the interference of outsiders in their functions. They objected to priests' disputing methods and content of instruction. They asked that examining committees for teacher certification be composed of teachers, following the practice of the professions of law and medicine and the practice that architects, seeking professional status, had demanded in 1846. A group of *instituteurs* in the Department of the Oise urged in 1842 that only experienced teachers be appointed to the position of primary school inspector.[23]

One inspector complained that teachers who attended short courses organized by the ministry used the occasion to escape the requirements of high moral conduct imposed upon them in their villages. They got drunk or at least drank excessively, which may be seen as another protest against the extraordinary outside interference in their private lives and a statement that they deserved to be treated like men of some standing. Another inspector warned that short courses were being used by abler teachers to inculcate "exaggerated" and "regrettable" pretensions in the teachers who attended. These actions and the articulated protests were not universal or constant, but from the late thirties onward reports of them recur with sufficient frequency in the records of the ministry and the press to indicate that the new *instituteurs* were forming a different perception of themselves and were trying to get it recognized by the state and public.[24]

By the latter thirties they had made some progress toward their goal. The Guizot law prescribed a minimum annual salary of 200 francs, about the equivalent of the earnings of an agricultural laborer. Student fees and free housing raised earnings somewhat but not enough to provide an adequate living or to win the respect of a money-oriented public. By 1845, however, 80 percent of the teaching corps received 500 francs or more annually. Pay was highest in the more urbanized departments. In Paris an *instituteur's* annual salary was 1,800 francs as early as 1836. The school inspector of the Department of the Var, which included the city of Toulon, reported one salary of 2,400 francs in 1847, though only a third of the teachers in the department received more than the statutory minimum of 200 francs. The average teacher's salary in Limoges in 1846 was 514 francs, and in the nearby town of Bellac nearly 150 francs higher. Rural teachers were still ill rewarded, and the *instituteurs'* principal complaint was against low pay. The Minister of Public Instruction proposed in 1846 that the minimum salary be raised to 600 francs, which was then probably about 20 percent higher than the average annual earnings of an industrial worker. In 1848 the *instituteurs*, behaving like self-interested professionals, supported the Republic, whose leaders promised higher pay for teachers, greater independence from local authorities, and free, compulsory primary education. In 1850 the Falloux Law did establish the 600-franc minimum salary proposed four years earlier and placed restrictions on outside work by teachers. The requirements of the government and the ambitions and pretensions of *normaliens* had combined to set the teachers on the way to achieving an identity and a public respect based on expert knowledge and service.[25]

The same thread of search for identity based on expertise or on occupation can be found running through the concerns and actions of both employers and workers of nascent large-scale industry. In January 1840 forty-five ironmasters joined to form the Comité des intérêts métallurgiques with a permanent secretary and headquarters. Established originally to combat the threats of cuts in protective tariffs on iron, the organization dealt with that and with many other problems common to management of the industry. It was the precursor of the Comité des forges, formed in 1864 by four members of the committee of 1840 and others, which became the powerful voice of the French iron and steel industries in the twentieth century. Manufacturers of heavy machinery, including François Cavé and Adolphe Schneider, formed a similar organization in 1840, as did coal-mine operators and sugar manufacturers. Cotton manufacturers of the eastern departments had a few years earlier joined in the Comité d'industrie cottonnière, and in 1842 woolen and linen manufacturers formed a similar permanent organization. Here, as Bertrand Gille has observed, are the true roots of "le grand syndicalisme patronal."[26]

The corporate organization that under the *ancien régime* embraced craftsmen of every trade had been destroyed by the French Revolution, and in the 1830s combinations of workers to influence wage rates or working conditions were still forbidden by law. But long-established traditions and practices were not easily rooted out by statute. Workers "remained intensely collective", and under Napoleon and the Restoration they again joined together in organizations similar in many ways to those that they and their fathers had known before 1789—mutual aid societies and *compagnonnages*. Tolerated by the Napoleonic and Restoration governments as long as they did not openly defy the laws against coalitions, they continued into the July Monarchy, and in the aftermath of the Revolution of 1830 and the continuing economic depression of the early thirties some of them evolved into incipient labor unions, representing and pressing their members' demands for higher wages or improved working conditions. In 1833 the early "unions" seem to have been active in planning and coordinating a wave of strikes that swept across France. In 1834, however, this nascent movement was struck down by an alarmed government, and for the remainder of the decade the labor movement survived in the essentially pre-Revolutionary mutual aid societies and *compagnonnages*, which engaged only in their traditional activities. There is evidence, however, of growing class consciousness—and resentment, born of disillusionment with the outcome of the Revolution of 1830—continuing through the thirties and into the forties, among a small group of intellectually inclined workers in Paris and Lyon.[27]

In 1840, tens of thousands of workers, tried by unemployment, wage cuts, and rising food costs in the depression years since 1837, went on strike to support demands for higher wages and changes in working conditions. In Paris by early September almost all branches of the city's industry were affected. The number of strikers was estimated as high as 100,000, an unprecedented number, and they used novel tactics to press their cause. They intimidated nonstrikers, advertised their grievances by peaceful demonstrations in the street, and organized communal kitchens to feed strikers and their families; and different crafts joined in supporting one another's demands. The government, unable or unwilling to recognize the economic roots of the strikes and demonstrations, attributed them, first, to the distribution of money among workers by foreign enemies, and then to the plotting of republican secret societies. Its response was repression. It made massive arrests among Parisian workers, many of whom subsequently received long sentences to prison or enforced residence.[28]

Later in the 1840s the vanguard of French workers continued to turn away from the well-worn paths of the eighteenth century and to venture onto ways opened by accelerating industrial change. Coal miners in the Loire Valley, confronted with large capitalist companies controlling most of the mines in the basin and employing hundreds of workers, began to perceive that persistence in their traditional roles left them at the mercy of impersonal, absentee employers. In February 1840 workers of the Compagnie générale des mines de Rive-de-Gier and of one other company had struck to protest a cut in wages. In traditional fashion they mounted no demonstrations and caused no disorders, but simply presented their grievances to the mayor, the subprefect, and *procureur du Roi*—the local representatives of the state—and asked for their intervention with the companies. The miners won public sympathy locally but failed to influence the mine owners, and after about three weeks they returned to work at the lower wage rates. Four years later they took a new course.[29]

In late March 1844 the newly formed Compagnie générale

des mines de la Loire proposed to reduce wages, and in April the miners at Rive-de-Gier again walked off their jobs. Two thousand of them struck, and this time they did not depend on the friendly intervention of authorities. They intimidated the hesitant, dispatching bands of emissaries armed with sticks and pistols throughout the basin to induce others to join them. They tried to prevent the stoking of boilers providing steam power to the mines and to block the delivery of forage to pit animals. Troops and gendarmes were immediately brought to the scene, and on the fifth day of the strike a crowd of miners ambushed a detachment of troops who were escorting some arrested strikers to Saint-Etienne. Despite their resort to violence and intimidation the miners retained the sympathy of the community. They were aided by strike funds collected in Lyon, and the *procureur-général* in Lyon heard of collections being made in Clermont, Grenoble, and Toulouse. For three weeks they kept the mines shut down and for another three and a half weeks kept them partially closed.[30] The *procureur-général* in Lyon, who represented the Ministry of Justice in the district where the strike occurred, reported to the minister in the strike's eighth day, "The workers of Rive-de-Gier acted with a solidarity that surprised everyone. They proved that they were perfectly organized."[31] Two days later he was alarmed by the effectiveness of their organization. He wrote to the minister, "This coalition, in contrast with the preceding ones, has taken on the character of a well-organized revolt."[32]

After the third week without pay, however, miners began straggling back to the mines, and by mid-May all were at work save those employed in mines damaged by strikers and not yet operative. The *procureur-général* continued to emphasize the unprecedented organization of the strikes and warned that a new kind of labor conflict lay ahead. A historian who in 1936 studied the Rive-de-Gier strike found in it evidence of a quite new sense of solidarity among its participants. More clearly than in the strike of 1840 they identified themselves as workers with no interests in common with their employers and united in common hostility to them.[33]

A year later workers in the naval arsenal at Toulon gave a

comparable novel demonstration of worker solidarity. In March 1845 almost all 2,500 of the arsenal's work force, for the first time in history, struck in support of demands for higher wages and changes in working conditions. They stayed out for a week and returned only when the maritime prefect promised to seek satisfaction of their demands. The next year the government announced that wages would be increased. Maurice Agulhon, writing recently on this strike,[34] declared, "A new personage, the working class, with its own body and its own will, erupted on the local political scene."[35]

Paris for a few years after the strikes of 1840 had been relatively free of overt labor unrest, but in June 1845 open protest resumed when between four thousand and five thousand carpenters struck in support of demands for higher wages, a ten-hour day, and changes in working conditions. They were joined in August by sawyers, and in September masons struck some employers. The strikers were well organized, and they revived the tactics of their predecessors half a decade earlier—street demonstrations, intimidation, and distribution of food to their needy families. They also used the press to publicize their cause and set up a strike fund, using contributions from their members who had resumed working with cooperating employers. The government again resorted to repression. It arrested strike leaders on charges of violating the law against coalitions; brought to trial and convicted, most of them were sentenced to prison terms of two to four months. Nonetheless, these strikes, like those of 1840 in Paris, revealed a growing sense of worker solidarity and their developing ability to organize and act in defense of common interests.[36]

One of the reactions of the giant Compagnie générale des mines de la Loire to the strike of 1844 was to introduce free medical and hospital care for its workers and their families and to subsidize the price of bread. During the troubles of 1848 the company sought to share available work among all its employees, took over support of the employees' mutual aid fund, and considered the establishment of a pension plan. Other large concerns offered similar benefits in the 1840s. Many sponsored mutual aid societies, and some matched—

or partially matched—their workers' contributions to the societies' funds. A few large companies instituted pensions for
widows and orphaned children and for aged workers with
long terms of employment. Subsidized housing was another
benefit; some large mining and metallurgical companies maintained primary schools for workers' children; and a few firms
offered advanced technical training to the most able youths.
These innovations, intended primarily to assure retention of
skilled workers essential to profitable operations, may also
have reflected a dawning recognition that workers were not
simply a commodity that could be discarded at will, but persons of individual value. Whatever the employers' motives,
the very existence of these novel benefits surely contributed
to the new industrial workers' development of their own identity in a changing world.[37]

In a less highly developed coal basin than the Loire, the
Aubin basin in south-central France, the miners of the Compagnie anonyme de houillères et fonderies de l'Aveyron at
Decazeville were in the 1840s beginning to evolve a new sense
of their identity. For a long time coal in this basin had been
mined by peasants who pieced out meager earnings from farming by extracting coal from the ground and selling it on the
open market, much as they took grain or potatoes from the
soil and sold them in the local markets. After the formation
of the company in 1826, followed by its growth into the eighth
largest coal producer in France in 1840, they became parts of
a large organization, full-time miners producing for the company or for its contractors. Farming was relegated to a supplementary occupation. In the depression of the latter forties
they cooperated with the company in cutting production costs,
including wages, in the hope of keeping the mines open: this
suggests that they identified with the company, seeing themselves as coal miners, not peasants, and as parts of the organization. Not until two decades later, when they went on
strike, did they match the independence and solidarity of their
fellows in the Loire basin, but the process of change had clearly
begun earlier.[38]

In the 1840s in Toulouse a new type of labor organization

appeared, replacing the traditional *compagnonnages*. The *compagnonnages* were secret fraternities of bachelor journeymen in particular crafts, and they were fiercely independent of one another. Their rivalry frequently exploded into brawls in the streets of Toulouse. The new organizations of the forties embraced workers from many different occupations, expressing a new sense of broader worker solidarity. Moreover, by the close of the decade Toulousain workers had formed their own clubs, newspapers, and electoral organizations. Some of this activity may be attributed to the vogue of association nurtured and spread by the February Revolution of 1848 and to the reestablishment of universal male suffrage, but the revision in "social solidarities" in Toulouse had begun earlier with the replacement of the *compagnonnages*. A related development occurred in Lyon about the same time. In 1843 the Société de l'union, nominally a mutual aid society of locksmiths but distinguished by possession of a central office, on the initiative of one of its members, Pierre Moreau, set up a committee to revise its statutes into a form more suitable to changed conditions in the forties. The statutes drawn up by the committee were adopted in 1846, and they stand as a significant and novel effort by workers themselves to form a strong, well-defined organization.[39]

In two matters literally superficial but symbolically perhaps quite significant—dress and portraiture—one can discern efforts at establishing new self-images, efforts made possible by the technological advances and economic developments of the time. Chapter II mentioned the consumer revolution of the 1840s and attributed it largely to the appearance on the market of low-cost cotton textiles. Flowered cotton dresses then began to replace the traditional black woolen dresses kept for ten years, and more slowly cotton clothes replaced the rough canvas smocks and trousers of peasants. An observer in 1844 wrote of a "virtual invasion of tulle and cotton lace," as mechanically produced lace came on the market. Not unrelated was the arrival in Paris in 1845 of Charles Frederick Worth, a young Englishman who had worked for several years in a fashionable clothier's shop in London's West End. In Paris he soon found a place in a women's apparel shop on the rue de Richelieu, beginning a career in France that would in the 1860s, after the opening of his own shop on the rue de la Paix, establish Paris as the capital of women's high fashion. Worth introduced into the making of women's clothes the tailoring developed by English tailors in the production of men's clothing, and the House of Worth became the first modern couture house. It flourished on the affluence of industrializing France and on the eagerness of women to identify themselves as ladies of wealth and taste.[40]

The craze for photographic portraits that began in the 1840s is perhaps another expression of the search for identity. In 1839 the French government acquired the newly perfected Daguerre process for making photographs and placed it in the public domain. A crowd of portrait photographers quickly took it up, and they did not lack for customers. In 1847 500,000 photographic plates were reported sold in Paris, and in 1849 100,000 daguerreotype portraits were made in the city. The business soon spread to almost every city and town of France, and it proved very popular throughout the country. Portraits, hitherto painted by artists, had been the privilege of the rich. Photography brought them within the means of thousands and soon of tens of thousands. In the forties a photographic portrait could be had for as little as ten francs, and two decades later the price was down to two francs. The eager purchase of them was perhaps an expression of the desire of newly affluent bourgeois to acquire the kind of permanently recorded identity hitherto reserved for the very wealthy.[41]

Visions of a New Society

IN PARIS of the 1840s there emerged into wide public awareness two bodies of ideas that for a century or more profoundly influenced the thinking and actions of Frenchmen and of much of the rest of the world. Auguste Comte then completed his basic work on positivism, the multivolume *Cours de la philosophie positive*, and Emile Littré began his influential popularization of it. In the same decade socialist thought and writing flowered in Paris as at no other time or place. There in these years utopian socialism came to maturity, and the ideology moved on to "scientific" socialism; and in the same years the ideas of socialism first significantly penetrated the working class.

The sixth and final volume of Comte's *Cours* appeared in 1842. Littré had first encountered the work two years earlier, when a friend lent him a volume of it. Greatly impressed by Comte's ideas, he at once began to spread word of them among his friends and by writing articles for the Parisian press. In 1845 he published his first book-length popularization, *Analyse raisonnée du Cours de philosophie positive d'Auguste Comte*, a readable, 100-page condensation of Comte's six volumes. This book, together with Littré's subsequent publication on the subject, contributed powerfully to making positivism the secular faith of the bourgeois Third Republic.[1]

Concern over poverty and the other social and economic ills of post-Revolutionary society, from which nineteenth-century socialism emerged, was not new in the 1840s. Even concern for the new problem of concentrated urban poverty, associated with expanding industry and the development of an industrial working class dependent solely on uncertain wages, had earlier begun to exercise French intellectuals. Comte Claude de Saint-Simon started to write and publish on the social question in the teens of the century, and after his death in 1825 a small band of his followers formed an organization and a newspaper in order to continue to develop his critique of existing society and his proposals for its reform.[2] In the 1820s and 1830s Charles Fourier in a series of volumes and in pamphlets set forth his attacks on laissez-faire capitalism, competition, and private property and offered his prescription for peaceful transformation of society and economy. He proposed the establishment of cooperative communities, which he called *phalanges*, where work would be a pleasure and the needs of all would be abundantly satisfied. After Fourier's death in 1837 Victor Considerant took over the leadership of his followers, and they continued to develop and publicize his ideas.[3] A more radical current was running, too: Filippo Buonarroti's account of the Babeuf "Conspiracy of Equals" of 1796, *Conspiracy pour l'égalité dite Babeuf*, was published in France in 1830, and in the next decade it won over many young radicals to a conspiratorial, revolutionary socialism.[4]

However important as precursors these and some other writings of the teens, the twenties, and the thirties may now seem to be, they were few in number and scattered in time. Then in 1840 "suddenly and dramatically, the social question exploded, showering the nation with a torrent of ideas," as Christopher Johnson puts it (*Utopian Communism in France*, p. 66). In that single year appeared Louis Blanc's *Organisation du travail*, Etienne Cabet's *Voyage en Icarie*, Pierre-Joseph Proudhon's *Qu'est-ce que la propriété*, Pierre Leroux's *De l'humanité*, Jean-Jacques Pillot's *Ni châteaux, ni chaumières*, the first of George Sand's social novels, *Le Compagnon du Tour de France*, and the first numbers of the monthly journal *L'Atelier*, edited by workers and advocating the Christian socialism of Pierre Buchez. Similar journals had been launched in the early 1830s, but they had proved ephemeral; *L'Atelier* survived for a decade and succumbed only in the postrevolutionary reaction in 1850.[5]

The year 1840 was one that could well nurture such a harvest. A long ministerial crisis, starting in March 1839, had continued into 1840. The fright raised by the Society of Seasons revolt in May 1839 had made possible the creation of a makeshift ministry in that month, but not until the formation of Soult-Guizot ministry in October 1840 was the crisis really resolved and the monarchy led by a strong ministry. For eighteen months the *juste milieu* of Louis-Philippe appeared to be incapable of governing the country. The economy had been in depression since 1837, and the working class had been hard hit by unemployment, reductions in wages, and rising food costs.[6] In 1840 a wave of strikes spread across the country. By early September in Paris tens of thousands, perhaps as many as a hundred thousand, had left their jobs. The growing number of strikers and the growing boldness of demonstrators in the streets so alarmed the government that it hastily reinforced the garrison in Paris, put into effect the newly devised Gérard Plan for military occupation of key points of the capital to forestall insurrection, and arrested hundreds of workers.[7] At the same time France was poised on the brink of a potentially disastrous war. The crisis in the Middle East, where France alone among the great powers supported the pasha of Egypt against the Ottoman sultan, culminated in the summer of 1840 in an agreement among the other four powers. The French public, encouraged by the prime minister, Adolphe Thiers, and the Parisian press, excitedly viewed it as a renewal of the anti-French coalition of 1814, an affront to French honor, and a threat to the national security that must be countered by war. Thiers used the occasion to resubmit to the chambers a project for the fortification of Paris that many on the left saw not as a measure of defense against foreign enemies but as an instrument of repression and containment of revolutionary Parisians. It was taken as yet another indication of the monarchy's fear of the working class and of its insensitivity to their grievances.[8]

Among the many socialist publications of that troubled year three are of special interest because of their lasting influence: Cabet's *Voyage en Icarie*, Blanc's *Organisation du travail*, and Proudhon's *Qu'est-ce que la propriété?* Cabet's book was a novel in which he described in a popular and appealing manner the organization and operation of an ideal socialist, or, as he called it, communist society.[9] The book found many readers among literate workers, who had been little attracted to the turgid prose or complicated arguments of more intellectual socialist publications. They liked the promise of Icaria, where, Cabet assured them, "in return for moderate labor, the Community . . . guarantees education, the possibility of marriage, food, housing; in a word, everything."[10] Cabet followed up the advantage that the book won for him and for the cause of social reform with further writings, with the establishment of a monthly journal, *Le Populaire*, directed to working class readers, and with active recruiting of followers among workers. By the mid-forties the Icarian movement had tens of thousands of members throughout France, and "communism" had become both a household word and the favored social theory and ultimate goal of contemporary revolutionaries. When Karl Marx wrote in 1848 that "a specter is haunting Europe—the specter of communism," he was implicitly paying homage to Etienne Cabet. The dreams of a French Icaria were destroyed by revolution and reaction in 1848, but Cabet's influence on the working class and socialist movements was crucial and enduring.[11] Christopher Johnson, the author of the standard work on Cabet and the Icarians, comes to this conclusion:

> . . . no historian can ignore the fact that this man . . . formed the first large communist working class "party" in European history. . . . But beyond the question of communism itself, Cabet did something else; he told the workers to emerge from their shell of apathy, to be conscious of their importance in society, and to recognize that through their collective action change could be wrought.[12]

The influential impact of Blanc's *Organisation du travail* was due, in large part, to Blanc's ability to take the ideas of more original men and to present them to his readers in succinct, comprehensible, and appealing form. He was no theorist or philosopher but a practicing journalist, and he first published the *Organisation du travail* in June and August 1840 as a series of articles in his own monthly, the *Revue de progrès politique, social et littéraire.* In September he republished them, slightly expanded, as a book. It was scarcely more than a pamphlet—131 small pages (16mo) in the first edition—inexpensive, and easy to read. The original printing of three thousand copies sold out in two weeks and an additional three thousand were printed. In 1847 it was in its fifth edition, in 1850 in its ninth. It was probably the single most influential socialist publication of the decade. Most of the book was devoted to a telling indictment of the existing competitive, capitalist system, which, Blanc warned, would bring ruin on all classes and lead to catastrophic war between Britain and France. (The book was published during the war scare of 1840.) In his final, brief chapter Blanc proposed a simple, peaceful, and seemingly practical way to replace this ruinous system with a cooperative society through the establishment, with state aid, of worker cooperatives. These cooperatives, which he called "social workshops," would assure work and security for all, and because of their superior productivity, he argued, they would eventually spread over the whole economy, eliminating private enterprise. Key words and phrases out of Blanc's little book—"organization of labor," "association"—became part of the working-class vocabulary in the 1840s, catchwords that expressed their aspirations for social and economic change. In 1848 they appeared on workers' banners in the great street demonstrations in Paris. Blanc himself became a member of the provisional government in February 1848, and the National Workshops, public works projects set up to cope with the problem of massive unemployment, were in name an acknowledgment of the popular appeal of Blanc's proposal of social workshops in 1840.[13]

Proudhon's *Qu'est-ce que la propriété?* is a classic attack on the institution of private property. It won immediate attention by the author's shocking answer to the question posed in the title. "What is property?" it asked. In the very first pages he replied, "Property is theft."[14] But Proudhon was more than a phrasemaker. Marx eventually broke with him and called him an apologist for the petty bourgeoisie, but Marx

praised *Qu'est-ce que la propriété?* as the first "ruthless and
. . . scientific investigation of the basis of political economy,
private property." It was, he added, a "great scientific advance,
. . . which revolutionized political economy."[15]

The years immediately following 1840 were only slightly
less prolific of socialist writing than 1840 itself. In 1841 Louis
Blanc published the first volume of his *Histoire des dix ans,
1830–1840*, an exposure, he intended, of both capitalism and
monarchy. In its preface he presented an interpretation of the
preceding regime, the Bourbon Restoration, which was Marxist before Marx. In the same year Cabet established *Le Populaire*, which became the most widely circulated socialist
periodical of the decade.[16] In June 1842 Eugène Sue's influential social novel, *Les Mystères de Paris*, began to appear in
daily installments in the Parisian newspaper, *Le Journal des
débats*. It was immensely popular, and for the next sixteen
months the installments, though written to entertain and sympathetic with liberal, laissez-faire ideology, introduced bourgeois readers to the frightening underworld of poverty and
violence in Paris. The book was widely read in Germany and
Russia as well, and Marx took it seriously enough to devote
part of *Die heilige Familie*, written in Paris in 1844, to discussion of it.[17] Also in 1842 Constantin Pecqueur, an eclectic
socialist who had been successively a Saint-Simonian, a Christian socialist follower of Pierre Buchez, and a Fourierist, published his most important book, *Théorie nouvelle d'économie
sociale et politique*, which Marx and Friedrich Engels apparently used when they wrote the *Communist Manifesto* five
years later.[18] Victor Considerant's *Manifeste de la démocratie
pacifique*, another precursor of Marxist analysis, appeared in
1843. In the same year Flora Tristan, both a socialist moved
by her observations of the miseries of the working class and
a feminist outraged by the discrimination against women that
she both experienced and observed, published her *L'Union
ouvrière*. In it she proposed the creation of a powerful, universal union of all workers, skilled and unskilled, male and
female, to establish a socialist society and to institute equality
for women.[19]

In 1845 Victor Hugo began to write *Les Misérables*, then under the title of *Jean Tréjean ou les Misères*, probably the most powerful single publication of the century in awakening literate French men and women to awareness of the frightening problems of poverty, exploitation, and oppression. In his fortress prison at Ham in the Somme Valley of northern France Louis-Napoleon Bonaparte, the pretender to the imperial throne, followed socialist writings, and there in 1844 he published his *Extinction du pauperisme*. Apparently inspired by the writings of Fourier and Blanc, it added nothing original to socialist thought, but it did demonstrate the influence of socialist ideas beyond the circles of Parisian and Lyonnais workers and intellectuals. It also revealed an astute politician's judgment of the political importance of the social problem and his conviction that it could be turned to political advantage. Indeed, the Bonapartism of Louis-Napoleon may be seen as another product of the intellectual ferment of the 1840s.[20]

The flowering of socialist ideology in Paris in the 1840s was not solely the work of the French socialists gathered there in those years. Many foreigners living in the city had an important part in it. France and Britain were then the most advanced countries in the world, and, compared with other large nations, each of them enjoyed wide freedom of inquiry, discussion, and publication. Subjects of less advanced countries looked to them for inspiration and example, and France, and especially Paris, because of their rich revolutionary tradition, held a special attraction for European radicals. Arnold Ruge, German socialist and an associate of Karl Marx, in 1843 called Paris "the cradle of the new Europe, the great laboratory where world history is formed and has its first source. . . . Even our philosophy will be able to triumph only when proclaimed in Paris and impregnated with the French spirit."[21] Marx, after living in Paris and studying the French Revolution and French socialist writings for several months, declared, "The day of the German resurrection will be heralded by the crowing of the Gallic cock."[22] A leading liberal journal in Lombardy, *Rivista europea*, in 1843 volunteered a similar judgment: "The geographical position of France in the civilized world, its means of communication with so many different peoples, the universality of its idiom, its political importance, have rendered it to some degree the arbiter and leader of the intellectual movement of Europe."[23] For the Russian socialist, Alexander Herzen, who came to Paris in 1847, "The name of Paris was bound up with all the noblest enthusiasms of contemporary humanity. I entered it with reverence as one used to enter Jerusalem and Rome."[24]

Many foreign intellectuals and writers came to Paris to observe, to study, to discuss, and to write. The Germans Karl Marx, Arnold Ruge, Heinrich Heine, Moses Hess, Karl Vogt, Lorenz von Stein; the Russians Mikhail Bakunin, Ivor Golovine, Alexander Herzen, and Nicholas Turgenev; the Pole Adam Mickiewicz; and others less well known were living in Paris at one time or another during the early and middle 1840s. There Marx and Engels became friends and collaborators. In August 1844 Engels stopped in Paris on his way home from England, where he had been collecting materials for his book, *Die Lage der arbeitenden Klass in England*, to talk with Marx, with whom he had had a cold and inconsequential meeting in Germany two years earlier. This time, in Paris, they discovered that they had come to hold similar views on a number of philosophical and economic issues. Engels stayed on for ten days of discussion and of planning a jointly written pamphlet, a project that materialized in 1845 as *Die heilige Familie*. This effort marked the beginning of four decades of fruitful and influential collaboration.[25]

Paris was also a refuge for a growing number of German workers, about thirty thousand in 1841, double that number by 1848. Early in the decade the Prussian government became concerned by reports that this colony of Germans was being infected by dangerous French socialist ideas, and it commissioned a young political economist, Lorenz von Stein, to investigate. His report, entitled *Der Sozializmus und Kommunismus des heutiger Frankreich*, appeared in 1843. A detailed examination of contemporary socialist thought in France, it was intended to inform, not to convert, but its effect was to increase and intensify the interest of European intellectuals, especially in Germany, in the writings and activities of French socialists. Mikhail Bakunin recorded in his memoirs that through it he learned for the first time of the works and ideas of Fourier, Cabet, Blanc, Proudhon, and their French contemporaries.[26]

The young Marx apparently took little interest in von Stein's book or in the French socialists, but after the Prussian government, in January 1843, suppressed the *Rheinische Zeitung*, the newspaper that he had been editing in Cologne, he decided that the strict Prussian censorship precluded continuation of his career as a radical journalist in the Rhineland. He then agreed to join Arnold Ruge, whose new Hegelian journal, *Deutsche Jahrbücher*, had just been suppressed in Saxony, to publish in Paris a political review to be called the *Deutsche-französische Jahrbücher*. He and his bride moved to Paris in October 1843 and took lodgings on the rue Vaneau in the present *Septième Arrondissement*, an ironically bourgeois address for the founder of scientific socialism! Only a single number of the *Jahrbücher* was published—in February 1844— before it collapsed under the weight of financial troubles, editorial differences between Marx and Ruge, and lack of support from French socialists. At the time the sole number attracted little interest in France or Germany, but its two articles by Marx, "Zur Judenfrage" and "Zur Kritik der Hegelschen Rechts Philosophie: Einleitung," eventually gave it a place of some importance in the history of Marxist thought.[27]

Marx and Ruge—and Engels as well—also contributed articles to the weekly *Vorwärts*, published in Paris and, for a few months in 1844 under the editorship of Lazarus Bernays, a German journalist, the only uncensored German-language, radical paper in the world. In response to mounting pressure from Prussia, the French government late in 1844 suppressed *Vorwärts* and ordered Bernays, Ruge, and Marx out of the country. Bernays and Ruge were in fact allowed to remain, and Marx might have, had he wished, but early in February he quietly left for Brussels, apparently satisfied that he had reaped what benefits he could from life and study in Paris.[28]

The influence of Marx's Parisian sojourn on the evolution of his thought and mission was profound. He arrived a young Hegelian philosopher; he left a social theorist. "The years 1843–45 are the most decisive in his life," wrote Isaiah Berlin: "in Paris he underwent his final intellectual transformation. At the end of it he had arrived at a clear position personally and politically: the remainder of his life was devoted to its development and practical realization."[29]

Once settled in Paris in 1843 Marx embarked on an intensive course of reading, first on the French Revolution, concentrating on its most radical stage under the National Convention, then in the French and English classical economists, and finally in French social reformers and theorists. He met and talked with Louis Blanc, P.-J. Proudhon, Pierre Leroux, and Mikhail Bakunin and mixed with the German radicals in Paris. He attended meetings of both French and German working-class groups, and in the Continent's largest city he saw for himself the poverty, misery, and degradation of a large urban proletariat, a revelation to a young man whose experience until then had been confined to the bucolic towns of the Rhineland and the university quarter of Berlin. From these encounters and from his readings and discussions in Paris he acquired a new appreciation of social problems. From them, too, came his conception of the proletariat as the revolutionary class that would liberate society in the final stage of the class struggle. The first classic exposition of Marxist "scientific" socialism in the *Communist Manifesto*, published early in 1848, was in essence a combination of Hegelian philosophy and Marx's perception of the role of the Parisian proletariat.[30]

During his stay in Paris Marx wrote—or completed—only three manuscripts, not including some short articles for *Vorwärts*. Though not among his most important works, they are significant in the evolution of his thinking. The first, "Zur Kritik der Hegelschen Rechts Philosophie: Einleitung," published in the single number of the *Deutsche-französische Jahrbücher*, presented for the first time his conception of the proletariat as the revolutionary class. The second, *Die heilige Familie*, Marx's first collaborative work with Engels, published in 1845, was an attack on the German Hegelians, which reflected his new understanding of French history and French social theory. It included the initial public exposition of some of the themes of his materialist conception of history. The third Parisian work, "Oekonomisch philosophische Manuskript aus dem Jahre 1844," sometimes called "The 1844 Manuscripts," is another landmark in the development of Marx's materialist interpretation of history. It was not published until 1932, but much of its essence was incorporated into *Das Kapital*, and it has been described as the first rough draft of that enormously influential book—a rather grand judgment perhaps for a manuscript that, when finally printed, came to only two hundred pages.[31]

While France in the 1840s was shaping the form of the socialism that would in a few decades shake Europe and the world, it was also nurturing social concern and reflection at the opposite end of the political spectrum—among the Catholic clergy and among bourgeois industrialists. This concern had limited practical consequences in the forties, but in time it contributed to the formation of policies and actions that tempered the impact of revolutionary socialism.

Most of the French clergy, still recruited from the aristocracy, the bourgeoisie, and the peasantry, knew little of the urban industrial working class, and those social disorders that they could not fail to notice they ordinarily attributed to "false teaching." Traditional charity remained their solution to undeniable poverty and misery. But a few bishops in industrial cities were moved to denounce not only the inhuman working conditions that they observed in their dioceses but also the laissez-faire system that produced such conditions and allowed them to continue. Archbishop Affre of Paris in his Easter sermon of 1843—half a century before Leo XIII's *Rerum novarum*—denounced industrial capitalism and free enterprise unrestrained by law or morality and the subjugation of workers to "the new slavery of pauperism." Cardinal Bonald of Lyon in 1842 and 1845 condemned employers for usurping the fruits of their workers' labor. In the northern textile region the archbishop of Cambrai in 1845 deplored the economic system that led to the "exploitation of man by man," and in 1846 he insisted that an adequate wage was one of the "rights" of man. The bishops of Rouen and Bordeaux openly expressed similar sentiments. The majority of the episcopate, however, remained silent, probably not even aware of the new social problem and its ominous implications for the Church.[32]

Some industrialists, realizing that a stable and economically secure labor force was a valuable economic asset, voluntarily took steps to improve the condition of their workers. The most common measures were provision of low-cost or even free housing, subsidizing the cost of food and other necessities, pensions, sickness benefits, and schools for workers' children. Instances of such paternalistic practices can be found as early as the teens of the century, but in the 1840s the practice became common, especially among larger firms. Peter Stearns estimates that more than two-thirds of the 650 firms employing more than fifty workers had such programs by 1848. He warns, however, that only a minority of workers were affected, that in many cases they were assessed fees to pay for benefits, and the services were often of marginal quality. On the other hand, some of the very largest companies did even more for their workers. Japy Frères et Cie., a large textile enterprise in Alsace, in 1842 opened a library and a kindergarten and two years later established a company bakery to serve its employees. Schneider at Le Creusot gave the commune a school building and land for a new church, and contributed substantially to the church's construction. The Compagnie générale des Mines de la Loire, after the strike at Rive-de-Gier in 1844, established free medical services for its workers and their families, and in 1846 it was committing about fifty francs annually per employee to fringe benefits. Already in gestation were less paternalistic and more advanced labor policies. In 1847 Emile Martin, the founder of the iron works at Fourchambault, the nation's third largest iron producer, proposed not only the introduction of a broad range of benefits for the company's workers but also that they share in the company's profits.[33]

By that year a growing number of educated Frenchmen had become aware of the problems of poverty and insecurity and of the paradox of growing national wealth accompanied by impoverishment of a large part of the population. Awareness had nurtured concern, and the problems had been analyzed by scores of writers and discussed in many parliamentary and academy debates; remedies, from the partial to the sweeping, had been proposed, and experiments with some of the more modest remedies had begun. These years may with reason be seen as France's social coming of age in the new economic world of the mid-nineteenth century.

New Departures in the Arts

IN 1986 the Fifth Republic will open a new museum of nine-teenth-century art, the Musée d'Orsay in the former Gare d'Orsay on the Left Bank. The Louvre's collection of "nine-teenth-century" French paintings will be moved across the river to the new galleries, leaving those of earlier centuries on the Right Bank. The date chosen as the break between all the preceding centuries of French painting and the new age of the nineteenth century is not at the chronological turn of the century but in the 1840s. The initial year of the Musée d'Or-say's collection will be 1848—and with good reason. In the forties came an artistic and literary flowering in France that matched the contemporaneous blossoming of socialist ideol-ogy. Young men then emerging on the Parisian scene moved onto untried paths and turned architecture, painting, fiction, and poetry in new directions. Their influence was powerfully felt in France for half a century and more. No other decade of the nineteenth century was so seminal in so many of the arts.

The critical economic and social upheavals that stimulated the burgeoning socialist theorizing of the forties contributed to these developments, too, even directly in the case of ar-chitecture, where the core innovation was the use of new materials, especially iron. Discerning young artists in France of the 1840s, perhaps like their counterparts in Vienna before 1914, saw that the world of their youth was doomed. France was beginning a social revolution; industrialization and the railroads would inevitably destroy the old agrarian, rural, hierarchical society. They were moved to find new modes of expression, and their art reflected both their interests in the emerging new world and their hopes and anxieties.

In the summer of 1843 ground was broken for the newly

authorized building of the Biliothèque Sainte-Geneviève in Paris. Nearly five years earlier the architect Henri Labrouste had been commissioned to design the building, his first major commission. His preliminary plans were ready in December 1839, but not until early 1843 did the Conseil des bâtiments civils give it final approval. Labrouste, forty-two years old in 1843, had been trained in the Ecole des beaux-arts in the 1820s and in Rome, but he became more interested in the structural aspects of architecture than in pure forms, which put him at odds with the traditionalists who dominated architecture in the Ecole des beaux-arts. Returning to Paris in 1830 he opened his own studio and quickly won a place as a leader of antiestablishment young architects. He advocated a return to functional rationalism, the influence of which had been diminishing among French architects of the time.[1] "In architecture," he wrote in November 1830, "form must always be appropriate to the function for which it is intended,"[2] an early expression of the modernists' dictum, "Form follows function."

The new Bibliothèque Sainte-Geneviève was to be the first library in France open to readers in the evening, and, though gas lamps would provide artificial illumination, Labrouste sought to make maximum use of natural light. Applying his interest in new, industrially produced building materials he built a neo-Renaissance stone shell around a light iron frame. The floor of the reading room, which occupied the entire second story, rested on iron girders, and slender iron columns supported the openwork iron arches of the barrel vaults that formed the ceiling. Continuous arcaded windows on all four sides and the delicate iron framing gave the room an extraordinarily light and open appearance. All of the iron elements in the building had been used earlier by architects and builders, for example, in bridges across the Seine, in the roof of the Halle aux Blés in Paris, and in Chartres Cathedral, replacing the wooden framework of the roof destroyed by fire in 1836. Labrouste's innovations in the Bibliothèque Sainte-Geneviève were, first, to build an entire major public building, from foundation to roof, on an iron frame, and second, to expose

Salle de lecture de la bibliothèque Sainte-Geneviève.

Fig. 1. Bibliothèque Sainte-Geneviève, Reading Room (Bibliothèque nationale, Paris)

the iron framing frankly and use it decoratively. In this structure, which still serves as a library of the University of Paris, Labrouste gave France its first lesson in the combined practical and aesthetic uses of iron in construction. It was a lesson and an example made possible at that time by recent technological advances and by the productive capacities of the more advanced French iron manufacturers, such as Schneider, which had installed its first steam hammer in 1839 and in 1840 had begun to supply iron girders to bridge builders.[3]

The building of the Bibliothèque Sainte-Geneviève, completed in 1850, marked the opening of a new age of construction, an age that brought to Paris a number of its great landmarks—the pavilions of the central markets, the train sheds of the new railway stations, and the Bibliothèque nationale's main reading room, designed by Labrouste himself. Later Parisian landmarks owing a debt to the Bibliothèque Sainte-Geneviève are the interior structures of the Grand Palais and the Petit Palais and, most renowned of all, the Eiffel Tower. Though initially used only in public or commercial buildings, iron during the Second Empire increasingly replaced wood for the framing of private houses in Paris, and structural elements for buildings became a specialty of the iron industry in the capital.[4]

Another architect who emerged on the French scene in the early 1840s, Eugène Viollet-le-Duc, exerted a profound influence on architecture, on architectural theory, and on popular tastes in the latter decades of the nineteenth century and in the twentieth century. Sir John Summerson, writing of him in 1949, declared, "He is the last great theorist in the world of architecture, and the modern architect still leans heavily on the truths which he expounded."[5]

Outside architectural circles, however, Viollet is now remembered as the great restorer of Gothic monuments in France. He received his first assignment to a restoration project in 1840 when, owing to the influence of Prosper Mérimée, then inspecteur générale des monuments historiques, he was appointed architect of the Church of the Madeleine at Vézelay. In the same year he was named an assisting architect on the restoration of the Sainte-Chapelle in Paris, and between 1842 and 1845 he received twelve additional commissions for restorations, including the Cathedral of Notre Dame in Paris and the Church of Saint-Sernin in Toulouse. Though active as theorist, teacher, writer, and practicing architect, he continued his work on restorations through the next three decades. Among his later projects were the cathedrals of Amiens and Reims, and Abbey Church of Saint-Denis, the ancient city of Carcassonne, and the Château de Pierrefonds. His example, his teaching, and his writings, beginning in 1844 with articles in the *Annales archéologiques*, were the principal architectural sources of the Gothic revival in France, and at Notre Dame, from 1844 to 1864, he trained the architects and craftsmen who gave the revival concrete expression in scores of restorations and new structures across the face of France.[6]

Viollet-le-Duc's own restorations have had enduring influence among the general public. The Sainte-Chapelle and Notre Dame of Paris, as restored by Viollet, probably more than any other structures shaped the late-nineteenth- and twentieth-century popular conceptions of medieval ecclesiastical architecture. Carcassonne became in the popular mind the quintessential medieval city and Pierrefonds the typical medieval castle. As late as 1967 the *Petit Larousse* still used a drawing of Pierrefonds as its example of a *château fort*.[7] Even now we see the Middle Ages to some extent through the eyes of this man of the 1840s. Many critics charge that it is a mistaken perception and that Viollet's restorations were more imaginative than historically authentic, but his enduring influence is undeniable.

Viollet-le-Duc was more than a restorer. Although he admired medieval architecture and believed that it had many lessons for the present, he did not hold that architecture should be exclusively or uncritically historical in form. Like Labrouste, he was a rebel against the architectural establishment based on the Ecole des beaux-arts and the Académie des beaux-arts. As a young man he had rejected his family's advice that he enroll in the Ecole des beaux-arts, and he received his training as an architect in the workshops of practicing architects. He valued Labrouste's rationalism and his pioneering work with iron, and in his own writing, teaching, and practice he was an influential advocate of ideas that Labrouste first applied in his design of the Bibliothèque Saint-Geneviève— notably the honest and imaginative use of new materials made available by developing industry. Viollet urged the use of iron even for externally visible framing, as Victor Baltard had done in the pavilions of the central markets in the fifties and sixties. The idea was embodied in a number of industrial and commercial buildings erected in Paris in the 1890s, and visitors to the city today find a recent example in the Pompidou Center, completed in 1977. Viollet advocated the employment of iron in decoration, and his detailed and often beautiful drawings were a source of inspiration for the *art nouveau* ironwork of the 1890s and the early twentieth century, some of which still ornaments Paris. *Art nouveau* architecture, which gave Paris a number of distinctive buildings—the Castel Béranger and the interior of the Au Printemps department store among others—had roots in the work and writings of Viollet-le-Duc. His influence carried into the twentieth century in another way, too. His student and disciple, Anatole de Baudot, following Viollet's advice on the use of new materials and applying principles of Gothic skeletal construction, around the turn of the century built the first reinforced concrete church in France, the Church of Saint-Jean de Montmartre.[8] August Perret, whose reinforced-concrete apartment block at 21*bis* rue Franklin, built in 1903, has been said to mark "the birth of modern architecture in Paris"[9] and who became one of the most prestigious French architects of the twentieth century, always maintained that he was both inspired and guided by Viollet's ideas. "Viollet-le-Duc was my real master," he declared.[10]

On the centenary of his death Viollet-le-Duc became the first architect to be honored by a one-man show in the national galleries of France.[11] A Parisian art critic, commenting on the show, held in the Grand Palais in 1980, called him "the only figure of world stature whom France has given to world architecture."[12]

Another rebel architect began the influential years of his long career in the same seminal forties. In 1840 César Daly founded the *Revue général de l'architecture et des travaux publiques* and for the next forty-nine years was its editor. The *Revue*, France's first illustrated architectural journal, was for half a century the country's most important architectural magazine. Daly, who had been trained both as an engineer—at the Ecole polytechnique of Douai—and as an architect—in Jacques Duban's *atelier* and at the Ecole des beaux-arts—personified the merger of traditional and contemporary elements of the new architecture. He made the *Revue* a journal for practicing architects but also used it to develop and to proselytize an architecture appropriate to the contemporary scientific and industrial age. In the 1830s, through his friendship with Victor Considerant, he had become a Fourierist, and he had been impressed by Fourier's belief that the design of the *phalanstère*, the great central residence building of his *phalange*, would have a crucial part in achieving the harmonious cooperative society that he foresaw. Although in the *Revue* Daly never openly mentioned his Fourierist connection, its pages reflected and, indirectly at least, espoused the idea that architecture has the power "to effect social good," that, properly applied, it can transform man and society. It was an idea that became an important component of the modernist movement in the 1920s.[13]

The decade of the forties was as important for painting as it was for architecture. In 1840 the young Gustave Courbet, age twenty-one, came to Paris from Franche-Comté, nominally to study law in preparation for taking his place in the respectable society of his bourgeois parents but actually to pursue his calling as an artist. The next few years were critically formative in the career of this man, who, probably more than any other, set French and much of western painting in the mid-nineteenth century on a new course. He broke decisively with the values of his Classical predecessors, and though at first—in the early narcissistic self-portraits, for example—he was influenced by Romantic conceptions of art, he soon turned in new directions and became the first great practitioner and advocate of realism.[14] Others were influential in this change, but, in the words of a recent critic, "the decisive blow was struck by Courbet. Modern art . . . was founded."[15]

In the second quarter of the nineteenth century the accepted subjects of painting, promulgated and sustained by the Ecole des beaux-arts and generally sanctioned by the Académie des beaux-arts and by the taste of many (though by no means all) collectors, were episodes from classical mythology, great historical events, and portraits of the wealthy and the well born (who alone could afford them). Exceptions to the prevailing taste can be found among early acquisitions of some of the great collectors of mid-century and in the bountiful production of French painters of the time. For example, small genre paintings that taught a moral lesson or told a quaint anecdote enjoyed some popularity, but the common man and episodes from daily life were not ordinarily considered appropriate subjects. Nonetheless, a waxing current of French thought did exalt the common man. The French Revolution had temporarily given him political importance, and the republican movement kept that tradition alive after 1815. The socialists of the thirties and forties had as their ultimate goal social justice and economic security for every man and, with some of them at least, for every woman. Some prescient contemporaries foresaw, too, that mounting productivity of industry would inevitably make industry dependent on a mass market, giving ordinary people an unprecedented importance as consumers. The establishment of the early *magasins de nouveautés* in Paris in the 1840s and their multiplication and expansion as department stores in the succeeding decades mark the democratization of the retail market. Popular histories of the French Revolution that began to appear in the 1840s—Louis Blanc's *Histoire de la Révolution française* (1847–1852), Jules Michelet's *Histoire de la Révolution française* (1847–1853), and Alphonse de Lamartine's *Histoire des Girondins* (1847–1848)—extolled the role of the common man, and Michelet's *Le Peuple*, published in 1846, was a paean to the French people. George Sand, Victor Hugo, and Eugène Sue found them worthy subjects of their novels. Félix Pyat and other "socialist dramatists" drew on them for characters in the thriving "people's theater." Young painters in Paris could scarcely have escaped the influence of ideas in such common currency.[16]

Courbet, as he declared a quarter of a century later, was a Fourierist when he came to Paris in 1840, and he read there the works of at least one other French socialist, P.-J. Proudhon, whose wide-ranging interests included art and its place in society. Proudhon almost certainly contributed to the shaping of Courbet's views on art, but his demonstrable influence came only in the late forties and in the fifties, when the two men became close friends. In Paris Courbet early became acquainted with Charles Baudelaire, art critic as well as poet, and his conception of the artist's role was surely influenced by Baudelaire's ideas. In his book, *Salon de 1846*, Baudelaire called on painters to "celebrate the heroism of modern life," and the contemporary author Champfleury (Jules Husson), a member of Courbet's and Baudelaire's circle in Paris in the forties, judged Courbet's great *Burial at Ornans* (first exhibited in 1851) to be a direct response to Baudelaire's appeal, even though Baudelaire was at the time he wrote thinking about Parisian subjects.[17]

Through the first half of the 1840s Courbet's paintings were conventional, offering no offense to accepted tastes, but in 1846 and 1847 he began to draw on popular imagery in Paris. The revolution in the capital the next year at first annoyed and repelled him, then puzzled him, and he began to look to the countryside for his subjects. In September 1849 he left Paris and for several months lived again in his native Franche-Comté.[18] Much of rural France, including the Franche-Comté, was then torn by bitter political conflict between radical republicans and conservative *notables* vying for the votes of the newly enfranchised peasantry. Courbet, in this environment, became increasingly interested in politics and increasingly sympathetic with the common man, and that interest and concern surely reinforced Baudelaire's advice of 1846. Within the year after Courbet's return to Ornans appeared the first great harvest of the formative years in Paris and of new concerns born of his recent experience—three paintings that T. J. Clark has called "the great trilogy of Realism": *Peasants of Flagey Returning from the Fair*, *The Stonebreakers*, and *Burial at Ornans*.[19] "They were truly daring and revolutionary," writes Linda Nochlin, the American authority on Courbet, "not merely in their subjects but . . . in their stylistic character."[20]

The *Burial at Ornans* is probably the most acclaimed of the three, and it may be taken as representative of the new school of painting that Courbet was creating. The subject is a common scene in the life of his native village. It tells no story, teaches no lesson. The people depicted in it are the village bourgeoisie, including members of his own family,

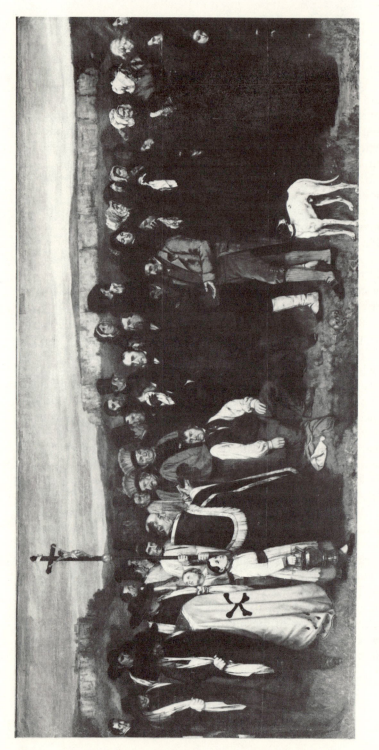

Fig. 2. Gustave Courbet, *Burial at Ornans* (Documentation photographique de la Réunion des musées nationaux, Paris)

most of them not long risen from the peasantry. He painted them not as ideal types but as they actually appeared, with all their warts and wrinkles and odd attire. Moreover, Courbet painted the scene not in the modest dimensions of genre paintings of the time but on a grand scale hitherto reserved for subjects drawn from antiquity or history. The painting, now hanging in the Louvre, measures about ten feet by twenty-two feet. Exhibited in the Salon of 1850 in Paris it raised a storm of protest among bourgeois viewers but appealed especially to provincial viewers, for in reproducing a rural life familiar to them it depicted something they could readily understand.[21]

In 1855 Courbet submitted fourteen of his paintings for exhibition at the Universal Exposition to be held in Paris that year. The jury accepted eleven of them but rejected three, including the *Burial at Ornans*. The indignant Courbet left the eleven in the official show but with financial help from friends erected a building on the avenue Montaigne near the exposition grounds and there mounted an exhibition of forty of his paintings, including *Burial at Ornans*, and four drawings. He christened the show *Réalisme*, and as a preface to the catalog he wrote a manifesto entitled "Le Réalisme," a proclamation of his artistic principles.[22] "To translate the customs, the ideas, the aspect of my time as I see them, . . ." he wrote, "in a word, to make art living, that is my object."[23] The show attracted few viewers, but with it "the great age of the avant garde" was launched.[24] For nearly a century thereafter—until World War II and the German occupation—Paris was the unchallenged capital of modern art. And in 1913 Guillaume Apollinaire, poet and champion of modern painting in pre-World War I France, wrote, "Courbet is the father of the new painters."[25]

To effect his break with artistic convention Courbet chose subjects from rural and village life, but the emerging urban world of industry and technology also contributed to the birth of "the great age of the avant garde."[26] Charles Baudelaire in his *Salon de 1846* deplored contemporary painters' neglect of the "beauty of circumstance." "Paris life," he declared, "is prolific in poetic and marvelous subjects."[27] His appeal bore fruit a decade and a half later in the work of Edouard Manet and his contemporaries. They were inspired by Napoleon III's rebuilding of Paris, begun in the 1850s, and by Baudelaire's advice first enunciated in 1846 and reiterated when he and Manet were friends in the early sixties. With Manet and the impressionists the city became "one of the most characteristic themes of modern art."[28]

Railway locomotives, trains, and stations, emerging as part of the common experiences in the 1840s, were dramatic expressions of a new age of speed and movement, and they soon began to find a place in contemporary literature and art. Alfred de Vigny in his Romantic poem, "La Maison du ber-ger," published in 1844 in the *Revue des deux mondes*, wrote of railroads with a mixture of admiration and dismay.[29] They had conquered time and space but were also diminishing man's capacity for experience. Yet he could write about them in poetic language:

> Que Dieu guide à son but la vapeur foudroyante
> Sur le fer des chemins qui traversent les monts,
> Qu'un Ange soit debout sur sa forge bruyante,
> Quand elle va sous terre ou fait trembler les ponts,
> Et de ses dents de fer dévorant ses chaudières,
> Transperce les cités et saute les rivières,
> Plus vite que le cerf dans l'ardeur des ses bonds![30]

In 1848 Théophile Gautier argued that contemporary art could achieve "a modern kind of beauty" with such subjects as locomotives, steamboats, and factory chimneys. Already, half a decade earlier, Honoré Daumier had made a series of lithographs of railroads, and Horace Vernet, heretofore conventional in his choice of subjects, in the mid-forties painted a locomotive, a steamboat, and factory chimneys into his ceiling paintings in the Salon de la Paix of the Palais Bourbon. Daumier, about the same time that he was doing his railway lithographs, produced a series of lithographs that he called *Histoire ancienne*, a biting satire on conventional paintings of Greek and Roman gods and heroes. He returned many times to railroads, doing oils, watercolors, and drawings of railway-carriage interiors and station scenes. A much-prized example is his *Third-class Railway Carriage* now in the Metropolitan Museum of Art in New York, valued as an authentic representation of train travel in the 1850s and as a work of art. Thomas Couture, Manet's teacher, won first prize in the Salon of 1847 with an enormous historical painting, *Romans of the Decadence*. Twenty years later he was telling his students that the railroad locomotive—a "grandiose and modern chariot"—and its drivers were fitting subjects for paintings. Manet himself became interested in railways and an admirer of railway engineers and firemen as modern heroes, and one of his most acclaimed paintings is *The Railroad* (1873). Claude Monet painted *The Train in the Country* in 1870–1871, and the paintings of his Argenteuil period, 1871–1878, include one of the railroad bridge of Argenteuil with passing train, *Train in the Snow*, and *The Train*. In the third impressionist show (1877) he exhibited seven canvases of the Gare Saint-Lazare in Paris.[31]

One cannot affirm with certainty that it was the railways that made possible the Parisians' "day in the country," an important element of the lives of thousands of them in the latter half of the nineteenth century, but they did make it easy and inexpensive and, for artists, opened up a new world of subjects. The impressionists' luminous paintings of scenes around the Ile-de-France remind us of this important interaction of technology and art. The railways did certainly bring the beaches of Normandy and the Channel coast into artists' ken and onto their canvases. The western and northern railways made these parts of France easily accessible to Parisians, and in the sixties the fashionable resorts that were developed there—Trouville, Deauville, Boulogne-sur-Mer—became popular subjects for painters. Manet painted scenes at Boulogne. Eugène Boudin, earlier a rural landscape painter, is now remembered chiefly as the painter of these seaside resorts and their wealthy vacationers.[32]

Yet another technological development of this age had important influence on French painting. As mentioned in Chapter IV, Daguerre's photographic process in December 1839 became freely available to the public, and in the next few months popular demand for his manual on its use required eight printings. Photographic portraits were increasingly popular in the forties, and books of photographs (actually engravings made from photographs, the process of reproducing photographs in print being still some decades in the future) of landscapes and architectural monuments found a ready market. For some artists photographs came to be a useful tool. Portrait painters used them in place of sketches. Manet worked from photographs for figures in his *Execution of the Emperor Maximilian*, and evidence suggests that Courbet used photographs for many of his paintings. But photography had more profound influences, and probably few artists of the time were wholly immune to them. At one extreme it led a part of the public to prize the accuracy of photographic representation and to expect similar accuracy in painting. Photographic standards, whether accepted or spurned, surely influenced the public's response to paintings of Ernest Meissonier (*The Barricade* [1848] and *1814: The Campaign of France* are examples). To more sophisticated viewers photographs made clear the difference between mechanical reproduction and artistic representation, and avant-garde artists and some discerning patrons spurned photographic realism. The painters of the latter nineteenth century who made the enduring reputations were not photographers with brush and palette but *impressionists*.[33]

One of the impressionists' most favored subjects—the *café-concert*, a café offering popular entertainment—appeared in Paris around 1840, first on the Champs Elysées and then along the boulevards. By the final quarter of the century it had become an established part of Parisian life. Manet's *A Bar at the Folies-Bergère* and *At the Café-concert* (1878), and Edgar Degas' *Café-concert* (1876–1877) and *The Café-concert of the Ambassadors* (1876–1877) have given it a secure place in the artistic heritage of France.[34]

In literature two giants appeared on the Parisian scene in the 1840s, Gustave Flaubert and Charles Baudelaire. In their writings both reflected a modern literary alienation that took shape under the July Monarchy. Traditional aristocratic literary sponsorship had disappeared, and writers had become dependent on the demands of an uncertain marketplace. At the same time growing industry and commerce were completing the political and cultural predominance of the bourgeoisie.[35] In the eyes of many artistic souls taste was being corrupted, the ugly was "developed to gigantic proportions," and mankind was being "moronized." "Speaking of industry," Flaubert asked a correspondent in 1853, "have you sometimes thought of the quantity of stupid professions it begets, and the vast amount of stupidity that must inevitably accrue from them over the years?"[36]

In the forties authors' perceptions of their function was changing. Romantic writers of the preceding decades, typified by Victor Hugo, saw themselves as prophets, as visionaries with special access to the truth, which they were able to reveal to readers. Balzac, writing the preface to *La Comédie humaine* in 1842, insisted that an author is properly not a visionary but a reporter, a "secretary." His own purpose, he said, was to depict the life he observed around him. "French society was going to be the historian; I had but to be the secretary."[37] In the very next year the catastrophic critical and popular failure of Hugo's Romantic drama of medieval lords of the Rhineland, *Les Burgraves*, seemed to place a bold exclamation point after Balzac's declaration. His counsel became part of the intellectual climate of Paris in the forties, and it contributed to shaping the ideas and eventually the writing of young literary figures then emerging.[38] Best-known among them is Gustave Flaubert.

Flaubert, aged twenty, came to Paris early in 1842 to study law. His father, a successful physician in Rouen, regarded medicine as the highest calling, but Gustave he judged to be unfit for medical training, and the son began his study of law feeling that he had been relegated to an inferior profession. The experience of law school only enhanced his distaste for the subject, and his interests and energies turned increasingly to literature, the passion of his school days in Rouen. The list of his writings in the 1830s compiled by Flaubert scholars includes some four score titles, none of them published except in obscure local journals. What the eminent Flaubertiste Jean Bruneau regarded as his juvenile period ended in 1842 with his completion of *Novembre*, a hundred-page Romantic novella.[39]

The next five years were decisive in shaping his literary talent and his subsequent contribution to French letters. Then his ideas of the world and of art were definitively fixed and his writing techniques perfected. He was leading the life of a not very diligent Parisian student during those years, broken by a serious illness, occasional sojourns in Normandy, and one trip to Italy. He read widely in the Greek and Latin classics, in French literature from the sixteenth century to his own time, and in the works of Shakespeare, Byron, Goethe, and Schiller. Between 1843 and 1845 he wrote his first novel, the first *Education sentimentale*, unpublished in his lifetime and not to be confused with the second and well-known *Education sentimentale*, published in 1869.[40]

Flaubert's experience after 1845—notably in the Revolution of 1848—and his reflection on it did, of course, influence the substance of his later work, but with the completion of the earlier *Education sentimentale*, Bruneau concludes, his formation as a novelist was complete; he was then prepared to write his great works of fiction, *Madame Bovary*, published in 1857, and the *Education sentimentale* of 1869. When he began *Madame Bovary*, a book that shaped both the form and the substance of the French novel for generations to come, he had largely mastered his techniques of narration, dialogue, description, and analysis. The manuscript novels written in his youth were narrative in form, but the narrative of the *Education* was more complex. In this book, too, he began to use dialogue as a subtle means of both narration and analysis; fully one-sixth of the text is given over to dialogue. His descriptions had become shorter, and they were distributed throughout the book and skillfully integrated into the text. In *Novembre* he had attempted some character analysis, but the *Education sentimentale* revealed for the first time his interest, so prominent in *Madame Bovary*, in analyzing the psychology of his characters. In the *Education*, too, one finds his satire of the bourgeoisie typical of his later, more well-known novels. In that germinal work, then, are the ideas on art and fiction and the techniques that in *Madame Bovary* and the second *Education sentimentale* would make Flaubert the most influential novelist of the latter half of the nineteenth century.[41] In the twentieth century he fell from critical favor in France, but, as Henri Peyre observed in mid-twentieth century, it is not easy for a contemporary novelist to create "a middle aged, dissatisfied, and tempted lady without conjuring up Emma Bovary."[42]

In poetry as well as in fiction the 1840s were seminal years. Between 1840 and 1845 the young Charles Baudelaire, who was to become (in the words of Henri Peyre) "the most influential of all modern poets,"[43] wrote most, if not all, of his greatest poems, *Les Fleurs du mal*. When they were published in 1857, they outraged the conventional morality and associated Baudelaire's name in the public mind with depravity and vice. But with them he made one of the great literary breaks with convention. He rejected both the subject matter and the forms of contemporary poetry. He dared to write openly on forbidden subjects—eroticism, perversion, decay, and darkest pessimism. He rejected the accepted forms and vocabulary of both Classical and Romantic poetry, and in his use of symbols he was the great precursor of the symbolist poets of the latter part of the century. The establishment found his poems scandalous, satanic, and blasphemous. When they were published, the government prosecuted him for offense against religion and against "public morality," and several of the poems were banned. Nonetheless, with *Les Fleurs du mal* he turned French poetry into new paths, and his influence was powerfully felt in France and in other Western countries for at least a century.[44]

The novels of Flaubert and the poetry of Baudelaire belong to high culture. In the realm of low or popular culture, too, the 1840s brought at least one innovation to French literature. There then appeared what has been called "industrialized literature," that is, fiction and occasionally history and memoirs produced by writers in uniform-length installments for the recently created mass-circulation daily newspapers in Paris. The repressive zeal of the July Monarchy, culminating in the September Laws of 1835, ended the great age of the political press in France. Those laws raised the caution money of Parisian dailies to 100,000 francs, instituted simpler judicial procedures in order to assure more convictions for violations of the press law, and increased the number of press offenses, offenses that could lead to heavier and damaging fines and prolonged suspension of publication. Publishing a political newspaper became an expensive and risky financial undertaking. Publishers and editors reduced the space devoted to politics in their papers and took care that such political articles as were published were more cautious—and usually less interesting—than in the past. This in turn made it difficult for papers whose readers had been held by political sympathies and loyalties to retain subscribers in sufficient numbers to cover operating costs.[45]

In 1836 a prescient journalist named Emile de Girardin concluded that there existed in Paris and elsewhere in France a body of readers with little interest in the rarefied world of high politics, and he established in the capital a new newspaper, *La Presse*, designed to appeal to them. It was to take no sides in politics. The cost of subscriptions was half the rate charged by established papers. Income lost in subscription fees Girardin planned to recoup in revenues from advertising, but years passed before advertising produced any substantial return. The requisite income was found by multiplying subscriptions. They were won and held by another of Girardin's innovations—the publication in *La Presse* of serialized novels, each day's installment appearing conspicuously at the bottom of the first page. By 1838 daily circulation exceeded 13,000 copies and by 1846 had risen above 21,000. Almost immediately Girardin had an imitator and competitor in the person of Armand Dutacq, who in 1836 founded *Le Siècle*. Vigorously promoted, its circulation mounted to more than 41,000 in 1841, many times the circulation of the traditional political papers.[46]

These figures, impressively large at the time, do not compare with those of the true mass-circulation dailies of the twentieth century. In 1910 *Le Petit Parisien* had a press run of 1.4 million, and in 1939 *Paris Soir* was printing 1.7 million copies daily. But *La Presse* and *Le Siècle* had made the initial break with traditional elitist journalism, and at the same time the application of the Guizot School Law of 1833 gave promise that in the future France would have millions of men and women who were literate but scarcely educated, among whom such papers could find masses of readers.[47]

The same masses also provided the growing clientele of popular, illustrated magazines that photography made widely appealing. The most celebrated and long-lived of these journals, *L'Illustration*, was founded in Paris in 1843. It was not the earliest illustrated magazine, nor was it originally a popular magazine. Its bookstall price of seventy-five centimes and annual subscription rate of thirty-six francs made it a journal of the well-to-do, and in the latter 1860s its press run was only eighteen thousand copies. By that time its low-cost imitators were effectively exploiting the popular market. *La Presse illustrée*, founded in 1858, selling for five centimes, had a press run of sixty thousand copies, and *Le Journal illustré*, fifty thousand. Their lineal descendant, *Paris-Match*, in the 1950s achieved a circulation of more than 1.8 million copies.[48]

The serial story soon became more than the financial foundation of the new popular journalism. Even long-established, conventional journals turned to serial stories to hold and increase their circulations, and editors competed for the work of popular authors. The staid *Journal des débats* began publication of serials in 1837, and in 1842–1843, when it published Eugène Sue's *Les Mystères de Paris*, it had impatient readers standing in line to pick up copies of each day's number. In 1844 the new owners of another long-established daily, *Le Constitutionnel*, anxious to bolster its circulation, paid Sue 100,000 francs for publication rights to his new novel, *Le Juif errant*. When it began to appear in the paper twenty thousand

Fig. 3. Honoré Daumier, *When the Newspaper Is Too Interesting* (Print Department, Boston Public Library)

new subscriptions poured in to the publisher. In 1845 *Le Constitutionnel* and *La Presse* together contracted with Alexander Dumas to take all his writings for the next five years in return for an annual retainer of 63,000 francs.[49]

The sensational popular success in the mid-forties of *Les Mystères de Paris*, a social novel of the Parisian underworld of poverty and crime, led other authors to follow Sue's example in hope of winning similar rewards. Adapting their creativity to the demands of the burgeoning mass market, they made the novel the dominant literary form. The growing market, moreover, enabled writers to support themselves by the sale of their writings, independent of both family wealth and the retainers of aristocratic patrons. The medium that gave them access to the market itself imposed a peculiar form upon the serial novel. Each uniform-length episode had to end with the action in a moment of suspense so as to assure that the reader, eager to learn what happened next, would not fail to buy the succeeding number of the paper.[50]

Dawning awareness of an emerging market for entertainment in print perhaps explains the appearance in the 1840s of the prototype of a medium that flourished in the mass culture of the twentieth century, the comic strip. The comic strips were the creation of a French-speaking Swiss resident in Geneva, Rodolphe Töppfer, and his first book of comics published in France appeared in 1839. Others followed in 1840 and 1846. In them he substituted for a text occasionally illustrated by drawings or engravings (a common format for books at the time) a continuous series of slightly changing drawings supplemented by brief, attached texts. His stories were simple, his characters uncomplicated, and his presentation enlivened by gags and surprises, all precursive of twentieth-century comic strips.[51]

For the historian, artistic tastes and styles are elusive subjects. One can point to no act of Parliament, no decisive military victory, no critical invention and say, Here and at this time and place art and taste turned in new directions. But in the 1840s in France the coincidence of accelerating economic change, social upheaval, intellectual effervescence in areas of

Fig. 4. Strip from Rodolphe Töpffer's *M. Pencil*, published in Paris and Geneva in 1840 (*Rodolphe Töpffer: M. Jabot, M. Crépin, M. Vieux Bois, M. Pencil . . .* [Editions Pierre Horay, Paris, 1975], p. 137)

widely felt social concern, and the innovations of a number of extraordinarily gifted individual artists, seen from the perspective of a century and a half, do indeed seem to make those years extraordinarily seminal, even decisive, in the evolution of architecture, painting, and literature. Certainly in 1860 the French artistic scene was distinctly different from what it had been in the 1830s, and the critical influences that effected the change were remarkably concentrated in the early and middle 1840s.

Toward a New Place
in the World

IN THE 1840s came the significant beginnings of a transformation of France's place in the world—her place in European alignments and alliances and her place in the wider area of imperial power and possessions. The centuries-old enmity with England was reversed, replaced with the first firmly based Franco-British entente. Although the entente of the forties was not sustained, the reversal then achieved sowed the seed of the French-British alliance that carried the two powers to victory in 1918 and survived in different form and with intermittent strains and disruptions to the present.[1] The forties, too, marked the effective beginning of the second French colonial empire. Between 1841 and 1847 French armed forces, moving out from the coastal enclaves held since 1830, conquered Algeria, and systematic settlement of the colony began. Around the world French officers and agents in those same years established footholds in West Africa, the South Pacific, and the Indian Ocean, while others were probing into Morocco, Mexico, and China. At the same time, on French initiative, the first Suez Canal company was formed, and the idea of a canal across the Isthmus of Panama received first serious consideration in France.

The primary objective of the Orleanist monarchy's foreign policy was, like that of the Bourbons in the teens and the twenties, the restoration of France to a position of equality among the great powers in Europe. The first step toward that end was perceived to be the establishment of an alliance, or at least an agreement, with another power. Probably to most Frenchmen England was the least likely of allies. In the preceding century and a half France and England had been at war eight times. Although Anglomania, expressed in the copying of English dress, the reading of Sir Walter Scott's novels, and attendance at performances of Shakespeare's plays, had flourished among the elite and the well-to-do of the Restoration, Anglophobia remained strong among the popular classes and even among the *notables*. Nonetheless, in the very earliest days of the new monarchy, Louis-Philippe, placed on the throne by the revolution that was the first great break in the settlement of 1815, urgently needed the support of England against the unsympathetic monarchies of central and eastern Europe. After the Belgian revolt against the Netherlands in August 1830, another rupture in the settlement of 1815, England needed French support to block intervention in Belgium by the eastern monarchies, which posed the threat of establishment of a strong military power in the Low Countries. The two western nations together arranged and enforced a bilateral settlement in Belgium, and the British government recognized Louis-Philippe as the king of the French. Louis-Philippe and Prince Talleyrand, his ambassador in London who had negotiated the agreement with England, as well as others in the government hoped that the agreement would lead to an alliance. But when in 1833 Talleyrand proposed it to Lord Palmerston, the British foreign secretary, Palmerston rejected the proposal, and his counterproposal, made a few months later, was unacceptable to the French. In the summer of 1834, Talleyrand, convinced that an alliance with England was impossible, resigned the ambassadorship and advised Louis-Philippe to seek an alliance on the Continent.[2]

In the succeeding years relations between the two countries deteriorated. "Our connection with England is so new, so contrary to all tradition that old habits [of hostility] reappear," Talleyrand warned in a letter to the duc de Broglie, his foreign minister.[3] After 1836 on neither side of the Channel did the address from the throne at the opening of Parliament include a reference to cordial relations between the two countries, and their rivalry became increasingly open and hostile in Spain and Portugal, in Greece, and in Belgium. In May 1840 the British government did make a friendly gesture in agreeing to the return of Napoleon's body to Paris from the British-held island of St. Helena, but only a few weeks later conflicting interests and policies in the eastern Mediterranean brought the two powers close to war.[4]

In the spring of 1839 Mehemet Ali, the pasha of Egypt, had seized the Ottoman province of Syria, posing, in Palmerston's judgment, a double threat to British interests. The British, ever sensitive to the security of the Mediterranean route to India, were anxious that the Ottoman Empire, the principal barrier against Russian penetration into the Mediterranean, not be weakened by partition, and they were also anxious that Egypt not become a large and powerful state athwart the British lifeline. Palmerston undertook to marshal the five major European powers into a joint effort to force Mehemet Ali to evacuate Syria, and all eventually agreed except France. The government of Louis-Philippe, seeking both strategic and economic advantage, had aided Mehemet Ali with loans and political support, and it was determined to prevent British humiliation of its protégé and frustration of its own policy. Adolphe Thiers, named first minister on 10 March 1840 with the expectation that he would take a hard line against Britain and the associated powers, pressed for direct negotiations between the Ottoman sultan and the pasha to settle the Syrian dispute, a course of action that would probably leave Mehemet Ali in possession of Syria. Palmerston suspected that Thiers was anticipating the establishment of a much enlarged and powerful Egypt, which would be a French ally, and he feared that the French, once firmly established at both ends of the Mediterranean—in Algeria and in Egypt—would then extend their influence to dominate all of the north coast of Africa, from Morocco to Syria. Thiers' belligerent stance—he declared that France would not accept the use of force against Mehemet Ali—confirmed Palmerston in his intransigence. On 15 July 1840 he obtained the signatures of representatives of Russia, Austria, and Prussia on an agreement to demand Mehemet Ali's immediate withdrawal from Syria and to use force against him if he should fail to heed their order.[5]

The negotiations leading to this agreement had been kept secret from the French, and to Louis-Philippe and Thiers word of it came as a surprise and a humiliation. When, at the end of July, Parisian newspapers published reports of the agreement, they aroused a storm of nationalist protest in France. The news came while the press and political orators, moved by preparations for the return of Napoleon's body to Paris, had been celebrating the victories and the glories of the emperor and of the *Grande Armée*. Now, in the eyes of the French, their old enemies had revived the anti-Napoleonic, anti-French coalition of 1814. Thiers, embarrassed by the collapse of his Near Eastern policy and fearful of denunciation by his foes as being "soft" on England, publicly took an uncompromising stand, called up army reserves, opened extraordinary military credits, and began the fortification of the capital. War fever in Paris and other cities was intense that summer and autumn. Lines of volunteers formed at recruiting stations. Columns of troops moved through the streets.[6] "We are in an extremity," exclaimed Alexis de Tocqueville to the Chamber of Deputies, "from which we must escape, even by war."[7]

But the prospect of war waged alone against the combined might of Europe and alarm at the intensity of popular belligerence brought second thoughts to the *notables* who ruled France. War might well end in defeat and greater humiliation, and it would certainly be costly and disruptive to the economy, finally recovering from prolonged depression. Moreover, the *notables*, recalling 1792–1795, associated war with revolution, which they feared more than war itself. The celebration of the tenth anniversary of the Revolution of 1830 came a few days after announcement of the agreement of 15 July, and an apprehensive government took the greatest of precautions to assure that it should not turn into another insurrection or another revolution. An unprecedented wave of strikes in Paris later that summer and in the fall fed revolutionary fears. The king was determined to avoid war, believing, with reason, that it involved unacceptable risks for the regime and the dynasty. On 8 October, Thiers, under pressure from the king, dispatched a note to the other powers proposing a compromise solution to the Syrian crisis, a solution close to that of 15

July. Nonetheless, he persisted in threatening war and continued to accelerate military preparations. When on 30 October he proposed to the king that he include in the forthcoming address to the opening of Parliament an allusion to the possibility of war, Louis-Philippe categorically rejected the proposal. Thiers resigned.[8]

The king called on Marshal Nicolas Soult and François Guizot to form a new ministry. Soult was chosen as an old and loyal friend, uncommitted to any party, on whom the king could count for unquestioning support. Guizot, recalled from the ambassadorship in London, took the foreign ministry, but he was in practice the effective head of the new council of ministers from the outset. The king chose him because of the affinity of Guizot's sympathies in domestic politics and in foreign affairs with those of the king himself. Guizot was convinced that in the mid-nineteenth century national power and security could no longer be achieved by war and conquest but only by growing economic strength. A profound conservative in domestic politics, he believed that France had achieved the best possible form of government and that the most serious threat to it came from war, which radicals could turn into revolution. In the autumn of 1840 he was committed to maintaining peace, and his first undertaking on coming to the foreign ministry was to resolve the crisis in the eastern Mediterranean. In July 1841 France joined with the other four powers in signing a convention that settled the dispute between the sultan and the pasha. That act implicitly dissolved the anti-French coalition of 15 July 1840.[9]

The Near Eastern Crisis had two side-effects that are now discernible as early manifestations of developments that, a few decades later, had profound consequences for France's position in Europe and for her national unity. Thiers' strident threats of war aroused German fears of renewed French aggression across the Rhine and revived aspirations for German national unity against the French threat. Prince Metternich, the Austrian chancellor, remarked in November 1840 that Thiers liked to be compared with Napoleon and that in Germany not only was the comparison apt but there Thiers had outdone Napoleon.[10] Alluding to the German liberation movement of 1813–1814, Metternich added, "It took him [Thiers] only a short time to lead Germany to a place where Napoleon had brought it by ten years of oppression."[11] That revival inspired a minor German poet, Max Scheckenburger, to write in 1840 "Die Wacht am Rhein," which, later set to music, became one of the great patriotic hymns of a united Germany. "Dear Fatherland, no danger thine," runs the chorus, "Firm stands thy watch along the Rhine." Indeed, the German historian of the July Monarchy, Karl Hillebrand, looking back from the vantage point of the 1880s, fixed the beginning of the German unification movement at 1 March 1840, the day that Thiers became president of the Council of Ministers![12]

Within France the Near Eastern Crisis contributed to the emergence of modern anti-Semitism. The growth of heavy industry and of capitalist enterprise during the July Monarchy revived the ancient image of the Jew as usurer. Jewish bankers, though outnumbered by Protestant bankers, were prominent in the financial oligarchy of the regime, and some early socialists, who deplored the consequences of the rise of capitalistic industrial society in which that oligarchy thrived, became anti-Semitic. Fourier called Jews "parasites" and "usurers" and termed their emancipation by the Revolution "shameful."[13]

A few months before the crisis provoked by Palmerston's agreement of 15 July anti-Jewish feeling had been stirred by an incident in the Near East. In February 1840, shortly after Mehemet Ali had taken Syria, a well-known Capuchin monk disappeared from his monastery in Damascus, and it was rumored that he had been murdered. Popular opinion blamed the Jews. France was the traditional protector of Roman Catholic Christians in the Ottoman Empire, and the French consul undertook an investigation. He had a number of Jews arrested and with brutal interrogations extracted confessions from some of them; he followed this with more arrests and more torture. An independent investigation by the Austrian consul in Damascus established that the charges against the Jews were groundless, but they continued to be victimized. European Jews, concerned with the plight of coreligionists, pressed their governments to intervene on their behalf. The Rothschilds joined this effort in Paris and in other capitals. Thiers, questioned in the Chamber of Deputies by a Jewish deputy on the French consul's handling of the affair, chided his questioner for putting Jewish interests before French interests and deplored the power of the Jews in European capitals. Conservative and Catholic papers joined in spreading anti-Jewish and anti-Rothschild charges.[14]

Anti-Semitic feeling generated by the Damascus affair combined with that nurtured by the war scare of 1840. Nationalists blamed bankers and other businessmen, who generally favored a peaceful settlement, for forcing the government to give in to England, and most bankers in France, it was claimed, were Protestants or Jews, the latter personified by the powerful Baron James Rothshchild. Thiers, seeking political advantage wherever he could find it, continued to appeal to anti-Semitic sentiments. Here, at the highest levels of government, appeared the association of Jews with international finance and with extranational loyalties. In 1846 a Fourierist writer, Alphonse Toussenel, published *Les Juifs, rois de l'époque: Histoire de la féodalité financière*, the first book to develop the thesis that the Jews through their financial power dominated France. It was followed by—and perhaps inspired—the publication of many anti-Jewish pamphlets and articles, and in them Toussenel's charge of Jewish domination was a recurring theme. In 1884 Edouard Drumont made it the thesis of his notorious book, *La France juive*, and it became firmly implanted in the popular nationalist mentality at the time of the Dreyfus affair.[15]

As foreign minister after October 1840 Guizot was more than a liquidator. France, he believed, should cease to be a "flaming meteor" in Europe. Instead it should become a "fixed star" in the European state system, and that, he thought, could best be achieved by alliance with Britain. He was an enthusiastic Anglophile. As a student early in the century in the then almost English city of Geneva he was introduced to Eng-

lish culture and became nearly as familiar with English literature as with French. Later, as a professor at the University
of Paris, he had lectured on English history, and in the 1820s
he edited a multivolume collection of sources on seventeenth-
century English history and wrote the two-volume *Histoire
de la Révolution d'Angleterre depuis l'avènement de Charles
Ier jusqu'à sa mort*. When he went to London in 1840 as Louis-
Philippe's ambassador, he was warmly received by the Whig
political magnates—Lord Holland, the duke of Devonshire,
and others—and by Whig intellectuals. The Tory leaders, then
out of power, were cordial, too, and he formed a close friendship with the earl of Aberdeen, the future foreign minister.
Guizot admired English parliamentary government, and he
and his friends—the duke de Broglie and Charles de Rémusat
among others—themselves landed aristocrats with a penchant
for elitist politics, felt a close kinship with the English ruling
class. Yet another bond of sympathy, rare in French-English
relations, was religion; Guizot was a Protestant.[16]

A foreign policy shaped by such pro-English views could
not be based on popular support. Anglophobia remained
strong in the popular classes, seemingly little influenced by
the internationalism of popular socialist writers. In the autumn of 1840 leftist newspapers, punning on Guizot's official
title, Ministre des affaires étrangères, mockingly called him
"Ministre des étrangères." The sympathies of the notables
were mixed, and they shifted with changes on the international
scene and in domestic politics. Most of them were, however,
eager to avoid war with Britain.[17]

Across the Channel popular opinion was probably as res-
olutely anti-French as it was anti-English in France, but among
the governing elite most were anxious to keep the country out
of war, and many shared Guizot's beliefs in the mutual benefits
to be gained by close cooperation between the two governments. A number of influential Whigs had opposed Palmerston's Mediterranean policy that led to estrangement with
France in 1840, and early in 1841 Palmerston himself made
some effort to soothe French feelings. More significant for
Guizot's aspirations, however, was the return of the Tories to

power in May 1841 with Guizot's good friend, Lord Aberdeen, as foreign secretary. Aberdeen, personally conciliatory in contrast to the combative Palmerston, was as anxious as Guizot to establish cordial relations between the two countries.[18]

On the French side the king shared his foreign minister's views on the English and, wanting to grow old peacefully on the throne and to assure the continuation of his dynasty, he supported Guizot's pressure for reconciliation with England. He had not forgotten that twice England had provided him and his family with a safe haven against the storms of war and revolution. Moreover, in the 1840s close family and personal ties, unmatched since the seventeenth century, connected the two ruling houses. Louis-Philippe's eldest daughter, Louise, was the wife of the Belgian King Leopold, Queen Victoria's uncle. In 1840 Leopold's nephew, Albert of Saxe-Coburg and Gotha, became the prince consort to Victoria. In the same year the queen's first cousin, Victoria of Saxe-Coburg and Gotha, married Louis-Philippe's second son, the Duc de Nemours. The two Victorias were very close; when the duchess died in 1847 the mourning queen declared, "We were like sisters." In the spring of 1843 Louis-Philippe's second daughter, Clementine, married another of Victoria's cousins, Prince August of Saxe-Coburg and Gotha. The queen early developed a personal liking for Louis-Philippe, and she much admired the family life of the Orléans.[19]

The tenor of French-British relations changed quickly after Aberdeen replaced Palmerston, but public opinion, the suspicions and hostility of diplomats, British apprehension of France's continuing pursuit of a Franco-Belgian customs union, and unresolved conflicts over enforcement of the international ban on the slave trade and over the royal succession in Spain restricted the new cordiality to personal relations between the two foreign ministers. The only practical consequence during the first year was the agreement on settlement of the Syrian-Egyptian problem and the removal of the immediate threat of war. In the summer of 1843, however, the cause of entente received a powerful boost when Queen Victoria on her own initiative proposed that she pay a visit to the French king. Not since 1520, when Henry VIII came to the Field of the Cloth of Gold, had an English monarch set foot on French soil. The king and Guizot were delighted by the proposal. In the years since Louis-Philippe had mounted the throne in the aftermath of the Revolution of 1830 not one foreign ruler had visited him. To the conservative monarchs of Europe he was still, after thirteen years, the "king of the barricades," raised to the throne by revolution in violation of the settlement of 1815. Visits by his two eldest sons to Berlin and Vienna had not been returned, and in 1842 the French suggestion that the king of Prussia, traveling to England for the baptism of Victoria's first child, cross French territory had been rebuffed. Victoria's visit would break the royal quarantine of the revolutionary regime and give Louis-Philippe and his dynasty a legitimacy that they had hitherto lacked.[20]

The royal visit to the Château d'Eu, Louis-Philippe's property in Normandy, in September 1843 provided the occasion both for personal and diplomatic talks and for the establishment of warm personal relations between the two monarchs and between their ministers. Three months later in December, speaking at the opening of the annual session of the chambers, Louis-Philippe referred to "the sincere friendship" that united him and the queen of England and to "the *entente cordiale* that now exists" between the two governments. Queen Victoria in her address to the opening of Parliament in January 1844 spoke of "friendly relations" between the two rulers and of "the good understanding" between their governments.

In 1841 Guizot had described France's international position as "isolation in an armed peace." After two and a half years in the foreign ministry he was able to have the king speak of "sincere friendship" and "an *entente cordiale*" with the ancient enemy.[21] "By early 1844," the British diplomatic historian Roger Bullen has written, "Anglo-French relations were on a new basis."[22] The two foreign ministers in close consultation tried to defuse existing conflicts and forestall the development of others. Both governments tempered their support of their respective candidates for the royal marriage matches in Spain, and Britain ceased to challenge French ascendancy in Madrid. When a French admiral occupied and announced the annexation of Tahiti, expelling the British consul, Guizot disavowed the annexation and had an indemnity paid to the consul. In response to British objections the French government stopped its military and naval operations against Morocco in 1844 and withdrew all its forces from Moroccan territory. Both monarchs continued to give strong support to the entente and to their pacifically inclined ministers. Louis-Philippe, accompanied by Guizot in October 1844, paid a state visit to Victoria and Albert at Windsor, the first French monarch ever to set foot voluntarily on English soil. The next year, after hearing Frederick William of Prussia propose a toast offensive to France, the queen and the prince consort altered the itinerary for their return home from Germany and pointedly came to Normandy to spend a day with Louis-Philippe and his family at Château d'Eu.[23]

Despite the cordiality at the top levels of government divisive differences remained or resurfaced—the marriages of the queen of Spain and her sister and access to Spanish markets, French tariffs on British industrial products, the Franco-Belgian customs union, conflicting interests in the islands of the South Pacific, and the rapid buildup of French naval power. Moreover, in both countries opposition to the entente continued strong, and out-of-office politicians made use of the opposition to discredit the incumbent governments. Palmerston in Britain, like Thiers in France, never retreated from his hostility to the policy of conciliation, and the entente did not long survive his return to the Foreign Office in June 1846. The particular occasion for its demise was the marriage in October 1846 of Louis-Philippe's son, the Duc de Montpensier, to Infanta Louisa, the sister of Queen Isabella of Spain and next in line for the throne. In British eyes this violated a gentlemen's agreement between the French and British cabinets on the marriages of Queen Isabella and her sister, and Palmerston bluntly denounced it as an attempt by the French to establish their influence over another state "by illegitimate means." Even Queen Victoria was disillusioned by what she regarded as Louis-Philippe's breach of faith, and she ceased to restrain Palmerston in his reversal of Aberdeen's policies. This petty dynastic squabble was itself scarcely a serious threat to the entente, but underlying it was the growing conflict between France and Britain over control of the Western Mediterranean. Any increase of French influence in Spain at the very time that the French were tightening their hold on the south coast of the Mediterranean in Algeria raised alarm in London.[24]

The *entente cordiale* was seemingly doomed, but seven years later the French and the British were allies, fighting side by side in the Crimea, with the monarchs again exchanging visits. That alliance, too, was short-lived, but neither the entente of the forties nor the alliance of the fifties was solely the ephemeral creation of few individuals or of passing circumstance. The two agreements were early, groping efforts at adaptation to fundamental changes then taking place in the balance of political and economic power in Europe. In the early 1830s the fortuitous and temporary coincidence of the need of both France and Britain for the other's support brought the two countries together in what is sometimes called their first entente. In the 1840s no sudden, isolated set of happenings effected their rapprochement. Then they were moved by the conviction that in the world of the mid-nineteenth century peace and closer economic ties would serve the interests of both and, on the French side, by the growing fear of Germany.

The potency of the French government's wish for closer links with Britain is suggested by its early railway projects. The first long-distance railway that the government proposed—in 1835—was for a line from Paris to Le Havre and Dieppe, which, the ministry's spokesmen said, British builders would continue from the south coast to London. The Minister of the Interior, in presenting the project to the Chamber of Deputies, recommended it on the grounds that it would bring Britain and France closer together.[25] "Certainly in this noble undertaking," he declared, "politics would benefit no less than industry and commerce."[26] The project never emerged from committee in the chamber, but three years later the government again proposed the construction of a Paris–Rouen–Le Havre–Dieppe railway, and this time the chambers approved. This line connecting with Britain became the first major railway concession in France. In its project for the long-awaited general railway law, presented to the chambers in 1842, the Guizot ministry placed at the top of its list of major lines, first, a railway from Paris to the Belgian border and to a French port on the Pas de Calais, and, second, a railway from Paris "to England" via a Channel port (in fact, the Paris–La Havre–Dieppe line already authorized but still incomplete).[27]

The minstry's urgent advocacy of the Paris–Belgium line stemmed in part from its growing concern with Germany. The Zollverein, the customs union formally established under Prussian leadership in 1834, brought a considerable measure of economic unity to a still politically divided Germany. It accustomed rulers of the individual German states to working together under Prussian leadership, and even then it appeared to some as a step toward political unification of Germany. French concern was not lessened by seeing across the Rhine the growing commitment of intellectuals to the cause of German unity.[28] When the newly appointed French ambassador to the Prussian court, the marquis de Dalmatie, left for his post in 1843, he carried with him a long instruction from Guizot, which concluded with the foreign minister's recommendation that he pay careful attention to "the German commercial union . . . so important in Prussian policy during the past 20 years."[29] In French eyes the union posed a threat to Belgian independence and, consequently, to French economic interests in Belgium and to the security of France's northeast frontier. In defending the proposal for the immediate construction of a rail line between Paris and Belgium the Minister of Public Works declared that he would not resign himself to Belgium's joining the Zollverein and that France must relentlessly make every effort to attach Belgium to France and to detach it from "that foreign association" which repeatedly tried to attract it into its orbit. His listeners understood the allusion to the Zollverein.[30] The prime minister, Marshal Soult, joining in the debate, said, "I see in that line to Belgium a political, strategic, and commercial importance that I perceive in no other line."[31]

The projected Paris–Strasbourg railway, which occupied third place in the government's priorities, also reflected the growing apprehension of Germany and concern for the security of the eastern frontier. In the debates on that line the commercial benefits expected from it were not neglected, but it won support in the chambers chiefly for its expected contribution to defense against Germany.[32]

One can see in these debates the growing realization that Germany was becoming a greater threat to French security and to French economic interests than the ancient enemy across the Channel. That apprehension of the 1840s, evolving in succeeding decades from apprehension to conviction, in the early twentieth century combined with a parallel conviction in Britain—nurtured especially by the naval policy of Wilhelmine Germany—to bring the two powers together as allies in two world wars.

While Guizot was turning France toward a new place in the alignment of European states, he was also launching his country on a new imperial course that in half a century would bring her an empire larger than that the Bourbons won and lost in North America and India before the Revolution. The beginnings of the second colonial empire were in North Africa. A French expeditionary force had conquered the city of Algiers and some adjoining hinterland in 1830 during the final days of the Bourbon Restoration in an action that was a hastily organized act of domestic politics, not a considered act of imperial expansion. For the new Orleanist regime after the July Revolution the conquest was an embarrassment and an inconvenience. The new political leaders had opposed the expedition to Algiers and had not applauded the news of its victory. In the summer and autumn, when the infant regime's very existence was threatened by enemies both foreign and domestic and it needed all the strength it could muster, the Algerian venture drained troops out of the Métropole. It alarmed the British, who opposed the establishment of France on the southern shore of the Mediterranean. Diplomatic and military prudence clearly called for evacuation of the French forces, but the ministry feared the political consequences of the patriotic and nationalist outcry likely to greet a decision to abandon the only French conquest since Napoleon's fall. For ten years Louis-Philippe's successive ministries failed to produce any coherent plans or sustained policies for the North African territories. Intermittent efforts at conquest, pacification, and limited settlement proved to be indecisive. At the decade's end native military resistance, violent, determined, and well led, was unsubdued; few French settlers had come; millions of francs had been spent; thousands of lives had been lost; and Algeria remained a festering and baffling sore.[33]

Algeria posed questions of imperial policy to which neither doctrine nor French experience with the colonies of the old empire offered ready answers. In French official circles the word "colony" still meant in 1840, as it had under the *ancien régime*, a spice island, a sugar island, or a trading post on a continental coast. These holdings were prized for their commercial value as sources of raw materials. Permanent settlement by Europeans was not intended. No patriotic or moral values attached to colonies, and no consideration was given to the interests or rights of native peoples. The Direction des colonies of the Ministry of the Navy held responsibility for administration of overseas territories, and in 1840 that office had only five employees above the clerical level. The newly acquired North African territories, which until 1839 did not even have a name, came under the Ministry of War, and that ministry in the 1830s had no coherent colonial policy. Algeria, indeed, fitted into no established patterns of imperial practice nor into the conceptions on which they were based. It was many times larger than any of the surviving old colonies. It had no one or two sought-after and easily exploited "colonial" products, such as sugar or spices, to be carried to European markets. Little was known of its mineral resources. Its agricultural products—cereals, olives, wine—would compete with French agriculture. The local population, better organized, led, and armed than natives of the old colonies, could not be ignored or easily intimidated.[34]

In January 1840 General Thomas Bugeaud, who had commanded troops in Algeria in 1836 and 1837 and was himself a member of the Chamber of Deputies, told the chamber that France must decide among three options in North Africa—total withdrawal, retention of a few holdings along the coast, or total conquest. Limited occupation, shared rule with the Arabs, and other half-measures, he warned, would inevitably fail. The *notables* who ruled France were divided on the choice he offered. Some feared the competition of Algerian agriculture. Others saw the possibility of new North African markets beneficial to France. Some high-ranking officers warned against the diversion of troops to Africa at the expense of French defenses at home. Other officers foresaw Bugeaud's third option multiplying the opportunities for promotion, a welcome change for an army underemployed since 1815. Guizot's interest in Algeria was primarily strategic. He viewed it as a site for the installation of French naval power on the south shore of the Mediterranean, and he was anxious to secure it. The king supported him, in part, it would seem, because he saw in Algeria the opportunity to win for his regime some military glory, for which he was not willing to risk war in Europe. In the final days of 1840 he appointed General Bugeaud governor of Algeria, charged him with applying his recommendation of total conquest, and gave him the authority and the materiel and men to accomplish it. By 1846 Bugeaud had under his command in North Africa 108,000 men, one-third of all the French army.[35]

In the six and a half years between February 1841 and June 1847, when Bugeaud gave up his command, he did conquer Algeria and defeated the charismatic leader of native resistance, Abd-el-Kadir, driving him into exile. In 1842 the government began the systematic colonization of pacified territories, an enterprise foreign to the conception of colonies that had prevailed in the preceding decade. Bugeaud would limit civilian settlement to a narrow coastal strip; inland he proposed the establishment of military colonies of soldiers or ex-soldiers, who would cultivate the soil and assure the continuing defense of newly acquired lands. The chambers ultimately rejected his proposal and prescribed settlement by civilians, but while Bugeaud remained in command in Algeria he continued to insist that inland settlement, even by civilians, be under military direction and that villages be organized as auxiliary military posts. To attract Europeans to an inhospitable land the government offered each settler twelve hectares (about twenty-six acres) of land, building materials, seeds, work animals, and tools. Between 1842 and 1846 nearly 200,000 European immigrants, fewer than half of them French, arrived in Algeria. Only about 15,000 settled outside coastal towns, but inland colonial villages with their white walled, tile-roofed, carefully aligned houses became a characteristic part of the Algerian landscape. Some few very large holdings were established, but Bugeaud opposed the granting of large tracts of land to colonizing companies, and that practice did not begin until the next decade. Big business interests were, however, already probing for economic opportunities in the newly secured territories. In 1845, or perhaps two years earlier (the record is not clear), Paulin Talabot, developer of the Marseille–Avignon and the Avignon–Lyon railways, apparently acting together with the Rothschilds, sent agents to Algeria to investigate opportunities in mining and timber. In that year the government granted the first mining and timber concessions, including one to the Talabot brothers, and a number of mining exploration permits. For most of the settlers life proved to be grim beyond all expectations, and more than 100,000 left between 1842 and 1846. Nonetheless, systematic settlement of Algeria by Europeans had begun. Not for more than a century would there again be serious consideration of French withdrawal from this centerpiece of the new colonial empire.[36]

The old colonies had never engaged popular emotions among the French people. They were commercial ventures, free of any involvement with national honor or prestige. The conquest of Algeria, its skirmishes magnified by the daily press into heroic battles, became associated in the public mind with national military glories (which had been in short supply for the French since the fall of Napoleon). This new possession in North Africa acquired a patriotic and national importance that the old colonies had never had. That emotional, even irrational, attachment lasted for more than a century, and in the 1950s and 1960s French men and women were fanatically shouting in the streets, "Algérie française!" and setting off plastic bombs to punctuate their convictions. The belief that France's destiny was somehow bound up with the possession of Algeria turned the debate over withdrawal into one of the most divisive issues of the French twentieth century.[37] And that hardy conviction did not die with the granting of Algerian independence in 1962. "Algiers as a key to French greatness and its future," wrote William B. Cohen in 1980, "continues, long after decolonization, to haunt the imagination of the French political elite."[38]

Bugeaud, a strong and opinionated man, left a lasting imprint on French colonial policy and practice. Young army officers who served under him in North Africa came to form a school of colonial officers who continued to practice his methods of warfare and repression (though modifying them as new experience accumulated) and copied his administrative organization for permanent control of native populations. They also shared his disdain for civilians and for civilian authority, for democracy, parliamentary government, and a free press, and, when they had risen in responsible commands, they remembered Bugeaud's defiance of orders from Paris with which he disagreed. They were a type that long survived in the new French empire, and it was they and their protégés who were largely responsible for French imperial expansion and colonization until the 1880s and, after that time, for colonial administration. General Louis Faidherbe, who expanded French holdings on the coast of Senegal into the colony of French West Africa, received his introduction into colonial warfare and administration as a young subaltern, just out of the Ecole polytechnique, assigned to service in Algeria under Bugeaud. One of Faidherbe's young officers in turn, Joseph Gallieni, developed Bugeaud's and Faidherbe's ideas on colonial rule and applied them in Madagascar and in Indochina. One of Gallieni's protégés was Hubert Lyautey, and through him Bugeaud continued to influence colonial policy in North Africa well into the twentieth century.[39]

While Bugeaud was making Algeria secure for colonization and the first substantial numbers of settlers were arriving, the navy's conception of colonies began to change. In 1844 the naval officer then serving as governor of the French trading posts in Senegal, L. E. Bouët-Willaumez, proposed that the French government, acting nominally to assure the security of these posts, extend its authority over all the adjoining territory. In support of his recommendation he cited the example of Algeria. The government in Paris nominally accepted Bouët-Willaumez's recommendation but did not act on it. Paris did, however, sanction the establishment in Senegal of a Direction des affaires extérieures to handle relations with native tribes in the territories adjoining the French posts. This, too, may have been inspired by the experience in Algeria, where French commanders had learned that native peoples could not simply be ignored or repressed or expelled. The establishment of the Direction des affaires extérieures, a first step toward French annexation of a kind of territory hitherto respected as independent, was a break with traditional French colonial policy heretofore followed by the Ministry of the Navy. The sequential steps to outright annexation came in the next two decades.[40]

Guizot opposed French colonization and settlement except in Algeria, and he valued that colony primarily as a base that strengthened France's presence in the Mediterranean. His first interest outside France was the defense and advancement of French interests in Europe, and his imperial policies were functions of that overriding concern. He did not want large overseas possessions for France, but he did see the other European powers staking out positions in oceans and on trade routes around the world, and in 1843 he declared to the Chamber of Deputies that France, too, must have "secure and strong maritime stations in parts of the world that are destined to become great centers of commerce and shipping, stations that will support our commerce, where it can come to take on supplies and seek refuge. . . . This is the policy that we are pursuing."[41] Guizot did not explicitly state that the bases could be used as staging points for expeditions inland from the sea or to neighboring islands, but this was clearly implied. Indeed, actions had preceded Guizot's announcement of his policy. In 1841 French naval forces had taken Nossi-Bé and nearby islands off the west coast of Madagascar, and Mayotte, one of the Comoro Islands to the northwest. In 1842 they occupied the Marquesas Islands and established protectorates over the Wallis and Futuna Islands and over Tahiti, all potentially valuable as sites of bases in the South Pacific. The next year Guizot sent a diplomatic mission to the Far East to find a port, outside the Chinese Empire, that could become a French base in the China Sea. In 1845 the mission reached an agreement for the lease of an island in the Sulu Archipelago (now part of the Commonwealth of the Philippines), but the ministry, anxious to avoid complicating the current negotiations for the Spanish marriages, dropped the project after Spanish officials in Manila objected to the establishment of French naval power so close to the Philippines.[42]

Elsewhere around the world in these seminal years the French were making their presence felt for the first time or in more insistent ways and taking actions that foreshadowed their later presence. In 1842 the navy, seeking a secure base in the western Indian Ocean, urged the total occupation of Madagascar, an island on which France had had a tenuous foothold since the seventeenth century. Guizot, eager not to alarm Britain, rejected the proposal, leaving it to the Third Republic and General Gallieni to carry out the proposal half a century later. In 1844, in an operation undertaken to stop further Moroccan aid to the native Algerian Leader, Abd-el-Kadir, French troops invaded Morocco, and French ships bombarded two of its Atlantic ports. The British protested, and entente prevailed over colonial interest. The French withdrew from Morocco after receiving commitments from the sultan to stop his support of the Algerians. On the other side of the world the French minister in Mexico in 1842 recommended the dispatch of a French expeditionary force to Mexico to overthrow the existing government and to establish a monarchy with a European prince on the throne. About the same time Michel Chevalier, a respected political economist, published a book entitled *L'Isthme de Panama: Examen historique et géograhie des differents directions suivants lesquelles on pourrait le percer* . . . , the first overt French expression of interest in a canal across Panama. The idea of a canal through the Isthmus of Suez had interested Napoleon, and in the 1830s it surfaced again among the Saint-Simonians. In the next decade one of them, Prosper Enfantin, was promoting the idea among engineers and financiers. He brought together representatives of French, British, and German interests, who in 1846 organized a company to explore the possibilities of building the canal. The enterprise was abandoned in 1848, but the French, acting alone, returned to it in the next decade, and in 1869 they celebrated the opening of the Suez Canal.[43]

Between 1840 and 1847 France had clearly turned into new diplomatic and imperial paths. A rapprochement with England had been achieved, and an English alliance had ceased to be unthinkable. Perception of the threat that was to dominate French foreign and military policy for a century—the threat of a united, Prussianized Germany—had been established in high places. Across the Mediterranean in Algeria the cornerstone of a new colonial empire had been firmly implaced, and around the world—in West Africa, Central America, China, and the South Pacific—the monarchy had started France on a course of colonial penetration and acquisition. The nation was moving into a new role in the world.

· CONCLUSION ·

TOWARD THE END of the "decisive years" the German socialist, Arnold Ruge, walking one day on the Champs Elysées,
looked up to see the king's carriage moving swiftly down the
avenue. Its cavalry escort covered it in front, in the rear, and
on the sides. The old king was slumped in the back seat, well
hidden, and Ruge noticed that the escorts had their weapons
cocked and ready to fire, not "just deployed in the usual
burlesque style."[1]

The guards' precautions were not unjustified: two attempts
had been made on Louis-Philippe's life in 1846 alone and
many more in earlier years. But the scene reported by Ruge
was symbolic, too. Louis-Philippe had been born in 1773
under the old regime. He had survived the perils of the Revolution (though his father had not) and long years of exile
during the Empire, and he had lived to mount the throne in
1830. The half-century of revolution, he then fervently hoped
and perhaps believed, was finally ended, and in his years as
king he had striven, using a combination of concession and
repression, to assure that revolution would not recur and to
safeguard the succession of his descendants to a secure throne.
In the early forties, with a congenial and sympathetic ministry
in power, the economy growing after the fluctuations of the
preceding decade, and an *entente cordiale* established with the
ancient enemy, Britain, the Orleanist regime and dynasty did
seem at last to be secure. But, as this book has emphasized,
economic development and its social and demographic consequences had begun to work a revolution more profound
than that of 1789. In the mid-forties discerning observers,
perhaps even Louis-Philippe himself, were coming to realize
that the old order was crumbling. The Prince de Joinville,
Louis-Philippe's third son, later remarked that the spring of
1846 had been the "critical period" for his father's government. The world, he said, was "moving on its axis," and it
required a political system and policies appropriate to new

conditions.[2] Louis-Philippe, far from being a stupid man, may well have understood as much, but grown old and weary, he hid behind a screen of guards, military and ideological, unable to bring himself to face the consequences of yet another revolution, this one more complex and baffling than the first, and ominous without precedent in its threats to established values and to long-cherished patterns of life and governance.

The emergence of revolutionary socialism and the accelerating changes in industry and in transportation, with their revolutionary implications for the concentration of population, for consumption habits, for the distribution of wealth, and for class distinctions and deference, were enough to alarm the old ruler surfeited with undesired change. But in the forties, as the preceding chapters have shown, came other developments possibly less immediately alarming to conservatives like Louis-Philippe but yet equally destructive to the old order—the extension of public education open to all, the acceptance by the state of the obligation to protect the welfare of industrial workers, and the replacement of class loyalties by professional loyalties. At the same time the grip of the *grands notables* on politics was breaking down. In the general election of 1842 half the candidates in Paris were from the middle bourgeoisie, not from the wealthy elite of proprietors, bankers, and wholesale merchants. The middle bourgeoisie no longer regarded the old elite as representing their interests. The election of 1846 returned to the chamber many new deputies who, though nominally conservatives, were more concerned with France's adaptation to economic and social change than with traditional political conflicts, and, finding the government's policies inadequate to the times, they expressed their disapproval by voting with the opposition on a number of important issues. Perhaps more ominous for the regime, from the latter thirties on, the lesser bourgeoisie were taking over the officers' positions in the Parisian national guard from the upper bourgeoisie, and the guard was becoming a militia of the middle and the petty bourgeoisie, a sector of the population unhappy with the established political system, which denied most of them the right to vote in national elections. The palace, seeing danger in this development, in 1840 discontinued royal reviews of the Parisian national guard.[3]

The accidental death in 1842 of the heir to the throne, the popular and liberally inclined Duc d'Orléans, brought the last great demonstration of popular sympathy for Louis-Philippe. That sad event's long-term effects, however, were damaging to the monarchy. The massive expression of sympathy led the king and the ministry to misjudge the strength of the regime and of the opposition. The choice of the king's conservative second son, the Duc de Nemours, as regent (to serve during the minority of the new heir to the throne, the four-year-old Comte de Paris), lost the regime the support of a large part of the dynastic left. Louis-Philippe and Guizot believed—or at least publicly pretended to believe—that France had achieved the optimum form of government—rule by an elite whose intelligence, education, and wealth made them the best of all possible representatives and defenders of the national interest. At the very time that they saw this brightest promise of the Revolution at last fulfilled, the foundations on which it rested were crumbling.

In a book such as this, concerned with the patterns of historical development, one must ultimately confront the problem of explanation. Why were the few years between 1840 and 1847 so extraordinarily active and creative and seminal? Answers suggest themselves more readily in some areas of change than in others. Certainly the preconditions of industrial takeoff had been building for half a century. The French Revolution had removed the principal barriers to free enterprise. Napoleon had provided reasonably efficient administrative and fiscal organizations. The prosperity of French agriculture through most of the years of the constitutional monarchy, beginning in 1814, permitted the accumulation of considerable capital, which banks and entrepreneurs were able to tap in the forties, and this capital helped to create and to sustain a growing demand for consumer goods. In rural areas waxing population created a labor supply exceeding the requirements of agriculture and provided a reservoir of manpower for industry. The technology essential for industrial expansion was available, and the Ecole polytechnique, the Ecole des mines, and the Ecole centrale des arts et manufactures supplied a corps of unmatched engineers.

In any explanation of the developments in the forties the construction of the railways and particularly the Railway Law of 1842 must be given important place. Without these the upsurge in industrial production would probably not have occurred when it did nor been sustained, once started. Had there been no railroad boom in the forties the adoption of new industrial technologies and the concentration of production and employment in large enterprises in the iron and machinery industries would not have come about. Without the railroads national markets would have developed in few commodities, and no revolution in individual mobility would have occurred before the coming of the automobile and the motor truck. The central government's coercive powers would not have been suddenly multiplied nor the economic outreach of Paris so quickly extended. A less mobile society would not have required the use of a common language throughout the country. Even the subject matter of art and literature would have been different without the trains, and the railways contributed to the shaping of foreign policies while becoming an instrument of them.

The creativity in social thought surely came as a response to economic change and to the distress associated with that change, and in the 1830s and the 1840s these seemed more threatening to established patterns of life and to the national well-being than in the past. The increased threat stimulated more reflection and discussion, and from reflection and discussion came more prescriptions for reform.

In the outburst of creativity in the arts the experience of twentieth-century Germany suggests a credible explanation. Imperial Germany had been hostile to innovation in the arts. After 1918 all restraints were lifted, and a flowering resulted that made the Weimar Republic one of the great ages of German art. Was the extraordinary creativity of the 1840s in France perhaps a delayed response to release from the restraints of Napoleonic censorship and preoccupation with the rude tasks of war and from the repressive effects of the Catholic revival in the teens and the twenties? These effects had not, of course, stifled Géricault or reduced Hugo to silence, but they were not as rebelliously destructive of established standards and tastes as were Courbet and Baudelaire and Flaubert.

Perhaps the vitality of these few years can be explained by the arrival at maturity in the early forties of men and women who had grown up in the decades after Waterloo and were less committed to the values of the *ancien régime* or of the Revolution than were their parents, a generation more willing to contemplate and accept alternatives to an agrarian, rural, elitist society. Some belonged to the so-called "Generation of 1830," a generation that, in the words of a French historian, "occupy a privileged place in our literature and in our history."[4] They emerged on the scene in 1830, when the Bourbon gerontocracy was overthrown, a generation full of enthusiasm, confidence, and hope, and they were still young in 1840. Louis Blanc was one of them; he was twenty-nine in 1840. Proudhon was thirty-one; Considerant, thirty-two; Michel Chevalier, thirty-four; George Sand, thirty-six; Eugène Schneider, head of the Le Creusot ironworks, thirty-five. Many of the innovators of the forties were even younger, and perhaps because they had passed beyond the optimistic illusions of the Generation of 1830, they were bolder in striking out in new directions. Karl Marx was twenty-five when he arrived in Paris in 1843. When Courbet came in 1840 he was twenty-one. Viollet-le-Duc was the same age. Flaubert and Baudelaire were then nineteen.[5]

Looking back over the first half of the nineteenth century one may with reason see the 1820s and 1830s as a period of working out the consequences of the Revolution of 1789 and the Napoleonic era, of the French people's adapting and learning to use new institutions, of experimentation with new technology from across the Channel, of groping for a new vocation on the international scene. By about 1840 this process was sufficiently advanced, domestic order sufficiently assured, and a new, less inhibited generation sufficiently established to permit the country to move ahead, unhampered by the confusions and conflicts of the twenties and thirties into an extraordinary period of innovation and growth.

CHAPTER I

1. *Le Moniteur universel* (Paris), 2–7 May, 13–16 July 1839.

2. Rosamonde Sanson, *Les 14 Juillet (1789–1975): Fête et consciences nationale* (Paris, 1975), pp. 19–21.

3. J.-C. Toutain, *La Population de la France de 1700 à 1959*, Cahiers de l'Institut de science économique appliquée, Series AF, 3 (Paris, 1963), pp. 47, 54; J.-C. Toutain, *Le Produit de l'agriculture française de 1700 à 1958*, vol. II, *La Croissance*, Cahiers de l'I.S.E.A., Series AF , 2 (Paris, 1961), pp. 200–01.

4. André Armengaud, *La Population française au XIXe siècle* (Paris, 1971), p. 22; Toutain, *Population*, p. 22; Louis Chevalier, *La Formation de la population parisienne au XIXe siècle* (Paris, 1950), p. 284.

5. France, *Annuaire statistique de la France*, LXXXIII (1978), p. 9.

6. André-Jean Tudesq, "Les Structures sociales du régime censitaire" in Jean Bouvier et al., eds., *Conjoncture économique, structures sociales: Hommage à Ernest Labrousse* (Paris, 1974), pp. 484, 486–87; André-Jean Tudesq, *Les Conseillers-généraux en France au temps de Guizot, 1840–1848*, (Paris, 1967), pp. 111–13, 120–21; André-Jean Tudesq, *Les Grands Notables en France (1840–1849): Etude historique d'une psychologie sociale* (Paris, 1964), I, pp. 357–58, 363–68, 377–78.

7. Tudesq, *Grands notables*, I, pp. 261–93, 352–62, 416; Tudesq, *Conseillers généraux*, pp. 162–68; André-Jean Tudesq, "Les Pairs de France au temps de Guizot," *Revue d'histoire moderne et contemporaine*, III (1956), pp. 272–75.

8. Tudesq, "Structures sociales," 485–86; Tudesq, *Grands Notables*, I, pp. 332–33.

9. Toutain, *Population*, p. 54.

10. Toutain, *Population*, p. 54.

11. Michel Morineau, *Les Faux-semblants d'un démarrage économique: Agriculture et démographie en France au XVIIIe siècle* (Paris, 1971), pp. 24, 30; E.J.T. Collins, "Labour Supply and Demand in European Agriculture, 1800–1880," in E. L. Jones and S. J. Woolf, eds., *Agrarian Change and Economic Development* (London, 1969), pp. 82, 86, 88; Abel Chatelain, "La Lente Progression de la Faux," *Annales: E.S.C.*, 11e Année (1956), p. 498.

12. Toutain, *Produit de l'agriculture*, II, p. 207.

13. Maurice Agulhon, Gabriel Desert, and Robert Specklin, *Apogée et crise de la civilisation paysanne, 1789–1914*, vol. III of Georges Duby and Armand Wallon, eds., *Histoire de la France rurale* (Paris, 1976), pp. 66, 75–76, 105, 109–10; Philippe Vigier, *La Monarchie de Juillet* (5th ed.; Paris, 1976), pp. 51–52; Abel Chatelain, *Les Migrants temporaires en France de 1800 à 1914* (Lille, 1977), I, p. 583.

14. Agulhon et al., *Apogée et crise*, pp. 67–71; Gilbert Garrier, *Paysans du Beaujolais et du Lyonnais, 1800–1970* (Grenoble, 1973), I, pp. 203, 210–13; Jean Merley, *La Haute-Loire de la fin de l'ancien régime aux débuts de la IIIe République* (Le Puy, 1974), I, p. 381; James R. Lehning, *The Peasants of Marlhes: Economic Development and Family Organization in Nineteenth-century France* (Chapel Hill, 1980), pp. 28–30; Etienne Juillard, *La Vie rurale dans la plaine de Basse Alsace; Essai de géographie sociale* (Strasbourg, 1953), pp. 313, 316; Peter Kriedte et al., *Die Industrialisierung vor der Industrialisierung: Gewerbliche Warenproduktion auf dem Land in der Formationsperiode des Kapitalismus* (Göttingen, 1977), pp. 66–67.

15. France, *Annuaire statistique*, LVIII (1951), p. 48.

16. Stendhal, *Vie de Henry Brulard*, Henri Martineau, ed. (Paris, 1949), I, pp. 247–48.

17. France, *Annuaire statistique*, XIII (1890), p. 519; Jean Egret, *La Pré-Révolution française (1787–1788)* (Paris, 1962), pp. 98, 161; J.-C. Toutain, *Les Transports en France de 1830 à 1965*, Cahiers de l'I.S.E.A., Series AF, 9 (Paris, 1967), p. 9.

18. Archives nationales, F¹⁷ 9310, Ministère de l'Instruction publique, Inspecteur des écoles primaires, Dépt. de l'Indre, Rapport général (15 Oct. 1843).

19. G. de Bertier de Sauvigny, *La Restauration* (Paris, 1955), p. 284.

20. François Crouzet, "Essai de construction d'un indice de la production industrielle au XIXᵉ siècle," *Annales: E.S.C.*, 25ᵉ Année (1970), p. 96.

21. Fernand Braudel and Ernest Labrousse, eds., *Histoire économique et sociale de la France* (Paris, 1976), III, pp. 508–12; Agulhon et al., *Apogée et crise*, pp. 67–70; France, *Annuaire statistique*, XIII (1890), p. 506; Jean Vial, *L'Industrialisation de la sidérurgie française, 1814–1864* (Paris, 1967), Annexe, p. 42.

22. J.B.A.M. Jobard, *Industrie française: Rapport sur l'exposition française de 1839* (Brussels, 1841–1842), pp. 168–69.

23. Bertrand Gille, "Les Problèmes techniques de la sidérurgie française au cours du XIXᵉ siècle," *Revue d'histoire de la sidérurgie*, II (1961), p. 34; Pedro Fraile, *The Diffusion of Iron Technology in Nineteenth Century France, Spain, and Italy* (M.A. thesis, Univ. of Texas at Austin, 1980), pp. 39, 43, 44–45, 46, 48, 49, graph between pp. 38 and 39; France, *Annuaire statistique*, LVIII (1951), p. 134; Maurice Lévy-Leboyer, *Les Banques européennes et l'industrialisation dans la première moitié du XIXᵉ siècle* (Paris, 1964), pp. 35–36; Jean-Bernard Silly, "La Disparition de la petite métallurgie rurale," *Revue d'histoire de la sidérurgie*, II (1961), pp. 47–49; Bertrand Gille, "Esquisse d'une histoire du syndicalisme patronal dans l'industrie sidérurgique française," *Revue d'histoire de la sidérurgie*, IV (1964), p. 224.

24. Lévy-Leboyer, *Banques*, p. 706; Reid G. Geiger, *The Anzin Coal Company, 1800–1833: Big Business in the Early Stages of the French Industrial Revolution* (Newark, Del., 1974), pp. 3–4, 7, 135; France, *Annuaire statistique*, LVIII (1951), p. 129.

25. Alexandre Moreau de Jonnès, *Statistique de l'industrie de la France* (Paris, 1856), pp. 135, 179–81; Paul Bairoch,

Révolution industrielle et sous-développement (4th ed.; Paris, 1974), pp. 295–97, 299–300; Henri Sée, *Histoire économique de la France* (Paris, 1939–1951), II, pp. 156, 158, 164; Charles Ballot, *L'Introduction du machinisme dans l'industrie française* (Paris, 1923), pp. 233–42; Sébastien Charléty, *La Monarchie de Juillet (1830–1848)* (Paris, 1921), p. 189.

26. Bairoch, *Révolution industrielle*, pp. 91, 92, 296, 300, 308; T.-J. Markovitch, *L'Industrie française de 1789 à 1964: Conclusions générales*, Cahiers de l'I.S.E.A., Series AF, 7 (Paris, 1966), p. 19; France, *Annuaire statistique*, LVIII (1951), p. 207; Moreau de Jonnés, *Statistique de l'industrie*, p. 84.

27. Bairoch, *Révolution industrielle*, pp. 323–25; Toutain, *Transports en France*, pp. 7–12; Roger Price, *The Modernization of Rural France: Communications Networks and Agricultural Market Structures in Nineteenth-century France* (London, 1983), pp. 36–45; Braudel and Labrousse, eds., *Histoire économique et sociale*, III, pp. 245–46.

28. Toutain, *Transports*, pp. 15–16, 55–56; Price, *Modernization of Rural France*, pp. 42–45.

29. Price, *Modernization of Rural France*, pp. 43–45; Braudel and Labrousse, eds., *Histoire économique et sociale*, III, 247–48.

30. Toutain, *Transports*, pp. 73–74; Price, *Modernization of Rural France*, pp. 28–36; Bairoch, *Révolution industrielle*, pp. 325–27; Gille, "Problèmes techniques de la sidérurgie française," p. 31; Silly, "Disparition de la petite metallurgie," p. 48.

31. Felix Rivet, *Navigation à vapeur sur la Saône et le Rhône (1783–1863)* (Paris, 1962), pp. 29–30, 97–98, 146, 174–75, 177; Price, *Modernization of Rural France*, p. 31.

32. Toutain, *Transports*, pp. 191–92, 252; Price, *Modernization of Rural France*, pp. 34–35.

33. France, *Annuaire statistique*, XXX (1910), "Résumé retrospectif," p. 195.

34. Alfred Picard, *Traité des chemins de fer: Economie, politique, commerce, finance ...* (Paris, 1887), I, pp. 4–6; Louis-Maurice Jouffroy, *L'Ere du Rail* (Paris, 1953), pp. 83–

84; Kimon A. Doukas, *The French Railroads and the State* (New York, 1945), p. 17; Arthur Dunham, "How the First French Railroads Were Planned," *Journal of Economic History*, I (May 1941), pp. 13–15; Alfred Picard, *Les Chemins de fer français: Etude historique sur la constitution et le régime du réseau: Débats parlementaires, actes législatifs . . .* (Paris, 1884), I, pp. 121, 141–48; Lévy-Leboyer, *Banques*, p. 623; Bertrand Gille, *Histoire de la Maison Rothschild* (Geneva, 1965), I, pp. 263–64.

35. Doukas, *French Railroads and the State*, p. 20; André Lefevre, *La Ligne de Strasbourg à Bâle: La Construction (1837–1846), les répercussions françaises et internationales* (Strasbourg, 1947), p. 20; E.-F. Talin d'Eyzac, *Histoire du chemin de fer de la Compagnie d'Orléans* (Paris, 1854), p. 20.

36. Braudel and Labrousse, eds., *Histoire économique et sociale*, III, 350–54; Jean Bouvier, *Un Siècle de la banque française* (Paris, 1973), pp. 79, 81; Guy P. Palmade, *French Capitalism in the Nineteenth Century* (New York, 1972), pp. 78–81, 106–09, 113; Bertrand Gille, *La Banque et le crédit en France de 1815 à 1848* (Paris, 1959), pp. 52–57, 63–70, 77–104, 114–18; Gille, *Histoire de la Maison Rothschild*, I, p. 233; Lévy-Leboyer, *Banques*, p. 423 n. 69; Louis Bergeron, *Banquiers, négociants et manufacturiers parisiens du Directoire à l'Empire* (Paris, 1978), pp. 9, 87, 299–307, 319.

37. Bairoch, *Révolution industrielle*, pp. 70, 117–19; Silly, "Disparition de la petite métallurgie," p. 49; Lévy-Leboyer, *Banques*, pp. 413, 444, 460–61, 700; Braudel and Labrousse, eds., *Histoire économique et sociale*, III, pp. 368–70.

38. Vigier, *Monarchie de Juillet*, pp. 45, 51–52; Palmade, *French Capitalism*, p. 45; Gille, *Banque et crédit en France*, pp. 127–28, 135–36.

39. Vigier, *Monarchie de Juillet*, pp. 46–50; Louis Bergeron, *Les Capitalistes en France, 1780–1914* (Paris, 1978), pp. 51–53; Tudesq, *Grandes Notables*, I, p. 429, 435, 474, 475; Maurice Agulhon, "Bourgeoisie ancienne et esprit d'entreprise au temps de la 'révolution industrielle' (d'après un exemple départmental)" in Jean Bouvier et al., eds., *Conjoncture éco-*

nomique, pp. 466–67; André-Jean Tudesq, "Structures sociales du régime censitaire," ibid., pp. 484–86; Adeline Daumard, *Les Bourgeois de Paris au XIXe siècle* (Paris, 1970), pp. 83–85, 80–82, 219.

40. André Jardin and André-Jean Tudesq, *La France des notables: L'Evolution générale, 1815–1848* (Paris, 1973), pp. 205, 207–08; Vigier, *Monarchie de Juillet*, p. 55; Braudel and Labrousse, eds., *Histoire économique et sociale*, III, pp. 222–23, 229–30; Jean-Pierre Aguet, *Les Grèves sous la Monarchie de Juillet (1830–1847)* (Geneva, 1954), pp. ix–xiii, xvi–xx; Ronald Aminzade, *Class, Politics, and Early Industrial Capitalism: A Study of Mid-nineteenth-century Toulouse, France* (Albany, N.Y., 1981), pp. 29–31, 70–73.

41. David H. Pinkney, *Napoleon III and the Rebuilding of Paris* (Princeton, 1958), pp. 6–8; G. de Bertier de Sauvigny, *Nouvelle Histoire de Paris: La Restauration, 1815–1830* (Paris, 1977), pp. 79, 377–79; Chevalier, *Formation de la population parisienne*, p. 284; Département de la Seine, Service de la Statistique municipale, *Recherches statistiques de la ville de Paris et la département de la Seine* (Paris, 1821–1860), V, Tableau 125.

42. Pinkney, *Rebuilding of Paris*, pp. 14–16; De Bertier de Sauvigny, *Nouvelle Histoire de Paris*, pp. 53, 54, 56–57.

43. Pinkney, *Rebuilding of Paris*, pp. 19–22; De Bertier de Sauvigny, *Nouvelle Histoire de Paris*, pp. 90–93.

44. Chevalier, *Formation de la population parisienne*, pp. 105–06.

45. Heinrich Heine, *Lutetia*, vol. XVI of *The Works of Heinrich Heine* (New York, n.d.), p. 360.

CHAPTER II

1. Walt W. Rostow, *The Stages of Economic Growth: A Non-communist Manifesto* (2d ed.; Cambridge, Eng., 1971), p. 7.

2. Jean Marczewski, "The Take-off Hypothesis and French Experience" in Walt W. Rostow ed., *The Economics of Take-*

off into Sustained Growth (New York, 1963), pp. 129, 131; Jean Marczewski, "Some Aspects of the Economic Growth of France, 1660–1958," *Economic Development and Cultural Change*, IX (1961), pp. 383–86; Maurice Lévy–Leboyer, "La Croissance économique en France au XIXᵉ siècle: Résultats préliminaires," *Annales: E.S.C.*, 23ᵉ Année (1968), pp. 788–89, 791, 793.

3. Hugues Neveux, "Analyse économique et histoire," *Revue d'histoire économique et sociale*, LII, 1 (1974), p. 113; François Crouzet, "Essai de construction d'un indice de la production industrielle au XIXᵉ siècle," *Annales: E.S.C.*, 25ᵉ Année (1970), pp. 56–99.

4. François Crouzet, "French Economic Growth in the Nineteenth Century Reconsidered," *History*, LIX (1974), p. 170.

5. Rostow, *Stages of Economic Growth*, p. 39.

6. Crouzet, "Essai," Tables 2 and 3.

7. François Perroux, "Prises de vues sur la croissance de l'économie française, 1780–1950," *Income and Wealth*, 5th series (1955), p. 63.

8. Jean Marczewski, *Le Produit physique de l'économie française de 1789 à 1913 (comparaison avec Grande Bretagne)*, Cahiers de l'I.S.E.A., Series AF, 4 (Paris, 1965), p. xcii.

9. J.-C. Toutain, *Le Produit de l'agriculture française de 1700 à 1958*, II, *La Croissance*, Cahiers de l'I.S.E.A., Series AF, 2 (Paris, 1961), pp. 164–65; Marczewski, "Some Aspects of Economic Growth," p. 325; Paul Bairoch, "Ecarts internationaux des niveaux de vie avant la Révolution industrielle," *Annales: E.S.C.*, 34ᵉ Année (1979), p. 154; Paul Bairoch, *Révolution industrielle et sous-développement* (4th ed.; Paris, 1974), p. 271.

10. Rostow, *Stages of Economic Growth*, pp. 210–13; Rostow, ed., *Economics of Take-off*, pp. 359–60.

11. Alexander Gerschenkron, *Economic Backwardness in Historical Perspective: A Book of Essays* (Cambridge, Mass., 1966), p. 36; Rostow, *Stages of Economic Growth*, p. 7; J.-C. Toutain, *Les Transports en France de 1830 à 1965*, Cahiers de l'I.S.E.A., Series AF, 9 (Paris, 1967), pp. 9, 74.

12. Maurice Lévy-Leboyer, *Les Banques européennes et l'industrialisation internationale dans la première moitié du XIXᵉ siècle* (Paris, 1964), pp. 374–75; Jean Vial, *L'Industrialisation de la sidérurgie française, 1814–1864* (Paris, 1967), pp. 85, 205; France, *Annuaire statistique*, LVIII (1951), p. 134.

13. Jean-Bernard Silly, "La Reprise du Creusot, 1836–1848," *Revue d'histoire des mines et de la métallurgie*, I (1969), pp. 233, 240, 245; Joseph Antoine Roy, *Histoire de la famille Schneider et du Creusot* (Paris, 1962), pp. 18–21, 31; Lévy-Leboyer, *Banques*, pp. 373 n. 156, 626 n. 142; Bertrand Gille, *Recherches sur la formation de la grande entreprise capitaliste (1815–1848)* (Paris, 1959), p. 88; Félix Rivet, *Navigation à vapeur sur la Saône et le Rhône (1783–1863)* (Paris, 1962), pp. 145, 146.

14. Lévy-Leboyer, *Banques*, p. 626 n. 1, 143 n. 144; Robert H. Locke, "Drouillard, Benoist et Cie. (1836–1856)," *Revue d'histoire de la sidérurgie*, VIII (1962) pp. 277, 280, 291, 293; Archives nationales, 60 AQ 1, Compagnie du chemin de fer de Paris à Orléans, Procès-verbaux du Conseil d'administration, I (14 Nov. 1838), p. 138.

15. Marcel Gillet, *Les Charbonnages du Nord de la France au XIXᵉ siècle* (Paris, 1973), pp. 36, 37, 38; Lévy-Leboyer, *Banques*, p. 626 n. 146.

16. Bairoch, *Révolution industrielle*, pp. 75, 85–93, 300; France, *Annuaire statistique*, LVIII (1951), p. 268; E.J.T. Collins, "Labour Supply and Demand in European Agriculture, 1800–1880," in E. L. Jones and S. J. Woolf, eds., *Agrarian Change and Economic Development* (London, 1969), p. 89; Fernand Braudel and Ernest Labrousse, eds., *Histoire économique et sociale de la France* (Paris, 1976), III, p. 484.

17. Braudel and Labrousse, eds., *Histoire économique et sociale*, III, p. 497; Rivet, *Navigation à vapeur sur la Saône et le Rhône*, pp. 116, 139; Bairoch, *Révolution industrielle*, p. 131; France, *Annuaire statistique*, LVIII (1951), p. 144; Vial, *Industrialisation*, pp. 40, 201; Lévy-Leboyer, *Banques*, pp. 371 n. 146, 373, 374 n. 158; Jules Burat, *Exposition de*

l'industrie française, année 1844, description méthodique (Paris, 1845), I, p. 26.

18. Braudel and Labrousse, eds., *Histoire économique et sociale*, III, pp. 259–60; Bairoch, *Révolution industrielle*, pp. 93–96; André Lefevre, *La Ligne de Strasbourg à Bâle: La Construction (1837–1846)* . . . (Strasbourg, 1947), pp. 20, 60; AN, 60 AQ 1, Cie. du chemin de fer, Paris–Orléans, P.-v., Conseil d'administration, I (1838), pp. 131, 146–48, 150, 164, 172; AN, 76 AQ 4, Chemin de fer de Paris à Rouen, Rapports du Conseil d'administration à l'assemblée générale des actionnaires (30 Nov. 1843), p. 6.

19. David H. Pinkney, "The Pacification of Paris: The Military Lessons of 1830" in John M. Merriman, ed., *France in 1830* (New York, 1975), pp. 196–98.

20. Crouzet, "Essai," pp. 62, 76, 83, Table 8b; Bairoch, *Révolution industrielle*, pp. 89, 91–92, 292, 300; Collins, "Labour Supply and Demand in European Agriculture," p. 89; R. Tresse, "Le Développement de la fabrication des faux en France de 1785 à 1827 et ses conséquences sur la pratique des moissons," *Annales: E.S.C.*, 10ᵉ Année (1955), p. 354; Vial, *Industrialisation*, p. 42; France, *Annuaire statistique*, LVIII (1951), p. 144; Ministre de la marine et des colonies, "Rapport au Roi," 2 Dec. 1845, in *Le Moniteur universel* (Paris), 20 Jan. 1846, p. 132.

21. Ernest H. Jenkins, *A History of the French Navy from Its Beginnings to the Present Day* (London, 1973), p. 292; A. Colin, *La Navigation commerciale au XIXᵉ siècle* (Paris, 1901), pp. 40–42, 54–55, Maurice Daumas, ed., *Histoire générale des techniques* (Paris, 1964–1979), III, pp. 341–43, 351; James Phinney Baxter III, *The Introduction of the Ironclad Warship* (Hamden, Conn., 1968), pp. 40, 60, 62–64; Ministre de la marine, "Rapport au Roi," 2 Dec. 1845, pp. 132, 134, 135; *Moniteur universel*, 10 July 1846, p. 2019.

22. Rostow, *Stages of Economic Growth*, p. 55; Marcewski, "Take-off Hypothesis," p. 129; François Caron, "Recherches sur le capital des voies de communication en France au XIXᵉ siècle . . ." in Pierre Léon et al., eds., *L'Industrialisation en Europe au XIXᵉ siècle* (Paris, 1972), p. 247; François Caron,

Histoire de l'exploitation d'un grand réseau français: La Compagnie d'un chemin de fer du Nord, 1846–1937 (Paris, 1973), pp. 57–58.

23. Braudel and Labrousse, eds., *Histoire économique et sociale,* III, p. 260; Bairoch, *Révolution industrielle,* p. 328 n. 26; Burat, *Exposition,* I, p. 36; Lefevre, *Ligne de Strasbourg à Bâle,* p. 51.

24. John H. Clapham, *The Economic History of Modern Britain* (2d ed.; Cambridge, Eng., 1930), I, pp. 386–87, 390–93; *Journal des chemins de fer* (Paris), 1re Année (1842), p. 22; Toutain, *Transports en France,* p. 144; A. G. Kenwood, "Railway Investment in Britain, 1825–1875," *Economica,* XXXII (1965), pp. 316–17; Henry Parris, "Railway Policy in Peel's Administration," *Bulletin of the Institute of Historical Research,* XXXIII (1960), p. 180.

25. Lévy-Leboyer, *Banques,* pp. 659–64, 671.

26. Louis-Maurice Jouffroy, *L'Ere du rail* (Paris, 1953), pp. 82–83; Toutain, *Transports en France,* pp. 8–9, 73; Arthur Young, *Travels in France and Italy During the Years 1787, 1788 and 1789* (Everyman Library, London, n.d.), pp. 9, 20, 28–29, 39, 40–42.

27. Jouffroy, *L'Ere du rail,* pp. 80, 83–84; Alfred Picard, *Traité des chemins de fer: Economie, politique, commerce, finance* (Paris, 1887), I, pp. 4–7; Lévy-Leboyer, *Banques,* p. 671.

28. Picard, *Traité des chemins de fer,* I, p. 8–11; *Moniteur universel,* 17 June 1842, p. 1513; *Moniteur des chemins de fer et de la navigation à vapeur* (Paris), 23 Apr. 1842, p. 26; Lévy-Leboyer, *Banques,* p. 672; Jouffroy, *L'Ere du rail,* p. 90.

29. Toutain, *Transports en France,* p. 183; François Caron, "Les Commandes des compagnies des chemins de fer en France, 1850–1914," *Revue d'histoire de la sidérurgie,* VI (1965), pp. 139–40.

30. *Journal des chemins de fer* (Paris), 2e Année (1843), pp. 499, 509, 649, 666, 690, 785; 3e Année (1844), passim. The tonnage of these orders can be only partially estimated. Early rails for French steam railroads were twelve or eighteen meters

in length and weighed twenty-five to thirty kilograms per meter. The first two orders of the Ministry of Public Works, for a total of 45,043 rails, would have amounted to at least 13,500 tons, perhaps as much as 24,500 tons. I have discovered no clue to the weight of rail chairs used on the early railways. —*Grande Encyclopédie Larousse* (Paris, 1975), p. 10109.

31. Lévy-Leboyer, *Banques*, pp. 677–82; Bertrand Gille, *La Banque et le crédit en France de 1815 à 1848* (Paris, 1959), pp. 349, 356; François Caron, "La Compagnie du Nord et ses fournisseurs (1845–1848)," *Revue du Nord*, XLV (1963), p. 350; François Caron, *Histoire de l'exploitation d'un grand réseau*, pp. 49–50; AN, 48 AQ 1, Chemin de fer du Nord, Procès-verbaux des assemblées générales, 28 Apr. 1846, p. 19; AN, 48 AQ 10, Chemin de fer du Nord, P.-v. des assemblées générales, 2 Dec. 1845, p. 14, 2 Jan. 1846, pp. 16, 30, 2 Feb. 1846, pp. 8, 16, 28 Apr. 1846, pp. 19, 20; AN, 48 AQ 3267–3272, Chemin de fer du Nord, Secrétariat, Enregistrement, Marchés, 1845–1848, passim.

32. AN, 13 AQ 33, Cie. du chemin de fer de Paris à Strasbourg, P.-v. des séances du conseil d'administration, 1845–1846, pp. 34, 60–61, 85, 90, 124–25, 134, 140–41, 162–83, 204–07, 221-25, 226–30, 231–34, 236–39, 254–57; AN, 13 AQ 34, Cie. du chemin de fer, Paris à Strasbourg, P.-v. des séances du conseil d'administration, 1847, pp. 289, 293–95, 299; Louis-Maurice Jouffroy, *Une Etape de la construction des grandes lignes de fer en France: La Ligne à la frontière d'Allemagne (1825–1852)* (Paris, 1932), II, pp. 60, 67, 123.

33. Caron, *Histoire de l'exploitation d'un grand réseau*, p. 53; AN, 13 AQ 33, Cie. du chemin de fer, Paris à Strasbourg, P.-v. des séances du conseil d'admin., 1845–1846, pp. 47–48, 134; Jouffroy, *Ligne de Paris à la frontière d'Allemagne*, II, p. 60; Jouffroy, *Etape de la construction des grandes lignes de fer*, III, pp. 60–61; Caron, "Compagnie du Nord," pp. 352–54.

34. France, *Annuaire statistique*, LVIII (1951), p. 134; Vial, *Industralisation*, Annexe, p. 9; Caron, "Commandes des chemins de fer," pp. 139–40; Caron, "Recherches sur la capital des voies de communication," p. 245; Roy, *Histoire de la*

famille Schneider, pp. 37, 137; Silly, "Reprise de Creusot," pp. 264–65; *Moniteur des chemins de fer* . . . , 18 June 1842, p. 9; Gille, *Banque et crédit*, pp. 350, 357; Jeanne Gaillard, *Paris, la ville, 1852–1870* . . . (Paris, 1977), p. 649; AN, 48 AQ 3267, Chemin de fer du Nord, Secrétariat, Enregistrement, Marchés, II, p. 135; Jeanne Gaillard, "Les Usines Cail et les métallurgistes de Grenelle," *Le Mouvement social*, xxxiii-xxxiv (1960–1961), pp. 35, 51; Théophraste (pseudonym of Louis Clot), *J.-F. Cail* (Paris, 1856), pp. 11, 13; Jules Gaudry, *Note sur François Cavé, constructeur de machines* (Paris, 1875), pp. 8–9, 13, 15; Lévy-Leboyer, *Banques*, p. 349 n. 25.

35. Caron, "Compagnie du Nord," p. 352; Caron, "Commandes des compagnies des chemins de fer," pp. 158–59; Lévy-Leboyer, *Banques*, pp. 697–98; Bertrand Gille, "La Sidérurgie française du XIXᵉ siècle avant l'acier," *Revue d'histoire de la sidérurgie*, VII (1966), pp. 258–59; Anon., "Les Crédits accordés à l'industrie sidérurgique au moment de la crise de 1848," *Revue d'histoire de la sidérurgie*, VI (1965), p. 191; Vial, *Industrialisation*, p. 37.

36. Caron, "Recherches," p. 247; Pedro Fraile, *The Diffusion of Iron Technology in Nineteenth Century France, Spain, and Italy* (M.A. thesis, Univ. of Texas at Austin, 1980), pp. 44–49; France, *Annuaire statistique*, LVIII (1951), p. 134; Emile Levasseur, *Histoire des classes ouvrières et de l'industrie en France de 1789 à 1870* (2d ed.; Paris, 1903–1904), II, p. 166; Guy Thuillier, *Georges Dufaud et les débuts du grand capitalisme dans la métallurgie en Nivernais au XIXᵉ siècle* (Paris, 1959), p. 91.

37. Fraile, *Diffusion of Iron Technology*, pp. 50–52; Vial, *Industralisation*, Annexe, p. 71.

38. Gille, *Recherches sur la grande entreprise*, pp. 29, 163; Thuillier, *Georges Dufaud*, pp. 169–70; Gille, "Sidérurgie française du XIXᵉ siècle," p. 258; Vial, *Industrialisation*, pp. 144–45; Bertrand Gille, *La Sidérurgie française au XIXᵉ siècle: Recherches historiques* (Geneva, 1968), p. 165; Jean-Bernard Silly, "La Disparition de la petite métallurgie rurale," *Revue d'histoire de la sidérurgie*, II (1961), pp. 49–50.

39. Vial, *Industrialisation*, pp. 144–45; Gerd H. Hardach,

"Le Problème de main d'oeuvre à Decazeville," *Revue d'histoire de la sidérurgie*, VIII (1967), p. 52; Roy, *Histoire de la famille Schneider*, p. 137.

40. J. Rolley, "Structure de l'industrie sidérurgique en France en 1845," *Revue d'histoire de la sidérurgie*, I (1960), 2ᵉ Trimestre, pp. 41, 51.

41. Lévy-Leboyer, *Banques*, p. 685; Pierre Guillaume, *La Compagnie des Mines de la Loire, 1846–1854: Essai sur l'apparition de la grande industrie capitaliste en France* (Paris, 1966), pp. 13–14; Pierre Guillaume, "Grèves et organisations ouvrières chez les mineurs de la Loire au milieu du XIXᵉ siècle," *Le Mouvement social*, XLIII (1963), p. 5.

42. Louis Bergeron, "French Industrialization in the Nineteenth Century: An Attempt to Define a National Way," paper presented at the Twelfth Annual Conference, Western Society for French History, Univ. of New Mexico, 26 Oct. 1984, pp. 10–16; Vial, *Industrialisation*, pp. 201–02, 205–07, 436; Silly, "Disparition de la petite métallurgie," pp. 49–50, 61; Rolley, "Structure de l'industrie sidérurgique, 1845," p. 51.

43. Jean Bouvier, *Un Siècle de banque française* (Paris, 1973), pp. 66–67; Tom Kemp, *Economic Forces in French History: An Essay on the Development of the French Economy, 1760–1914* (London, 1971), pp. 123, 124, 127; Braudel and Labrousse, eds., *Histoire économique et sociale*, III, pp. 368–69, 395; Léon Faucher, "Des projets de loi sur les chemins de fer," *Revue des deux mondes*, new series, 13ᵉ Année (1843), vol. 2, pp. 359–60; David S. Landes, "Vieille Banque et banque nouvelle: La Révolution financière du dix-neuvième siècle," *Revue d'histoire moderne et contemporaine*, III (1956), p. 314; Adeline Daumard, ed., *Les Fortunes françaises au XIXᵉ siècle* (The Hague, 1974), pp. 159, 164, 230–33; Charles F. Freedeman, *Joint-stock Enterprise in France, 1807–1867: From Privileged Company to Modern Corporation* (Chapel Hill, 1979), pp. 69–70.

44. Braudel and Labrousse, eds., *Histoire économique et sociale*, III, pp. 368–69, 394–95; Lévy-Leboyer, *Banques*, pp. 699, 702; Toshihiro Tanaka, "Note on the Relationship Between the English Interests and the French Interests in French

Railway Companies of the 1840s," *Journal of Economics of Fukuoka University*, XXVII (1982), pp. 305, 310–12.

45. Toutain, *Transports en France*, pp. 8, 45, 55, 79–80, 109, 156, 160, 165, 276–79; Caron, *Histoire de l'exploitation d'un grand réseau*, pp. 57–58.

46. Toutain, *Transports en France*, p. 144; Alexandre Moreau de Jonnès, *Statistique de l'industrie de la France* (Paris, 1856), pp. 13, 65–66; Jules Michelet, *Le Peuple* (2d ed.; Paris, 1846), pp. 79–81; France, *Annuaire statistique*, LVIII (1951), p. 207.

47. Michelet, *Le Peuple*, p. 80.

48. Gaillard, *Paris, la ville*, pp. 343 n. 3, 441, 530; Chambre de commerce de Paris, *Statistique de l'industrie à Paris . . . 1847–1848: Résultats généraux* (Paris, 1851), Part 1, pp. 108–09; J.-C. Toutain, *La Consommation alimentaire en France de 1789 à 1964*, Cahiers de l'I.S.E.A., V, no. 11 (Geneva, 1971), p. 1946; Price, *Modernization of Rural France*, p. 305. The influence of the railways on the structure of agricultural markets in France in the nineteenth century is explored in detail in Roger Price's new book, *The Modernization of Rural France* (London, 1983).

49. Ted W. Margadant, *French Peasants in Revolt: The Insurrection of 1851* (Princeton, 1979), pp. 338–44; Charles Tilly, "How Protest Modernized in France" in William O. Aydelotte et al., eds., *The Dimensions of Quantitative Research in History* (Princeton, 1972), pp. 208–18, 224–26, 247–50; Charles Tilly, Louise Tilly, and Richard Tilly, *The Rebellious Century, 1830–1930* (Cambridge, Mass., 1975), pp. 41, 46, 48, 50–51, 54–55. See also Ted W. Margadant's review article, "Tradition and Modernity in Rural France During the Nineteenth Century," *Journal of Modern History*, LVI (1984), p. 667-97.

CHAPTER III

1. Roger Price, *The Modernization of Rural France: Communications Networks and Agricultural Market Structures in Nineteenth-century France* (London, 1983), pp. 47–55.

2. Pierre Léon in Fernand Braudel and Ernest Labrousse, eds., *Histoire économique et sociale de France* (Paris, 1976), III, p. 241.

3. Braudel and Labrousse, eds., *Histoire économique et sociale*, III, p. 250; J.-C. Toutain, *Les Transports en France de 1830 à 1965*, Cahiers de l'I.S.E.A., Series AF, 9 (Paris, 1967), pp. 73–75, 117; Price, *Modernization of Rural France*, p. 29–34, 35–36, Félix Rivet, *Navigation à vapeur sur la Saône et le Rhône (1783–1863)*, (Paris, 1962), pp. 29, 146, 161, 164; Stendhal, *Travels in the South of France*, Elisabeth Abbott, trans. (New York, 1970), pp. 51, 55.

4. Toutain, *Transports*, pp. 7–9, 11; Braudel and Labrousse, eds., *Histoire économique et sociale*, III, pp. 243, 245–46; Paul Bairoch, *Révolution industrielle et sous-développement* (4th ed.; Paris, 1974), pp. 323–25; Georges-Eugène Haussmann, *Mémoires* (4th ed.; Paris, 1890–1893), I, pp. 67–71.

5. Toutain, *Transports*, pp. 9, 11, 271; Bairoch, *Révolution industrielle*, pp. 248, 325; Braudel and Labrousse, eds., *Histoire économique et sociale*, III, p. 248; Price, *Modernization of Rural France*, pp. 36–42, 262–63; Alain Corbin, *Archaïsme et modernité en Limousin au XIXᵉ siècle, 1845–1880* (Paris, 1975), pp. 119–20; France, *Annuaire statistique*, XXX (1910), "Résumé retrospectif," p. 55.

6. L. de Lavergne, *Economie rurale de la France depuis 1789* (Paris, 1860), p. 442, quoted in Toutain, *Transports*, p. 9.

7. Braudel and Labrousse, eds., *Histoire économique et sociale*, III, pp. 246–47; Price, *Modernization of Rural France*, pp. 39–42, 269–70.

8. *Annuaire du Départment de la Corrèze*, 1827, p. 146, quoted in Corbin, *Archaïsme et modernité en Limousin*, p. 120.

9. Corbin, *Archaïsme et modernité en Limousin*, pp. 119–24, 128–29, 1022.

10. Toutain, *Transports*, pp. 15–16, 55, 56–57; Braudel and Labrousse, eds., *Histoire économique et sociale*, III, p. 254; Bairoch, *Révolution industrielle*, pp. 329–30.

11. Toutain, *Transports*, pp. 15, 46, 148–49, 159–60; Bairoch, *Révolution industrielle*, pp. 329–30; Braudel and La-

brousse, eds., *Histoire économique et sociale*, III, pp. 254, 266–67.

12. France, *Annuaire statistique*, XXX (1910), "Résumé rétrospectif," p. 55; Toutain, *Transports*, pp. 45, 79, 144–45, 248–49; Braudel and Labrousse, eds., *Histoire économique et sociale*, III, pp. 268–69.

13. Chambre de commerce de Paris, *Statistique de l'industrie à Paris* . . . *1847–1848* (Paris, 1851), Part 1, p. 38; Chambre de commerce de Paris, *Statistique de l'industrie à Paris* . . . *1860* (Paris, 1864), p. XX; Louis Chevalier, *La Formation de la population parisienne au XIXᵉ siècle* (Paris, 1950), p. 284.

14. André Armengaud, *La Population française au XIXᵉ siècle* (Paris, 1971), pp. 73–75; Braudel and Labrousse, eds., *Histoire économique et sociale*, III, pp. 217–20, 231; France, *Annuaire statistique*, I (1878), pp. 17, 19; Etienne Juillard, *La Vie rurale dans la plaine de Basse Alsace: Essai de géographie sociale* (Strasbourg, 1953), pp. 291–92; Joseph Antoine Roy, *Histoire de la famille Schneider et du Creusot* (Paris, 1962), p. 38.

15. Charles H. Pouthas, *La Population française pendant la première moitié du XIXᵉ siècle* (Paris, 1956), pp. 32–37, 201; Armengaud, *Population au XIXᵉ siècle*, pp. 24–25, 63–65; J.-C. Toutain, *La Population de la France de 1700 à 1959*, Cahiers de l'I.S.E.A., Series AF, 3 (Paris, 1963), pp. 54–56; Paul Hohenberg, "Migrations et fluctuations démographiques dans la France rurale, 1836–1901," *Annales: E.S.C..*, 29ᵉ Année (1974), p. 474; Georges Dupeux, "La Croissance urbaine en France au XIXᵉ siècle," *Revue d'histoire économique et sociale*, LII (1974), pp. 180, 182–84, 186.

16. Armengaud, *Population au XIXᵉ siècle*, p. 33.

17. Armengaud, *Population au XIXᵉ siècle*, pp. 63-64; André Armengaud, *La Population française au XXᵉ siècle* (Paris, 1965), pp. 102–03; Toutain, *Population*, pp. 54–56, 200; France, *Annuaire statistique*, LXXII (1966), p. 23.

18. Braudel and Labrousse eds., *Histoire économique et sociale*, III, pp. 224–26; Armengaud, *Population au XIXᵉ siècle*, pp. 67, 69–70; Bairoch, *Révolution industrielle*, pp.

296–97, 307–09, 311; Pouthas, *Population française*, pp. 205–15, 224–25; Juillard, *La Vie rurale . . . Basse Alsace*, pp. 270, 276; Pierre Sorlin, *La Société française, 1840–1914* (Paris, 1969–1971), I, p. 39; Roger Brunet, *Les Campagnes toulousaines: Etude géographique* (Toulouse, 1965), pp. 386, 391; Gilbert Garrier, *Paysans du Beaujolais et du Lyonnais, 1800–1970* (Grenoble, 1973), pp. 212–13; Lawrence Wylie et al., *Chanzeaux: A Village in Anjou* (Cambridge, Mass., 1966), pp. 176–77.

19. Abel Chatelain, *Les Migrants temporaires en France de 1800 à 1914: Histoire économique et sociale des migrants temporaires des campagnes françaises au XIXe siècle et au début du XXe siècle* (Lille, 1977), pp. 813, 1105; E.J.T.C. Collins, "Labour Supply and Demand in European Agriculture, 1800-1880," in E. L. Jones and S. J. Woolf, eds., *Agrarian Change and Economic Development* (London, 1969), pp. 65–66; Braudel and Labrousse eds., *Histoire économique et sociale*, III, p. 225.

20. Marcel Blanchard, "La Politique ferroviaire du Second Empire," *Annales d'histoire économique et sociale*, VI (1934), p. 531.

21. Armengaud, *Population au XIXe siècle*, p. 69; Braudel and Labrousse, eds., *Histoire économique et sociale*, III, p. 225.

22. Braudel and Labrousse, eds., *Histoire économique et sociale*, III, p. 298; Pierre Rousseau, *Histoire des techniques* (Paris, 1962), pp. 356–57; Charles Singer et al., eds., *A History of Technology*, vol. IV, *The Industrial Revolution, 1750–1850* (Oxford, 1958), p. 646; Maurice Daumas, ed., *Histoire générale des techniques* (Paris, 1964–1979), III, pp. 421–22; Roger Price, *Economic Modernization of France, 1730–1880* (New York, 1975), p. 26.

23. *Moniteur universel*, 11 May 1842, p. 1082; Stewart Edwards, *The Paris Commune of 1871* (London, 1971), p. 320; France, Ministère des travaux publiques, *Album statistique graphique de 1900* (Paris, 1906), plate 39; Roger Price, "Techniques of Repression: The Control of Popular Protest in Mid-nineteenth-century France," *Historical Journal*, XXV

(1982), pp. 876–77; Alfred Picard, *Traité des chemins de fer: Economie, politique, commerce, finance* . . . (Paris, 1887), I, pp. 135–40; Louis Girard, *Nouvelle Histoire de Paris: La Deuxième République et le Second Empire, 1848–1870* (Paris, 1981), p. 42; Louis Girard, *La Garde nationale, 1814–1871* (Paris, 1964), p. 318; Jean Vidalenc, "La Province et les journées de juin," *Etudes d'histoire moderne et contemporaine*, II (1948), pp. 101–02, 105–07, 111–12, 141; Charles Tilly and Lynn Lees, "Le Peuple de juin 1848," *Annales: E.S.C.*, 29ᵉ Année (1974), p. 1068.

24. Jeffrey Kieve, *The Electrical Telegraph in the U.K.: A Social and Economic History* (New York, 1973), p. 46; Braudel and Labrousse, eds., *Histoire économique et sociale*, III, pp. 284, 286–87; Price, *Modernization*, p. 26; France, *Annuaire statistique*, XXX (1910), "Résumé rétrospectif," p. 64.

25. Claude Bellanger et al., eds., *Histoire générale de la presse française*, vol. II, *De 1815 à 1870* (Paris, 1969), p. 25; France, *Annuaire statistique*, III (1910), "Résumé rétrospectif," pp. 10, 12, 62, 63; Patrick Hamilton, *A Hundred Years of Postage Stamps* (2d ed.; London, 1940), p. 33.

26. Bellanger et al., eds., *Histoire de la presse*, II, p. 25; Price, *Economic Modernization*, pp. 53–54; Braudel and Labrousse, eds., *Histoire économique et sociale*, III, pp. 454–55; Jean-Pierre Aguet, "Le Tirage des quotidiens de Paris sous la Monarchie de Juillet," *Revue suisse d'histoire*, X (1960), p. 264.

27. Anthony Sutcliffe, "Capital of Europe: Paris in the Nineteenth Century," Unpublished MS, p. 7; Louis Chevalier, *La Formation de la population parisienne au XIXᵉ siècle* (Paris, 1950), p. 108; Girard, *Nouvelle Histoire de Paris, 1848–1870*, pp. 205, 208–09, 214.

28. Braudel and Labrousse, eds., *Histoire économique et sociale*, III, p. 369; Bertrand Gille, *Histoire de la Maison Rothschild* (Geneva, 1965), I, pp. 355–56; Tashihiro Tanaka, "Note on the Relationship Between the English Interests and the French Interests in French Railway Companies of the 1840s," *Journal of Economics of Fukuoka University*, XXVII, no. 2 (1982), pp. 292–93, 295, 311.

29. André-Jean Tudesq, *Les Grands Notables en France (1840–1849): Etude historique d'une psychologie sociale* (Paris, 1964), I, pp. 262, 234, II, pp. 651–52, 655–56, 667–68, 856, 860, 869, 1231; André Jardin and André-Jean Tudesq, *La France des notables* (Paris, 1973), II, pp. 221–22.

30. Braudel and Labrousse, eds., *Histoire économique et sociale*, III, p. 272; Kimon Doukas, *The French Railroads and the State* (New York, 1945), pp. 22–23.

31. *Moniteur universel*, 20 July 1837, p. 1868.

32. Louis Gueneau, "La Législation restrictive du travail des enfants," *Revue d'histoire économique et sociale*, XV (1927), pp. 497–98, 501–03; Braudel and Labrousse, eds., *Histoire économique et sociale*, III, pp. 784–85; Tudesq, *Grands Notables*, II, p. 595; Jeanne Gaillard, *Paris, la ville, 1852–1870* . . . (Paris, 1977), pp. 412–14.

33. Jean-Baptiste Duroselle, *Les Débuts du Catholicisme social en France (1822–1877)* (Paris, 1951), p. 229.

34. *Moniteur universel*, 7 July 1838, pp. 1897–98, 25 Dec. 1839, 2187–88; Gérard Bleaudonu and Guy Le Gauffey, "Naissance des asiles d'aliénés," *Annales: E.S.C.*, 30ᵉ Année (1975), pp. 96–98, 118; C. Lanteri-Laura, "La Chronicité dans la psychiatrie moderne," *Annales: E.S.C.*, 27ᵉ Année (1972), pp. 560–61.

35. Charles Tilly, "How Protest Modernized in France" in William O. Aydelotte et al., eds., *The Dimensions of Quantitative Research in History* (Princeton, 1972), pp. 195, 225–26; Charles Tilly, "The Changing Place of Collective Violence" in Melvin Richter, ed., *Essays in Theory and History: An Approach to the Social Sciences* (Cambridge, Mass., 1970), pp. 139–40, 149, 154; Price, "Techniques of Repression," pp. 876–77, 887.

36. Tilly, "How Protest Modernized," p. 226.

37. Ted W. Margadant, *French Peasants in Revolt: The Insurrection of 1851* (Princeton 1979), pp. 336–44; Eugen Weber, "Comment la politique vint aux paysans: A Second Look at Peasant Politization," *American Historical Review*, LXXXVII (1982), pp. 359–64, 377.

38. Jardin and Tudesq, *France des notables*, II, p. 220; Weber, "Comment la politique vint aux paysans," p. 388.

39. André-Jean Tudesq, "Les Chefs de cabinet sous la Monarchie de Juillet: L'Exemple d'Alphonse Génie" in Michel Antoine et al., *Origines et histoire des cabinets des ministres* (Geneva, 1975), pp. 39, 42–44, 49; Guy Thuillier, *Bureaucratie et bureaucrats en France au XIXe siècle* (Geneva, 1980), pp. 478–98.

40. Antoine Prost, *Histoire de l'enseignement en France, 1800–1967* (Paris, 1968), pp. 90–92, 104–05, 108; Roger Thabault, *Mon Village, ses hommes, ses routes, son école* (Paris, 1945), pp. 80–81; Corbin, *Archaïsme et modernité en Limousin*, I, pp. 336–40; André Thuillier, *Economie et société nivernaises au début du XIXe siècle* (Paris, 1974), p. 372; François Furet and Jacquet Ozouf, *Lire et écrire: L'Alphabétisation des français de Calvin à Jules Ferry* (Paris, 1977), I, pp. 138–39, 147–48; Mary Jo Maynes, "Work or School? Youth and the Family in the Midi in the Early Nineteenth Century" in Donald N. Baker and Patrick J. Harrigan, eds., *The Making of Frenchmen: Current Directions in Higher Education in France, 1679–1979* (Waterloo, Ont., 1980), pp. 115–27; Louis Trenard, *Salvandy et son temps, 1795–1856* (Lille, 1968), pp. 353, 355, 356; James Smith Allen, *Popular French Romanticism: Authors, Readers, and Books in the 19th Century* (Syracuse, N.Y., 1981), p. 165; France, Ministère de l'instruction publique, *Statistique comparée de l'enseignement primaire, 1829–1877* (Paris, 1880), pp. 78–79; P. M. Jones, "An Improbable Democracy: Nineteenth Century Elections in the Massif Central," *English Historical Review*, XCVII (July 1982), p. 534.

Recent studies by Raymond Grew, Patrick Harrigan, and James Whitney have revealed that rapid increases in primary school enrollments and in the number of schools began in the 1820s, well before the passage of the Guizot law, and by implication they discount that law's direct influence on either enrollments or the number of schools. Their data do show, however, a marked acceleration in rate of growth in the first few years after the passage of the law. Moreover, they find that the increase in enrollments became general throughout the country only in the three decades *after* 1837.—Raymond Grew, Patrick J. Harrigan, and Jaems B. Whitney, "La Scolarisation en France, 1829–1906," *Annales: E.S.C.*, 39ᵉ Année (1984), p. 117, "The Availability of Schooling in Nineteenth-Century France," *Journal of Interdisciplinary History*, XIV (1983), pp. 30-32.

41. Furet and Ozouf, *Lire et écrire*, I, pp. 180, 275–76, 308–13; Thabault, *Mon Village*, pp. 79–80; Trenard, *Salvandy*, p. 356; Archives nationales, F¹⁷ 9306, Ministre de l'instruction publique, Inspecteur primaire du Département du Puy-de-Dôme, Rapport général, 1839–1840 (15 Oct. 1840); Inspecteur prim. du Dépt. de la Seine-Inférieure, Rapport gén. [n.d., probably 1837–1838 or 1838–1839]; Mary Jo Maynes, "Work or School?" p. 102; Thuillier, *Economie et société*, pp. 372–73.

42. France, *Annuaire statistique*, XI (1888), pp. 414–15, XXX (1910), "Résumé rétrospectif," p. 19; France, Ministère de l'instruction publique, *Statistique rétrospective: Etat récapitulatif indiquant par département le nombre de conjoints qui ont signé l'acte de mariage au 17ᵉ, 18ᵉ et 19ᵉ siècles* ("Enquête Maggiolo") (Paris, 1879), pp. 3, 5.

43. Furet and Ozouf, *Lire et écrire*, I, pp. 137–44, 147–53; François Furet and Jacques Ozouf, "Trois Siècles de métissage culturel," *Annales: E.S.C.*, 32ᵉ Année (1977), 491–93; Corbin, *Archaïsme et modernité*, p. 331; Thabault, *Mon Village*, pp. 130, 133; Guy Thuillier, *Aspects de l'économie nivernaise au XIXᵉ siècle* (Paris, 1966), p. 292; Adeline Daumard, *Les Bourgeois de Paris au XIXᵉ siècle* (Paris, 1970), p. 285.

44. Pierre-Jakez Hélias, *The Horse of Pride: Life in a Breton Village* (New Haven, 1978), p. 135.

45. France, *Annuaire statistique*, XXX (1910), "Résumé rétrospectif," pp. 13, 22.

46. Guy Thuillier, *La Promotion sociale* (2d ed.; Paris, 1969), pp. 13, 14–16; AN, F¹⁷ 9351, Résumé de l'inspection des écoles primaires ... visitées pendant l'année scolaire 1835–36; F¹⁷ 9310, Ministère de l'instruction publique, In-

specteur des écoles primaires, Dépt. de la Nièvre, Rapport
gén., 1843 (16 Dec. 1843); Sous-inspecteur du Dépt. de
l'Haute-Vienne, Rapport gén., 1845–1846 (4 Sept. 1846); Inspecteur prim. du Dépt. du Var, Rapport gén., 842–43, Rapport gén., 1846–1847; Inspecteur prim. du Dépt. du Nord,
Situation de l'instruction primaire, 1 Oct. 1847.

47. Maurice Agulhon, *La République au village: Les Populations du Var de la Révolution à la Seconde République*
(Paris, 1970), p. 194.

48. Quoted in Edouard Baratier, ed., *Histoire de la Provence*
(Toulouse, 1969), p. 535.

49. Agulhon, *République au village*, pp. 190–94, 203–04;
Baratier, *Histoire de la Provence*, p. 535; Furet and Ozouf,
Lire et écrire, I, pp. 324–44; Furet and Ozouf, "Trois siècles
de métissage culturel," p. 491.

50. Ruth L. White, *"L'Avenir" de La Mennais: Son Rôle
dans la presse de son temps* (Paris, 1974), pp. 174–75; Charles
S. Phillips, *The Church in France, 1789–1848: A Study in
Renewal* (New York, 1966), pp. 289–91; Marvin L. Brown,
Jr., *Louis Veuillot, French Ultramontane Catholic Journalist
and Layman, 1813–1883* (Durham, N.C., 1977), pp. 64, 66,
73–74; Maurice Crubellier, *Histoire culturelle de la France,
XIXe–XXe siècle* (Paris, 1974), p. 89; *Dictionnaire biographique français* (Paris, 1933–), II, p. 370; G. H. Tavard,
"Assumptionists," *New Catholic Encyclopedia* (New York,
1967), I, p. 975.

CHAPTER IV

1. Pierre-Joseph Proudhon, *Carnets* (8th ed.; Paris, 1960–
1968), I, p. 47.

2. W. J. Reader, *Professional Men: The Rise of the Professional Classes in Nineteenth-century England* (London, 1966),
pp. 161–66; Burton J. Bledstein, *The Culture of Professionalism: The Middle Class and Development of Higher Education in America* (New York, 1976), pp. 83–92; Robert H.

Wiebe, *The Search for Order, 1870–1920* (New York, 1967), pp. vii–viii, xiv, 111.

3. Société des gens de lettres, *Au Service des écrivains de notre temps* (Paris, 1971), p. 1; Robert Escarpet, *Sociologie de la littérature* (5th ed.; Paris, 1973), pp. 8, 54–55.

4. *Gazette des hôpitaux* (Paris), 10 June 1845, pp. 269–70, 9 Nov. 1845, p. 541; George D. Sussman, "The Glut of Doctors in Mid-nineteenth-century France," *Comparative Studies in Society and History*, XIX (1977), pp. 288–89; Louis Mazoyer, "Catégories d'âge et groupes sociaux: Les Jeunes Générations françaises de 1830," *Annales d'histoire économique "et sociale*, 10ᵉ Année (1938), pp. 396–97, 408–09; Louis trenard, "Les Etudes médicales sous Louis-Philippe" in *Actes du 91ᵉ Congrès des Sociétés savantes* (Rennes, 1966), Section d'histoire moderne et contemporaine, III, pp. 167, 171, 186–90; George Weisz, "The Politics of Medical Professionalization in France, 1845–1848," *Journal of Social History*, XII (1978), pp. 5–7; Louis Trenard, *Salvandy et son temps, 1795–1856* (Lille, 1968), p. 794.

5. *Gazette des hôpitaux*, 9 Nov. 1845, p. 543, 11 Nov., p. 545; Trenard, "Etudes médicales," pp. 184, 186–87.

6. *Gazette des hôpitaux*, 17 June 1845, p. 281, 5 Aug., p. 361, 7 Aug., pp. 366–67, 23 Aug., p. 388, 1 Nov., p. 509, 2 Nov., p. 516, 11 Dec., p. 604; Trenard, "Etudes médicales," p. 190; Jacques Léonard, *La Médicine entre les pouvoirs et les savoirs* (Paris, 1981), pp. 213–14.

7. *Gazette des hôpitaux*, 1 Nov. 1845, p. 509, 9 Nov., p. 541, 11 Nov., p. 545, 13 Nov., pp. 549–51, 15 Nov., p. 555.

8. Weisz, "Politics of Medical Professionalization," pp. 8, 10; Trenard, "Etudes médicales," p. 191; *Gazette des hôpitaux*, 9 Dec. 1845, p. 598, 27 Jan. 1846, p. 44.

9. *Gazette des hôpitaux*, 7 Nov. 1845, p. 536, 8 Nov., p. 538.

10. *Gazette des hôpitaux*, 15 Nov. 1845, p. 557, Trenard, "Etudes médicales," pp. 191, 194, 211, 213–14; Trenard, *Salvandy*, pp. 794–96; Weisz, "*Medical Profession*," pp. 13, 22–23; *Le Moniteur universel* (Paris), 22 June 1847, p. 1676.

11. *Gazette des hôpitaux*, 5 Nov. 1845, p. 521, 6 Nov., p.

529, 15 Nov., p. 556, 25 Nov., p. 513, 9 Dec., p. 558, 27 Jan. 1846, p. 43, 19 Feb., p. 83, 2 June, pp. 253–54, 27 Oct., p. 501.

12. *L'Union médicale: Journal des intérêts scientifiques et pratiques moraux et professionnels* (Paris), *Prospectus* [n.d.]; Letter soliciting subscriptions, 20 June 1846; *L'Union médicale*, 2 Jan. 1847, pp. 1–2.

13. M. Birr, "La Profession d'architecte à travers les âges" in Institut technique du bâtiment et des travaux publics, *Circulaire*, series A, no. 5 (10 Feb. 1944), pp. 3–4; Roger de Saint-Chamas, *L'Architecte* (Paris, 1957), pp. 19, 20; Société centrale des architectes, *Observations presentées par la Société sur la nécessité d'un diplôme d'architecte* (Paris, 1847), pp. 1, 3–4, 7–14, 18.

14. Terry Shinn, "Des Corps de l'Etat au secteur industriel: Genèse de la profession d'ingénieur, 1750–1920," *Revue française de sociologie*, XIX (1978), pp. 39–40, 47–48, 53, 56–57; Société centrale des ingénieurs civils, *Compte rendu*, I (Mar.–May 1848); Société des ingénieurs civils de France, *Mémoires et compte-rendu*, 51ᵉ Année (1898), p. xv; Société des ingénieurs civils de France, *Soixantenaire, 1848–1908* (Paris, 1908), pp. 17–18, 23, 30; John Hubbell Weiss, *The Making of Technological Man: The Social Origins of French Engineering Education* (Cambridge, Mass., 1982), pp. 86, 215–16, 277.

15. Guy Thuillier, *Bureaucratie et bureaucrats en France au XIXᵉ siècle* (Geneva, 1980), pp. xii–xiii, 177–92; Clive Church, *Revolution and Red Tape: The French Ministerial Bureaucracy, 1770–1850* (Oxford, 1981), pp. 237, 293, 300–01.

16. Thuillier, *Bureaucratie*, pp. 471–98.

17. Vincent Wright, "L'Ecole nationale d'administration de 1848–1849: Un Echec révélateur," *Revue historique*, CCLV (1976), pp. 21–42; Church, *Revolution and Red Tape*, pp. 302, 306.

18. Paul Gerbod, *La Condition universitaire en France au XIXᵉ siècle* (Paris, 1965), pp. 10–12, 21, 23, 141, 143, 169, 175, 184–85; Paul Gerbod, "Associations et syndicalismes

universitaires de 1828 à 1928 (dans l'enseignement secondaire public)," *Le Mouvement social*, LV (Apr.–Jun. 1966), pp. 9–10.

19. *Bulletin des lois du Royaume de France*, IXe Série, 1e Partie, *Lois*, 2e Semestre 1833, pp. 254–56; Antoine Prost, *Histoire d'enseignement en France, 1800–1967* (Paris, 1968), p. 140; Peter V. Meyers, "Professionalization and societal Change: Rural Teachers in Nineteenth Century France," *Journal of Social History*, IX (1976), p. 542; AN, F[17] 9307, Rapport sur la situation de l'instruction publique dans le Dépt. d'Indre-et-Loire, 1 Aug. 1839.

20. AN, F[17] 9306, Inspecteur prim., Dépt. du Puy-de-Dôme, Rapport gén., 1838–1839, 10 Jan. 1840; F[17] 9307, Rapport sur la situation de l'instruction publique dans le Dépt. d'Indre-et-Loire, 1 Aug. 1839; F[17] 9311, Inspecteur prim., Dépt. de Saône-et-Loire, Rapport gén., 1845–1846, 15 Nov. 1846; F[17] 10293, Recteur de l'Académie de Lyon au Ministre de l'instruction publique, 8 June 1847.

21. Meyers, "Professionalization," p. 543; René Lemoine, *La Loi Guizot, 28 juin 1833: Son Application dans le Département de la Somme* (Abbeville, 1933), pp. 174–76; Alain Corbin, *Archaïsme et modernité en Limousin au XIXe siècle, 1845–1880* (Paris, 1975), I, pp. 341, 343–49; AN, F[17] 9306, Inspecteur prim., Dépt. des Basses-Pyrénées, Rapport gén., 1838–1839, 7 Dec. 1839; Inspecteur prim., Dépt. du Puy-de-Dôme, Rapport gén., 1837–1838, 30 Nov. 1838; AN, F[17] 9307, Inspecteur prim., Dépt. de la Sarthe, Rapport gén., Nov. 1839; Inspecteur prim., Dépt. de Seine-et-Marne, Considération générale sur l'ensemble de l'instruction primaire dans le département, Dec. 1838; Inspecteur prim., Dépt. de l'Aisne, Rapport gén., 1839–1840; F[17] 9311, Inspecteur prim., Dépt. du Bas-Rhin, Rapport gén., 1846; Inspecteur prim., Dépt. de l'Ain, Rapport gén., 1846, 4 Jan. 1847.

22. Prost, *Enseignement en France*, pp. 137–38; Meyers, "Professionalization," pp. 545–46; Félix Ponteil, *Histoire de l'enseignement en France: Les Grandes Etapes, 1789–1964* (Paris, 1966), pp. 201–02; AN, F[17] 9306, Inspecteur prim., Dépt. de l'Yonne, Rapport gén., 1837–1838, 7 Dec. 1838;

Inspecteur prim., Dépt. de Seine-Inférieure [n.d., probably 1837–1838 or 1838–1839]; Inspecteur prim., Dépt. des Basses-Pyrénées, Rapport gén., 1838–1839, F¹⁷ 9310, Inspecteur prim., Dépt. du Cher, Rapport gén., 1842–1843, 15 Oct. 1843; F¹⁷ 9311, Inspecteur prim., Dépt. de la Meuse, Rapport gén., 1846; Trenard, *Salvandy*, p. 664; *Bulletin des lois*, IXᵉ Série, 15 (1837), pp. 785–88.

23. AN, F¹⁷ 9307, Inspecteur prim., Dépt. de Seine-Inférieure, Rapport gén., 1839–1840; Inspecteur prim., Dépt. de la Sarthe, Rapport gén., Nov. 1839; Inspecteur prim., Dépt. de l'Aisne, Rapport gén., 1838–1839, 15 May 1840; Inspecteur prim., Dépt. des Pyrénées-Orientales, Rapport gén., 1839–1840, 27 Oct. 1840; Inspecteur prim., Dépt. de la Dordogne, Rapport gén., 1839–1840, 24 Dec. 1840; Inspecteur prim., Dépt. de l'Oise, Rapport sur l'instruction primaire, 1839–1840; F¹⁷ 9311, Inspecteur prim., Dépt. de Tarn-et-Garonne, Rapport triennale, 1844–1846, 15 Jan. 1847; Inspecteur prim., Dépt. de la Mayenne, Rapport gén., 1845–1846; F¹⁷ 10302, Les Instituteurs primaires communaux du Canton de Liancourt (Oise) à Messieurs les membres de la Chambre des députés, 25 May 1847; F¹⁷ 10309, Inspecteur prim., Dépt. du Var, Rapport sur l'état de l'instruction primaire, 1846–1847, 20 Oct. 1847; *L'Echo des écoles primaires: Journal des instituteurs* (Paris), I (1818), pp. 572–73, 575–77, 629; *L'Emancipation de l'enseignement: Journal politique, scientifique et littéraire* (Paris), 27 May 1848.

24. AN, F¹⁷ 9311, Inspecteur prim., Dépt. de la Haute-Garonne, Rapport gén., 1845–1846; Inspecteur prim., Dépt. de la Meuse, Rapport gén., 1846; Inspecteur prim., Dépt. de l'Isère, Observations à la statistique de 1846.

25. Prost, *Enseignement de France*, pp. 140–41; AN, F¹⁷ 9306, Inspecteur prim., Dépt. des Deux-Sèvres, Rapport gén., 1837–1838; F¹⁷ 9310, Inspecteur prim., Dépt. des Bouches-du-Rhône, Rapport gén., 1842–1843; Inspecteur prim., Dépt. de la Nièvre, Rapport gén., 1843, 16 Dec. 1843; F¹⁷ 9351, Résumé de l'inspection des écoles primaires, 1835–1836; F¹⁷ 10309, Inspecteur prim., Dépt. de la Haute-Vienne, Rapport gén., 1845–1846, 4 Sept. 1846; Inspecteur prim., Dépt de la

Nièvre, Rapport gén., 1847; Inspecteur prim., Dépt. de la Meurthe, Rapport gén., 1846, 29 Jan. 1846, 29 Jan. 1847; Inspecteur prim., Dépt. de la Var, Rapport gén., 1846–1847, 20 Oct. 1847; Sous-inspecteur prim., Dépt. de la Haute-Vienne, Rapport gén., 1845–1846, 4 Sept. 1846; Peter V. Meyers, "Teachers in Revolutionary France: The *Instituteurs* in 1848" in *Consortium on Revolutionary Europe, Proceedings 1977* (Athens, Ga., 1978), pp. 154–55; Meyers, "Professionalization," pp. 546–48.

26. Bertrand Gille, *Recherches sur la formation de la grande entreprise capitaliste (1815–1848)* (Paris, 1959), pp. 129–30, 134, 135–36, 142, 144; Bertrand Gille, "Esquisse d'une histoire du syndicalisme patronale dans l'industrie sidérurgique française," *Revue d'histoire de la sidérurgie*, IV (1964), pp. 219–21, 223, 226–27; Peter N. Stearns, "Patterns of Industrial Strike Activity in France During the July Monarchy," *American Historical Review*, LXX (1965), pp. 392–94.

27. Fernand Braudel and Ernest Labrousse, eds., *Histoire économique et sociale de la France* (Paris, 1976), III, pp. 804, 808–13; William H. Sewell, Jr., *Work and Revolution in France: The Language of Labor from the Old Regime to 1848* (Cambridge, Eng., 1980), pp. 162–67, 194–220; Jacques Rancière, *La Nuit des prolétaires* (Paris, 1981), passim.

28. Braudel and Labrousse, eds., *Histoire économique et sociale*, III, p. 814; Jean-Paul Aguet, *Les Grèves sous la Monarchie de Juillet (1830–1847): Contribution à l'étude du mouvement ouvrier français* (Geneva, 1954), pp. 202, 204, 206–07, 211–20; Octave Festy, "Le Mouvement ouvrier à Paris en 1840," *Revue des sciences politiques*, XXX (1913), pp. 67–78, 228, 230–36.

29. AN, BB[18] 1376, Procureur général, Lyon, au Ministre de la justice, 23, 26, 28 Feb., 1, 18 Mar. 1840; BB[18] 1420, Proc. gén., Lyon, au Min. de la justice, 30 May 1844; Pierre Guillaume, "Grèves et organisations ouvrières chez les mineurs de la Loire au milieu du XIXe siècle," *Le Mouvement social*, XLIII (Apr.–Jun. 1963), p. 5.

30. Aguet, *Grèves sous la Monarchie de Juillet*, pp. 269–

71; AN, BB¹⁸ 1420, Proc. gén., Lyon, au Min. de la justice, 1, 3, 4, 5, 5 (11 P.M.), 6, 7, 18 Apr., 18, 21 May 1843.

31. AN, BB¹⁸ 1420, Proc. gén., Lyon, au Min. de la justice, 8 Apr. 1843 (9 A.M.).

32. AN, BB¹⁸ 1420, Proc. gén., Lyon, au Min. de la justice, 10 Apr. 1843.

33. AN, BB¹⁸ 1420, Proc. gén., Lyon, au Min. de la justice, 19, 23 (4:30 P.M.), 30 Apr., 1, 3, 5, 10, 11, 14, 18 May 1844; Eugène Tarlé, "La Grande Coalition des Mineurs de Rive-de-Gier en 1844," *Revue historique*, CLXXVII (1936), pp. 250, 259, 277; Guillaume, "Grèves et organisations ouvrières," p. 16.

34. Maurice Agulhon, *Une Ville ouvrière au temps du socialisme utopique: Toulon de 1815 à 1851* (Paris, 1970), pp. 163–64, 167–73, 179.

35. Agulhon, *Une Ville ouvrière*, p. 179.

36. Braudel and Labrousse, eds., *Histoire économique et sociale*, III, p. 814; Aguet, *Grèves sous la Monarchie de Juillet*, pp. 301–10.

37. Pierre Guillaume, *La Compagnie des Mines de la Loire, 1846–1854: Essai sur l'apparition de la grande industrie capitaliste en France* (Paris, 1966), pp. 151–55; Bertrand Gille, "La Sidérurgie française du XIXᵉ siècle avant l'acier," *Revue d'histoire de la sidérurgie*, VII (1966), p. 253; Peter N. Stearns, *Paths to Authority: The Middle Classes and the Industrial Labor Force in France, 1820–1848* (Urbana, Ill., 1973), pp. 93–96; Christian Devilliers and Bernard Huet, *Le Creusot: Naissance et développement d'une ville industrielle, 1782–1914* (Seyssel, 1981), pp. 53, 54.

38. Donald Reid, *The Miners of Decazeville: A Genealogy of Deindustrialization* (Cambridge, Mass., 1985), pp. 10, 16–17, 20, 23, 26–29, 44–46.

39. Ronald Aminzade, *Class, Politics and Early Industrial Capitalism: A Study in Mid-nineteenth-century Toulouse, France* (Albany, N.Y., 1981), pp. 70–76; Jacques Marillier, "Pierre Moreau, L'Union," *Actualité de l'histoire*, V (Oct. 1953), pp. 6, 9–10.

40. Maurice Crubellier, *Histoire culturelle de la France,*

XIXᵉ–XXᵉ siècle (Paris, 1974), pp. 197–98; Roger Thabault, *Mon Village, ses hommes, ses routes, son école* (Paris, 1945), pp. 39–40; Amy Latour, *Kings of Fashion* (London, 1958), pp. 58–97, 100–21.

41. Helmut Gernsheim and Allison Gernsheim, *L.J.M. Daguerre (1787–1851), the World's First Photographer* (Cleveland, Oh., 1956), pp. 72, 88–89, 110, 118–19; Theodore Zeldin, *France, 1848–1945* (Oxford, 1973–1977), II, pp. 455–56.

CHAPTER V

1. D. G. Charlton, *Secular Religions in France, 1815–1870* (Oxford, 1963), pp. 46–54; D. G. Charlton, *Positivist Thought in France During the Second Empire* (Oxford, 1959), pp. 24–25; Stanislas Aquarone, *The Life and Works of Emile Littré, 1801—1881* (Leyden, 1958), pp. 24–27, 205; Gordon Wright, *France in Modern Times: From the Enlightenment to the Present* (3d ed.; New York, 1981), pp. 242–43, 296–99, 303.

2. Frank E. Manuel, *Prophets of Paris* (Cambridge, Mass., 1962), pp. 111–13, 151–52, 158–62; Ernest Labrousse, *Le Mouvement ouvrier et les idées sociales en France de 1815 à la fin du XIXᵉ siècle* (Paris, n.d.), I, pp. 51–55, II, pp. 113–16.

3. Nicholas V. Riasanovsky, *The Teachings of Charles Fourier* (Berkeley, 1969), pp. 8–10, 42–43, 139–40; Labrousse, *Mouvement ouvrier*, II, pp. 117–18, III, pp. 145–47; Manuel, *Prophets of Paris*, p. 200.

4. Elizabeth L. Eisenstein, *The First Professional Revolutionary: Filippo Michele Buonarroti (1761–1837): A Biographical Essay* (Cambridge, Mass., 1959), pp. 65, 68, 73–74; Christopher H. Johnson, *Utopian Communism in France: Cabet and the Icarians, 1839–1851* (Ithaca, N.Y., 1974), pp. 68–70.

5. Charles Louandre, "De la production intellectuelle en France depuis quinze ans," *Revue des deux mondes*, new se-

ries, 17ᵉ Année (1847), vol. 20, p. 279; Claude Bellanger et al., eds., *Histoire générale de la presse française*, vol. II, *De 1815 à 1871* (Paris, 1969), pp. 131–32, 237.

6. Labrousse, *Mouvement ouvrier*, I, pp. 30–38; Bertrand Gille, *La Banque et le crédit en France de 1815 à 1848* (Paris, 1959), pp. 337–44.

7. Octave Festy, "Le Mouvement ouvrier à Paris de 1840," *Revue des sciences politiques*, XXX (1913), pp. 67–68, 77, 78, 231–32, 238; Jean-Pierre Aguet, *Les Grèves sous la Monarchie de Juillet (1830–1847): Contribution à l'étude du mouvement ouvrier français* (Geneva, 1954), pp. 166–228; David H. Pinkney, "Pacification of Paris: The Military Lessons of 1830," in John M. Merriman, ed., *France in 1830* (New York, 1975), pp. 197–98.

8. Patricia O'Brien, "*L'Embastillement de Paris*: The Fortification of Paris During the July Monarchy," *French Historical Studies*, IX (Spring 1975), pp. 66, 80–81; Johnson, *Utopian Communism*, pp. 76–77.

9. The book was first published in Paris in 1839 as *Voyage et aventures de Lord William Carisdall en Icarie*, nominally a translation of an English text by one Francis Adams. Few copies were distributed. Subsequent editions appeared as *Voyage en Icarie: Roman philosophique et social* by Etienne Cabet. David Owen Evans, *Social Romanticism in France, 1830–1848* (Oxford, 1951), p. 140; Pierre Meyer, review of Etienne Cabet, *Oeuvres*, I, *Voyage en Icarie* in *Le Mouvement social*, IX (Jan.–Mar. 1976), p. 117.

10. Cabet, *Voyage*, quoted in Johnson, *Utopian Communism*, p. 49.

11. Johnson, *Utopian Communism*, pp. 18–19, 78, 145–53, 185–206, 261, 291; Labrousse, *Mouvement ouvrier*, III, pp. 147–49.

12. Johnson, *Utopian Communism*, p. 297.

13. Leo Loubere, *Louis Blanc: His Life and His Contribution to the Rise of French Jacobin Socialism* (Evanston, Ill., 1961), pp. 8–14, 22, 31–39, 247; Labrousse, *Mouvement ouvrier*, III, pp. 149–54; Louis Blanc, *Organisation du travail* (5th ed.; Paris, 1848), reprinted in J.A.R. Marriott, *The French*

Revolution of 1848 in Its Economic Aspect (Oxford, 1913), I.

14. Pierre-Joseph Proudhon, *Qu'est-ce que la propriété?* in *Oeuvres complètes* (new ed.; Paris, 1926), pp. 131–32.

15. Lloyd S. Kramer, *Exiles in Paris: European Intellectuals and the French Experience, 1830–1848* (unpublished diss., Cornell Univ., Ithaca, N.Y., 1983), pp. 255–56.

16. Loubère, *Louis Blanc*, p. 55; Louis Girard, "Les Problèmes français" in Max Beloff et al., eds., *L'Europe du XIXᵉ et du XXᵉ siècle: Problèmes et interpretations historiques* (Milan, 1959–1967), I, p. 522; Johnson, *Utopian Communism*, pp. 78, 148–53.

17. Jean-Louis Bory, *Eugène Sue: Le Roi du roman populaire* (Paris, 1962), p. 243; Paul Thureau-Dangin, *Histoire de la Monarchie de Juillet* (2d ed.; Paris, 1884-1892), VI, pp. 75–76; Edward R. Tannenbaum, "The Beginnings of Bleeding Heart Liberalism: Eugène Sue's *Les Mystères de Paris*," *Comparative Studies in Society and History*, XXIII (1981), pp. 491–93, 500; A. R. Vidler, *A Century of Social Catholicism, 1820–1920* (London, 1964), p. 17; Auguste Cornu, *Karl Marx et Frédéric Engels: Leur Vie et leur oeuvre*, vol. III, *Marx à Paris* (Paris, 1962), pp. 239–41.

18. Jean-Pierre Ferrier, *La Pensée politique de Constantin Pecqueur* (Paris, 1969), pp. 8–11, 176–77, 181; Evans, *Social Romanticism*, p. 64.

19. Hubert Bourgin, *Victor Considerant, son oeuvre* (Paris, 1909), p. 76; Maurice Dommanget, *Victor Considerant: Sa Vie, son oeuvre* (Paris, 1929), pp. 24–25; Jean Baelen, *La Vie de Flora Tristan: Socialisme et feminisme au 19ᵉ siècle* (Paris, 1972), pp. 165–69, 221–24; S. Joan Moon, "Feminism and Socialism: The Utopian Synthesis of Flora Tristan" in Marilyn Boxer and Jean Quaetert, eds., *Socialist Women: European Feminism in the Nineteenth and Twentieth Centuries* (New York, 1978), pp. 21–25, 34–40. *L'Union ouvrière* (3d ed.; 1844) is now available in English translation: Flora Tristan, *The Worker's Union*, Beverly Livingston, ed. and trans. (Urbana, Ill., 1983).

20. Elliott M. Grant, *The Career of Victor Hugo* (Cam-

bridge, Mass., 1946), p. 138; F. A. Simpson, *The Rise of Louis Napoleon* (3d ed.; London, 1950), p. 371; Stuart L. Campbell, *The Second Empire Revisited: A Study in French Historiography* (New Brunswick, N.J., 1978), pp. 5–8, 199.

21. Quoted in David McLellan, *Karl Marx: His Life and Thought* (New York, 1973), p. 62.

22. Quoted in Kramer, *Exiles in Paris*, p. 221.

23. Quoted in Kent R. Greenfield, *Economics and Liberalism in the Risorgimento: A Study in Nationalism in Lombardy, 1814–1848* (Baltimore, 1934), p. 307.

24. Quoted in Edward Hallett Carr, *The Romantic Exiles: A Nineteenth-century Portrait Gallery* (New York, 1933), p. 29.

25. Cornu, *Marx et Engels*, III, pp. 177, 196–97; McLellan, *Karl Marx*, p. 131. For an interesting discussion of the fruitful interaction between exiles in Paris and the Parisian environment in the 1830s and 1840s see Lloyd S. Kramer, "Exile and European Thought: Heine, Marx, and Mickiewicz in July Monarchy Paris," *Historical Reflections/Réflexions historiques*, XI (1984), pp. 45–70.

26. Cornu, *Marx et Engels*, III, pp. 6–7; Jacques Grandjonc, *Marx et les communistes allemands à Paris, 1844: Contribution à l'étude du Marxisme* (Paris, 1974), p. 12; McLellan, *Karl Marx*, pp. 55, 97 n. 2; David McLellan, *The Young Hegelians and Karl Marx* (New York, 1969), pp. 36–37; Kramer, *Exiles in Paris*, pp. 233–34; H. E. Kaminiski, *Bakounine: La Vie d'un révolutionnaire* (Paris, 1938), p. 55; Mikhail Bakunin, *The Confession of Mikhail Bakunin* . . . (Ithaca, N.Y., 1977), p. 35.

27. McLellan, *Karl Marx*, pp. 53–54, 60–64, 79–80, 98; Kramer, *Exiles in Paris*, pp. 222–23, 227, 231–32; Karl Marx, *Economic and Philosophic Manuscripts of 1844* (16th ed.; Moscow, n.d.), pp. 14–15.

28. Boris Nicolaievsky and Otto Maenchen-Helten, *Karl Marx: Man and Fighter* (London, 1973), pp. 88–91; McLellan, *Karl Marx*, pp. 135–36; Grandjonc, *Marx et les communistes allemands*, pp. 39, 86–95.

29. Isaiah Berlin, *Karl Marx: His Life and Environment* (4th ed.; Oxford, 1978), p. 60.

30. Berlin, *Karl Marx*, pp. 63–66; McLellan, *Karl Marx*, pp. 86–87, 97, 104, 180–87; Kramer, *Exiles in Paris*, pp. 221–22, 235, 236, 248, 253–54, 259–62, 313–14; Cornu, *Marx et Engels*, III, pp. 6–8, 9, 11–12, 255; Nicolaievsky and Maenchen-Helten, *Karl Marx*, pp. 86, 87.

31. Cornu, *Marx and Engels*, III, pp. 12–13, 87-88, 135–36, 172, 177, 198, 199, 247, 248, 255; Karl Marx, *Manuscrits de 1844, économie politique et philosophie* (Paris, 1962), pp. 7–9, 14–15.

32. Vidler, *A Century of Social Catholicism*, pp. 28–29, 54–55; Paul Droulers, "Catholicisme et mouvement ouvrier en France aux XIXe siècle: L'Attitude de l'Episcopat" in François Bédarida and Jean Maitron, eds., *Christianisme et monde ouvrier, Le Mouvement social*, no. 1 (Paris, 1975), pp. 40–41; Jean Bruhat, "Anticléricalisme et mouvement ouvrier en France avant 1914" ibid., p. 105.

33. Peter N. Stearns, *Paths to Authority: The Middle Class and the Industrial Labor Force in France, 1820–1848* (Urbana, Ill., 1973), pp. 89–103; Joseph Antoine Roy, *Histoire de la famille Schneider et du Creusot* (Paris, 1962), p. 38; Guy Thuillier, *Aspects de l'économie nivernaise au XIXe siècle* (Paris, 1966), pp. 286–87.

CHAPTER VI

1. David T. Van Zanten, "Henri Labrouste," *Macmillan Encyclopedia of Architects* (New York, 1982), II, p. 594; Neil Levine, "The Book and the Building: Hugo's Theory of Architecture and Labrouste's Bibliothèque Ste-Geneviève" in Robin Middleton, ed., *The Beaux-arts and Nineteenth-century French Architecture* (Cambridge, Mass., 1982), pp. 146–47.

2. Siegfried Giedion, *Space, Time, and Architecture: The Growth of a New Tradition* (5th ed., rev.; Cambridge, Mass., 1967), p. 219, quoting a letter by Labrouste.

3. Van Zanten, "Labrouste," p. 594; Levine, "Book and Building," pp. 155, 169; Giedion, *Space, Time, and Architecture*, pp. 220–21; M. Dubuisson et al., *L'Expansion du machinisme*, vol. III of Maurice Daumas, ed., *Histoire générale des techniques* (Paris, 1968), pp. 481, 484, 485; Henry-Russell Hitchcock, *Architecture: Nineteenth and Twentieth Centuries* (2d ed.; Baltimore, 1963), pp. 119–20, 123–24; Pierre Lavedan, *French Architecture* (Baltimore, 1956), pp. 24, 214; Marcel-Joseph Bulteau, *Déscription de la Cathédrale de Chartres* (Chartres, 1850), pp. 32–33.

4. Giedion, *Space, Time, and Architecture*, pp. 222–27; Jeanne Gaillard, *Paris, la ville, 1852–1870 . . .* (Paris, 1977), pp. 69–70, 474.

5. Sir John Summerson, ed., *Eugène Emmanuel Viollet-le-Duc* (London, 1980), p. 7.

6. R. D. Middleton, "Eugène Emmanuel Viollet-le-Duc," *Macmillan Encyclopedia of Architects*, IV, pp. 324–26, 331; France, Réunion des musées nationaux, *Viollet-le-Duc* (Paris, 1980), pp. 35, 57–58, 73, 82–84, 105, 114, 130–33.

7. *Petit Larousse* (Paris, 1967), p. 195.

8. Middleton, "Viollet-le-Duc," p. 325; France, *Viollet-le-Duc*, pp. 31–32, 375–78; Nikolaus Pevsner, *The Sources of Modern Architecture and Design* (New York, 1968), pp. 16, 95, 137; Nikolaus Pevsner, *Ruskin and Viollet-le-Duc: Englishness and Frenchness in the Appreciation of Gothic Architecture* (London, 1969), pp. 32, 34; Jean-Claude Delorme, *L'Ecole de Paris: 10 architectes et leurs immeubles, 1905–1937* (Paris, 1981), pp. 12–15; Jacques Grégoire Watelet, "Art Nouveau and the Applied Arts in Belgium" in *Art Nouveau Belgium France* (Houston, 1976), pp. 120, 123; François Loyer, "Art Nouveau in Architecture in France," ibid., pp. 382, 385, 398; Donald Drew Egbert, *Social Radicalism and the Arts, Western Europe: A Cultural History from the French Revolution to 1968* (New York, 1970), pp. 141–42; Peter Collins, *Concrete: The Vision of a New Architecture: A Study in Auguste Perret and His Precursors* (New York, 1969), pp. 113, 115.

9. Delorme, *Ecole de Paris*, p. 22.

10. Collins, *Concrete*, pp. 155, 173, 279–80.

11. France, *Viollet-le-Duc*, p. 6.

12. Pierre Schneider, "Viollet-le-Prophète," *L'Express* (Paris), 22 Mar. 1980, p. 12.

13. Hélène Lipstadt, "César Daly," *Macmillan Encyclopedia of Architects*, I, pp. 492–93; Hélène Lipstadt, "César Daly: Revolutionary Architect?" *A D [Architectural Design]*, XLVIII (1978), pp. 18–19; Ann Lorenz Van Zanten, "Form and Society: César Daly and the *Revue générale d'architecture*," *Oppositions*, VIII (Spring 1977), pp. 137–38; Anthony Vidler, "The Dream of a New Architecture," ibid., p. 135; Egbert, *Social Radicalism and the Arts*, p. 141; Nicholas V. Riasanovsky, *The Teachings of Charles Fourier* (Berkeley, 1969), pp. 43–46.

14. Jack Lindsay, *Gustave Courbet: His Life and Art* (Bath, Eng., 1973), p. 16.

15. Lindsay, *Courbet*, p. ix.

16. Albert Boime, "Entrepreneurial Patronage in Nineteenth-century France" in Edward C. Carter et al., eds., *Enterprise and Entrepreneurs in Nineteenth- and Twentieth-century France* (Baltimore, 1976), pp. 140, 143; James Henry Rubin, *Realism and Social Vision in Courbet and Proudhon* (Princeton, 1980), pp. 4, 10–11.

17. Egbert, *Social Radicalism and the Arts*, pp. 196–97; Rubin, *Realism and Social Vision*, pp. 4, 131; Lindsay, *Courbet*, p. 31; T. J. Clark, *The Absolute Bourgeois: Artists and Politics in France, 1848–1851* (London, 1973), p. 181; T. J. Clark, "A Bourgeois Dance of Death: Max Buchon on Courbet," *Burlington Magazine*, CXI (1969), p. 211; Charles Baudelaire, *Salon de 1846* in *Art in Paris, 1845–1862: Salons and Other Exhibitions Reviewed by Charles Baudelaire* (Greenwich, Conn., 1975), p. 119; T. J. Clark, *The Image of the People: Gustave Courbet and the Second French Republic, 1848–1851* (Greenwich, Conn., 1973), p. 127; Rubin, *Realism and Social Vision*, pp. 16–20.

18. Clark, *Image of the People*, pp. 39–41, 43, 49–51.

19. Clark, *Image of the People*, pp. 48–49, 51, 78, 86–87, 113–15.

20. Linda Nochlin, *Gustave Courbet: A Study of Style and Society* (New York, 1976), p. 127.

21. Clark, *Image of the People*, pp. 114–16; Clark, "Bourgeois Dance of Death," pp. 208–09; Meyer Schapiro, "Courbet and Popular Imagery: An Essay on Reaction and Naiveté," *Journal of the Warburg and Courtauld Institutes*, IV (1940–1941), pp. 181–82, 184–85; Nochlin, *Courbet*, pp. 132–46.

22. Lindsay, *Courbet*, pp. 135–39; Egbert, *Social Radicalism and the Arts*, p. 190; France, Ministère de la culture et de l'environment, *Gustave Courbet (1819–1877)* (Paris, 1977), pp. 31–32.

23. France, Min. de la culture et de l'environment, *Gustave Courbet*, p. 77.

24. Hilton Kramer, "France's New Culture Palace," *New York Times Magazine*, 23 Jan. 1977, p. 13.

25. *Les Peintres cubistes: Méditations esthétiques* (Paris, 1913), quoted in Nochlin, *Courbet*, p. 231.

26. Linda Nochlin has argued that Courbet was the first avant-garde painter in the original sense of the term, which implies being both artistically and politically progressive. In a more recent sense of the term, which includes the concept of alienation, Manet was the pioneer. —"The Invention of the Avant-garde: France, 1830–1880," *Art News Annual*, XXXIV (1968), pp. 12, 16.

27. Baudelaire, *Salon de 1846*, p. 119.

28. Peter Gay, *Art and Act: On Causes in History—Manet, Gropius, Mondrian* (New York, 1976), pp. 88–89; Theodore Reff, *Manet and Modern Paris* (Washington, D.C., 1982), pp. 13, 23, 33.

29. *Revue des deux mondes*, new series, 14ᵉ Année (1844), pp. 302–13.

30. May God guide to her goal the quick-thundering steam
On the ways of iron that run over hills,
May an angel stand watch upon her dinning forge,
When she goes below ground or makes tremble the spans,
And devouring her cauldrons with her own iron teeth,

She penetrates cities and leaps over torrents
More rapid than the buck in the heat of his jump!
Translation by James Winchell from the text in Alfred de
Vigny, *Oeuvres complètes* (Paris, 1964), I, p. 125.

31. Reff, *Manet and Modern Paris*, pp. 53–57, 60; *Selections from the Armand Hammer Daumier Collection* (Los Angeles, 1976); Robert N. Beetem, "Horace Vernet's Mural in the Palais Bourbon: Contemporary Imagery, Modern Technology, and Classical Allegory During the July Monarchy," *Art Bulletin*, LXVI (1984), pp. 254–55, 261–69; A.J.D., "Plafond du Salon de la Paix à la Chambre des Députés par M. Horace Vernet," *L'Illustration*, X (25 Dec. 1847), pp. 263–64; Howard P. Vincent, *Daumier and His World* (Evanston, Ill., 1968), pp. 101–05, 207; K. E. Maison, *Honoré Daumier: Catalogue raisonné of the Paintings, Watercolours and Drawings* (London, 1968), I, pp. 109, 141-42, 148–49, II, pp. 96–97, 99–106; Gay, *Art and Act*, pp. 75, 87–88; France, Ministère de la culture et de la communication, *Hommage à Claude Monet (1840–1926)* (Paris, 1980), pp. 95–96, 146–47, 159–63; Joel Isaacson, *Claude Monet* (Oxford, 1978), p. 79; William C. Seitz, *Claude Monet* (New York, n.d.), p. 32.

32. *A Day in the Country: Impressionism and the French Landscape* (Los Angeles, 1984), pp. 33, 35–41, 43–49, 138–43, 273–78; Reff, *Manet and Modern France*, pp. 150–59.

33. Helmut Gernsheim and Allison Gernsheim, *L.J.M. Daguerre (1787–1851), The World's First Photographer* (Cleveland, Oh., 1956), p. 104; Theodore Zeldin, *France, 1848–1945* (Oxford, 1973), II, pp. 455–57; Harry Levin, *The Gates of Horn: A Study of Five French Realists* (New York, 1963), p. 69; Aaron Scharf, *Art and Photography* (Baltimore, 1974), pp. 55–56, 66–75, 129, 131–36; Constance Cain Hungerford, "Ernest Meissonier's First Military Paintings," *Arts Magazine*, LIV, no. 5 (Jan. 1980), pp. 89–90, 104; Reff, *Manet and Modern Paris*, p. 73.

34. Reff, *Manet and Modern Paris*, pp. 73–93.

35. César Graña, *Bohemian Versus Bourgeois: French Society and the Man of Letters in the Nineteenth Century* (New York, 1964), pp. xii, xiv, 87, 91–94, 108–10; Roger L. Wil-

liams, *The Horror of Life* (Chicago, 1980), pp. ix–x, 111–13; Arthur Mitzman, "Roads, Vulgarity, Rebellion, and Pure Art: The Inner Space in Flaubert and French Culture," *Journal of Modern History*, LI (1979), pp. 515, 521.

36. Flaubert to Louise Colet, 14 Aug. 1853, in Francis Steegmuller, ed., *The Letters of Gustave Flaubert, 1830–1857* (Cambridge, Mass., 1970), I, p. 196.

37. Honoré de Balzac, *La Comédie humaine* (Paris, 1945–1952), I, p. 7.

38. Balzac, *La Comédie humaine*, I, p. 4–7; Elliott M. Grant, *The Career of Victor Hugo* (Cambridge, Mass., 1946), pp. 120–22, 249; Hubert Juin, *Victor Hugo* (Paris, 1980), I, pp. 853–54.

39. Benjamin F. Bart, *Flaubert* (Syracuse, N.Y., 1967), pp. 31, 36, 42–43, 49–50, 62–66; Steegmuller, ed., *Letters of Flaubert*, I, pp. xii, 14; Jean-Paul Sartre, *L'Idiot de la famille: Gustave Flaubert de 1821 à 1857* (Paris, 1971), I, pp. 13–51; Jean Bruneau, *Les Débuts littéraires de Gustave Flaubert, 1831–1845* (Paris, 1962), pp. 2, 11, 15.

40. The first *Education sentimentale* did not appear in print until 1910–1911, when it was published serially in the *Revue de Paris*. Its first publication as a book was in English translation, *The First Sentimental Education* (Berkeley, 1972).

41. Bruneau, *Débuts littéraires de Flaubert*, pp. 9–11, 383–89, 391–92, 420–37, 557–58, 584; Bart, *Flaubert*, pp. 89–97, 105–06; Levin, *The Gates of Horn*, p. 69; Michel Raimond, *Le Roman depuis la Révolution* (Paris, 1967), pp. 81, 82, 86.

42. Henri Peyre, *The Contemporary French Novel* (New York, 1955), p. 12.

43. Henri Peyre in *Encyclopedia Americana* (New York, 1973), III, p. 367.

44. Enid Starkie, *Baudelaire* (New York, 1933), pp. 83–101, 251, 254, 258–67; Henri Peyre, *Connaissance de Baudelaire* (Paris, 1951), pp. 155–70; Ernest Raynaud, *Ch. Baudelaire: Etude biographique et critique* . . . (Paris, 1922), pp. 150, 163.

45. Claude Bellanger et al., eds., *Histoire générale de la presse française*, vol. II, *De 1815 à 1871* (Paris, 1965), pp.

111–15, 119, 122; Irene Collins, *The Government and the Newspaper Press in France, 1814–1881* (London, 1959), pp. 82–83; Jean-Pierre Aguet, "Le Tirage des quotidiens de Paris sous la Monarchie de Juillet," *Revue suisse d'histoire*, X (1960), pp. 229–32.

46. Bellanger et al., eds., *Histoire de la presse*, II, pp. 114–15, 119–20; Aguet, "Tirage des quotidiens," pp. 231–32, 235–36; Pierre Albert, Gilles Feyel, and Jean-François Picard, *Documents pour l'histoire de la presse nationale aux XIXᵉ et XXᵉ siècles* (Paris, n.d.), pp. 14, 18; Joanna Richardson, "Emile Girardin, 1806–1881: The Popular Press in France," *History Today*, XXVI (1976), p. 813.

47. Bellanger et al., eds., *Histoire de la presse*, II, p. 356, III, *De 1871 à 1940* (Paris, 1972), pp. 137, 234, 296; Albert et al., *Documents*, pp. 58, 72.

48. Bellanger et al., eds., *Histoire de la presse*, II, pp. 110, 300–02, 311, V, *De 1858 à nos jours* (Paris, 1976), p. 384.

49. Collins, *Government and the Press*, pp. 90–91; Bellanger et al., eds., *Histoire de la presse*, II, pp. 120–22; Paul Thureau-Dangin, *Histoire de la Monarchie de Juillet* (Paris, 1884–1892), VI, pp. 70, 73, 75, 77.

50. David Owen Evans, *Le Roman social sous la Monarchie de Juillet* (Paris, 1936), pp. 7, 18, 45, 82–83; Peter Brooks, "A Man Named Sue," *New York Times Book Review*, 30 July 1978, pp. 3, 26–27.

51. Maurice Crubellier, *Histoire culturelle de la France, XIXᵉ–XXᵉ siècle* (Paris, 1974), pp. 85–86, 109; Pierre Couperie et al., *A History of the Comic Strip* (New York, 1968), p. 11; François Caradec, "La Littérature en estampes" in *Rodolphe Töppfer, M. Jabot, M. Crépin . . .* (Paris, 1975), pp. 5, 7, 10; "Bande dessinée: Töppfer avait tout inventé," *L'Express* (Paris), 19–25 Jan. 1976, pp. 60–61.

Chapter VII

1. Stanley Mellon, "Entente, Diplomacy, and Fantasy," *Reviews in European History*, II (Sept. 1976), pp. 376–80.

2. Roger Bullen, "France and the Problem of Intervention

in Spain, 1834–1836," *Historical Journal*, XX (1977), pp. 363–73; Douglas Johnson et al., eds., *Britain and France: Ten Centuries* (London, 1980), p. 274; Paul Thureau-Dangin, *Histoire de la Monarchie de Juillet* (Paris, 1884–1892), II, pp. 393–94.

3. Thureau-Dangin, *Histoire*, II, p. 377.

4. Roger Bullen, *Palmerston, Guizot and the Collapse of the "Entente Cordiale"* (London 1974), pp. 16–17, 29 n. 15.

5. John H. Gleason, *The Genesis of Russophobia in Great Britain: A Study of the Interaction of Policy and Opinion* (Cambridge, Mass., 1950), pp. 226–27; Pierre Renouvin, *Histoire des relations internationales*, vol. V, *Le XIXe Siècle*, part 1, *De 1815 à 1871* (Paris, 1954), pp. 120–22.

6. Renouvin, *Histoire*, V, Part 1, p. 122; Thureau-Dangin, *Histoire*, IV, pp. 221, 247, 271, 281–82; André-Jean Tudesq, *Les Grands Notables en France (1840–1849): Etude historique d'une psychologie sociale* (Paris, 1964), I, pp. 485, 493; Adeline Daumard, *Les Bourgeois de Paris au XIXe siècle* (Paris, 1970), p. 341; Charles de Rémusat, *Mémoires de ma vie* (Paris, 1958–1967), III, pp. 452, 455; Heinrich Heine, *Lutetia*, vol. XV of *The Works of Heinrich Heine* (New York, n.d.), pp. 128, 136, 151, 156.

7. *Le Moniteur universel* (Paris), 1 Dec. 1840, p. 2349.

8. Tudesq, *Grands Notables*, I, pp. 493–94, 498–99, 500; Daumard, *Bourgeois de Paris*, pp. 338, 342; Renouvin, *Histoire*, V, Part 1, pp. 123–24; Thureau-Dangin, *Histoire*, IV, pp. 283–86, 303–05, 330–50; Rémusat, *Mémoires*, III, pp. 395–401; Jean-Pierre Aguet, *Les Grèves sous la Monarchie de Juillet (1830–1847): Contribution à l'étude du mouvement ouvrier français* (Geneva, 1954), pp. 194–228.

9. Thureau-Dangin, *Histoire*, IV, pp. 353–56; Renouvin, *Histoire*, V, Part 1, pp. 124–25; Douglas Johnson, *Guizot: Aspects of French History, 1787–1874* (London, 1963), pp. 267–68, 270.

10. Thureau-Dangin, *Histoire*, IV, p. 321.

11. Quoted from Metternich's *Mémoires* in Thureau-Dangin, *Histoire*, IV, p. 321.

12. Pierre Chalmin, "Quelques repères pour une histoire

sociale de l'armée française au XIXe siècle," *Actualité de l'histoire*, XXII (Feb. 1958), p. 27.

13. George Lichtheim, "Socialism and the Jews," *Dissent*, XV (July–Aug. 1968), pp. 317, 319–24; Zosa S. Szajkowski, "The Jewish Saint-Simonians and the Socialist Anti-Semites in France," *Jewish Social Studies*, IX (1947), pp. 46–52, 55–59.

14. Bernhard Blumenkranz, ed., *Histoire des Juifs en France* (Toulouse, 1972), pp. 333–34, 339; S. Posener, *Adolphe Crémieux* (Philadelphia, 1940), pp. 95–105; Anka Muhlstein, *Baron James: The Rise of the French Rothschilds* (New York, 1983), pp. 115–20, 123–26; *Moniteur universel*, 3 June 1840, pp. 1257–58.

15. Blumenkranz, *Histoire des Juifs*, p. 312; Muhlstein, *Baron James*, pp. 116–20, 128, 145; Alphonse Toussenel, *Les Juifs, rois de l'époque: Histoire de la féodalité financière* (Paris, 1845), pp. 174–78. Despite the outburst of anti-Semitism in 1840 the situation of French Jews improved during the July Monarchy. In 1831 the state extended to rabbis its practice of paying the salaries of the clergy of the Catholic and Protestant churches, and in 1846 the Court of Cassation ended the requirement that Jews involved in judicial proceedings take a special oath, the *More Judaico*, the last surviving remnant of legal discrimination against Jews in France. The decades of the Orleans monarchy were, moreover, a period when Jews in France were becoming increasingly integrated into French society and when old prejudices against them seemed to be diminishing.—Blumenkranz, *Histoire des Juifs*, pp. 307, 313, 317; Phyllis Cohen Albert, *The Modernization of French Jewry: Consistory and Community in the Nineteenth Century* (Hanover, N.H., 1977), pp. 28, 37–41.

16. Johnson, *Guizot*, pp. 292, 321; Charles Pouthas, *La Jeunesse de Guizot (1787–1814)* (Paris, 1936), pp. 111–14; Charles Pouthas, *Guizot pendant la Restauration: Préparation de l'homme d'état (1814–1830)* (Paris, 1923), p. 327; Rémusat, *Mémoires*, I, p. xviii; François Guizot, *Mémoires pour servir l'histoire de mon temps* (new ed.; Paris, 1872), V, pp. 133–39, 146–62; Tudesq, *Grands Notables*, II, p. 753;

Georges Renard, "L'Influence de l'Angleterre sur la France depuis 1830," *La Nouvelle Revue*, XXXVI (Sept.–Oct. 1885), p. 47.

17. Tudesq, *Grands Notables*, II, pp. 752–53, 763, 780; Daumard, *Bourgeois de Paris*, p. 343; Thureau-Dangin, *Histoire*, IV, p. 356.

18. Gleason, *Genesis of Russophobia*, pp. 238–39, 254, 271; John Richard Hall, *England and the Orleans Monarchy* (London, 1912), pp. 327, 331–32; Bullen, *Palmerston, Guizot*, p. 21–22, 25, 55–56, 61.

19. *Almanach de Gotha*, 93° Année (1846), pp. 1–3, 27–29, 30–31; Thureau-Dangin, *Histoire*, V, 191-92; T.E.B. Howarth, *Citizen-king: The Life of Louis-Philippe, King of the French* (London, 1961), p. 336.

20. Bullen, *Palmerston, Guizot*, pp. 27–28; Thureau-Dangin, *Histoire*, V, pp. 190–91, 201; Renouvin, *Histoire*, V, Part 1, p. 185.

21. Thureau-Dangin, *Histoire*, V, pp. 193–200, 219–20, 227; Bullen, *Palmerston, Guizot*, p. 29 n. 15; *Moniteur universel*, 29 Dec. 1843, p. 2589.

22. Bullen, *Palmerston, Guizot*, p. 25.

23. Renouvin, *Histoire*, V, Part 1, pp. 182–84; Rémusat, *Mémoires*, IV, pp. 78, 93; Hall, *England and the Orleans Monarchy*, pp. 347–48, 355, 367, 371; Bullen, *Palmerston, Guizot*, pp. 29, 39–40, 66; Thureau-Dangin, *Histoire*, V, pp. 418–20, 455–57.

24. Renouvin, *Histoire*, V, Part 1, pp. 182–86; Bullen, *Palmerston, Guizot*, pp. viii–ix, 53, 59, 68, 126–28, 145, 147–49, 334–36; James Phinney Baxter III, *The Introduction of the Ironclad Warship* (Hamden, Conn., 1968), p. 65; Michel Chevalier, "Des Rapports de la France et de l'Angleterre à la fin de 1847," *Revue des deux mondes*, new series, 18ᵉ Année (1848), vol. 21, p. 519; Hall, *England and the Orleans Monarchy*, p. 393.

25. Alfred Picard, *Les Chemins de fer français: Etude historique sur la constitution et le régime du réseau . . .* (Paris, 1884), I, p. 25; *Moniteur universel*, 3 April 1835, pp. 722–23.

26. *Moniteur universel*, 3 April 1835, p. 723.

27. *Moniteur universel*, 19 April 1842, pp. 847, 850; 30 April 1842, p. 966.

28. Renouvin, *Histoire*, V, Part 1, pp. 78–79, 163–65; *Moniteur universel*, 6 May 1838, p. 1159, 11 May 1838, p. 1203, 8 Feb. 1842, p. 254.

29. France, Ministère des affaires étrangères, Correspondance politique, Prusse, vol. 297 (June–Dec. 1843).

30. *Moniteur universel*, 8 May 1838, p. 1159; 11 May 1838, p. 1203.

31. *Moniteur universel*, 9 May 1838, p. 1174.

32. Louis-Maurice Jouffroy, *Une Etape de la construction des grandes lignes de chemin de fer en France: La Ligne à la frontière d'Allemagne (1825–1852)* (Paris, 1932), I, pp. 9, 10, 249; II, pp. 219–21.

33. Charles-André Julien, *Histoire de l'Algérie contemporaine*, vol. I, *La Conquête et les débuts de la colonisation (1827–1871)* (Paris, 1964), I, pp. 64, 163; Christian Schefer, *L'Algérie et l'évolution de la colonisation française* (Paris, 1928), pp. 76–78, 121, 168–69, 215–20, 311; Henry Blet, *Histoire de la colonisation française* (Paris, 1946–1950), II, pp. 112–24, 135–36.

34. Schefer, *Algérie*, pp. 14, 23, 32-33, 35; *Almanach royal et national* (1840), pp. 136–37; D. Bruce Marshall, *The French Colonial Myth and Constitution-making in the Fourth Republic* (New Haven, 1973), p. 26; Julien, *Histoire de l'Algérie*, II, p. 251; Anthony Thrall Sullivan, *Thomas-Robert Bugeaud, France and Algeria, 1784–1849: Politics, Power and the Good Society* (Hamden, Conn., 1983), pp. 61, 75.

35. Tudesq, *Grands Notables*, II, pp. 803, 806–07, 809, 811, 819–22; Charles-André Julien, *Les Techniciens de la colonisation (XIXe–XXe siècles)* (Paris, 1946), pp. 60–61; Blet, *Histoire*, II, pp. 142, 143; Howarth, *Citizen-king*, pp. 277–78; Sullivan, *Bugeaud*, pp. 67–68, 73.

36. Blet, *Histoire*, II, pp. 143, 150, 153, 156–58, 186; Julien, *Techniciens de la colonisation*, pp. 61, 73; Schefer, *Algérie*, pp. 347–50; Julien, *Histoire*, II, pp. 217–19, 230–35, 250, 266; Sullivan, *Bugeaud*, pp. 142–52; Bertrand Gille, *Recherches sur la formation de la grande entreprise capitaliste*

(1815–1848) (Paris, 1959), pp. 108–09; Bertrand Gille, *Histoire de la Maison Rothschild* (Geneva, 1965), I, pp. 388–89.

37. Schefer, *Algérie*, pp. 32–33; Tudesq, *Grands Notables*, II, p. 803; Marshall, *French Colonial Myth*, pp. 31, 50–51.

38. William B. Cohen, "Legacy of Empire: The Algerian Connection," *Journal of Contemporary History*, XV (1980), p. 120.

39. R. Delavignette and Charles-André Julien, *Les Constructeurs de la France d'outre-mer* (Paris, 1946), pp. 200–01; Julien, *Histoire*, pp. 212–13; Sullivan, *Bugeaud*, pp. 164–70; Marshall, *French Colonial Myth*, pp. 24, 33–37; William B. Cohen, *Rulers of Empire: The French Colonial Service in Africa* (Stanford, 1971), pp. 7–12, 16.

40. Schefer, *Algérie*, pp. 434, 436, 485, 486.

41. *Moniteur universel*, 1 April 1843, p. 649.

42. Johnson, *Guizot*, p. 292; Schefer, *Algérie*, pp. 384–85, 533; Bernard Schnapper, "La Politique des 'points d'appui' et la fondation des comptoirs fortifiées dans le Golfe de Guinée, 1837–1843," *Revue historique*, 85ᵉ Année, vol. CCXXV (Jan. 1961), 99–100; Blet, *Histoire*, II, pp. 106–07; Bernard d'Harcourt, "Négociations relatives à un projet d'établissement colonial français en 1845," *Revue d'histoire diplomatique*, I (1887), pp. 526, 528–29.

43. Blet, *Colonisation*, I, pp. 113–16, II, pp. 57–58, 75–77, 106–07, 148, 179–80, 239, III, pp. 186–88; Rémusat, *Mémoires*, IV, p. 78 n. 1; Nancy Nichols Barker, *The French Experience in Mexico, 1821–1861: A History of Constant Misunderstanding* (Chapel Hill, 1979), p. 104; Michel Chevalier, *Isthme de Panama: Examen historique et géographique des différentes directions suivant lesquelles on pourrait le percer et des moyens d'employer* (Paris, 1844); Gille, *Recherches sur la grande entreprise*, p. 111.

Conclusion

1. Quoted in Boris Nicolaevsky and Otto Maenchen-Helfen, *Karl Marx: Man and Fighter* (London, 1973), p. 71.

2. Charles Rémusat, *Mémoires de ma vie* (Paris, 1958–1967), IV, pp. 92–93.

3. Robert L. Koepke, "The Failure of Parliamentary Government in France, 1840–1848," *European Studies Review*, IX (1979), p. 446; Adeline Daumard, *Les Bourgeois de Paris au XIXᵉ siècle* (Paris, 1970), pp. 310–16; André-Jean Tudesq, *Les Grands Notables en France (1840–1849): Etude historique d'une psychologie sociale* (Paris, 1964), II, pp. 670–71, 679, 685, 905–06; Louis Girard, *La Garde nationale*, 1814–1871 (Paris, 1964), pp. 279, 281–82.

4. Louis Mazoyer, "Catégories d'âge et groupes sociaux: Les Jeunes Générations françaises de 1830," *Annales d'histoire économique et sociale*, 10ᵉ Année (1938), p. 385.

5. Anthony Esler, "Youth in Revolt: The French Generation of 1830" in Robert J. Bezucha, ed., *Modern European Social History* (Lexington, Mass., 1972), pp. 303, 326; Mazoyer, "Catégories d'âge," pp. 385, 399–402, 406–07.

· BIBLIOGRAPHY ·

ARCHIVES

Archives de France
  Archives d'entreprises
      13 AQ 33, 34, Cie. du chemin de fer de Paris
  à Strasbourg, 1845–47
      48 AQ 1, 10, 3267, Chemin de fer du Nord, 1845–88
      60 AQ 1–2, 173, Cie. du chemin de fer de Paris
  à Orléans, 1838–52
      76 AQ 4, Chemin de fer de Paris à Rouen, 1843–55
  Ministère de justice
      BB¹⁸ 1376 (Dossiers 7697–8008), 1420, 1421
  Ministère des travaux publics
      F¹⁷ 9306, 9307, 9310, 9311, 9351, 10224, 10286,
      10302, 10293, 1832–49
  Archives de la Ministère des affaires étrangères
      Correspondance politique, Prusse, vol. 297, June–De-
      cember 1843

OFFICIAL PUBLICATIONS

Almanach royal et national, An MDCCCXL (1840)
Annuaire statistique de la France, I (1878), XI (1888), XIII
    (1890), XXX (1910), LVIII (1951), LXXII (1966).
Bulletin des lois du Royaume de France, 1833.
France, Ministère de l'instruction publique, *Statistique de l'en-*
    seignement primaire, II, *Statistique comparée de l'en-*
    seignement primaire, 1829–1877. Paris, 1880. 528 pp.
France, Ministère de l'instruction publique, *Statistique re-*
    trospective: Etat récapitulatif et comparatif indiquant

département des conjoints qui ont signé l'acte de mariage au 17ᵉ, 18ᵉ eu 19ᵉ siècles ("Enquête Maggiolo"). Paris, 1879. 8pp.

Seine, Département de la, Service de la statistique municipale, *Recherches statistiques sur la ville de Paris et le département de la Seine,* vol. IV. (Paris, 1829). 87 pp., 145 tableaux.

SERIALS

Annales des ponts et chaussées: Mémoires et documents (Paris), I (1841), VII (1847).
L'Echo des écoles primaires: Journal des instituteurs (Paris), 1837–1843.
L'Emancipation de l'enseignement: Journal politique, scientifique et littéraire (Paris), 27 May 1848.
Gazette des hôpitaux civils et militaires (Paris), 2d series, I–IX (1839–1848).
Journal des chemins de fer et des progrès industriels (Paris), I–VI (1842–1847).
Moniteur des chemins de fer et de la navigation à vapeur (Paris), I (April–October 1842). Ceased publication October 1842.
Le Moniteur universel (Paris), 1835, 1838, 1840–1847.
Revue d'histoire de la sidérurgie (Nancy), I–IX (1960–1968).
Revue d'histoire des mines et de la métallurgie (Nancy), I–IV (1969–1972). Continuation of *Revue d'histoire de la sidérurgie.* Ceased publication 1972.
Société des ingénieurs civils de France, *Mémoires et compte-rendu.* Paris, 1848——.
L'Union médical: Journal des intérêts scientifiques et pratiques, moraux et professionnels (Paris), 1847. *Prospectus,* n.d., and letter soliciting subscriptions, 2 January 1847.

Books and Articles

Aguet, Jean-Pierre. *Les Grèves sous la Monarchie de Juillet (1830–1847): Contribution à l'étude du mouvement ouvrier français.* Geneva, 1954, 406 pp.

Aguet, Jean-Pierre. "Le Tirage des quotidiens de Paris sous la Monarchie de Juillet," *Revue suisse d'histoire,* X (1960), pp. 216–86.

Agulhon, Maurice. "Bourgeoisie ancienne et esprit d'entreprise au temps de la 'révolution industrielle' (d'après un exemple départemental)" in Jean Bouvier et al., eds., *Conjoncture économique, structures sociales: Hommage à Ernst Labrousse* (Paris, 1974) pp. 465–75.

Agulhon, Maurice. *La République au village: Les Populations du Var de la Révolution à la Seconde République.* Paris, 1970. 543 pp.

Agulhon, Maurice. *Une Ville ouvrière au temps du socialisme utopique: Toulon de 1815 à 1851.* Paris, 1970. 368 pp.

Agulhon, Maurice, Gabriel Desert, and Robert Specklin. *Apogée et crise de la civilisation paysanne, 1789–1914,* vol. III of Georges Duby and Armand Wallon, eds., *Histoire de la France rurale.* Paris, 1976. 571 pp.

A.J.D. "Plafond du Salon de la Paix à la Chambre des Députés par M. Horace Vernet," *L'Illustration,* X (25 Dec. 1847), pp. 263–64.

Albert, Pierre, Gilles Feyel, and Jean-François Picard. *Documents pour l'histoire de la presse nationale aux XIXe et XXe siècles.* Paris, n.d. 341 pp.

Albert, Phyllis Cohen. *The Modernization of French Jewry: Consistory and Community in Nineteenth Century.* Hanover, N.H., 1977. 450 pp.

Alembert, Jean d'. *Mélanges de littérature, d'histoire et de philosophie.* New ed.; Amsterdam, 1770. 4 vols.

Allen, James Smith. *Popular French Romanticism: Authors, Readers, and Books in the 19th Century.* Syracuse, N.Y., 1981. 280 pp.

Aminzade, Ronald. *Class, Politics, and Early Industrial Cap-*

italism: A Study of Mid-nineteenth-century Toulouse, France. Albany, N.Y., 1981. 334 pp.

Anonymous. "Les Crédits accordés à l'industrie sidérurgique au moment de la crise de 1848," *Revue de l'histoire de la sidérurgie,* VI (1965), pp. 191–99.

Antoine, Michel et al. *Origines et histoire des cabinets des ministres.* Geneva, 1975. 181 pp.

Aquarone, Stanislas. *The Life and Works of Emile Littré, 1801–1881.* Leyden, 1958. 217 pp.

Armengaud, André. *La Population française au XIXe siècle.* Paris, 1971. 121 pp.

Armengaud, André. *La Population française au XXe siècle.* Paris, 1965. 126 pp.

Baelen, Jean. *La Vie de Flora Tristan: Socialisme et feminisme au 19e siècle.* Paris, 1972. 253 pp.

Bairoch, Paul. "Ecarts internationaux des niveaux de vie avant la Révolution industrielle," *Annales: E.S.C.,* 34e Année (1979), pp. 145–71.

Bairoch, Paul. *Révolution industrielle et sous-développement.* 4th ed.; Paris, 1974. 360 pp.

Baker, Donald N. and Patrick J. Harrigan, eds. *The Making of Frenchmen: Current Directions in Higher Education in France, 1679–1979.* Waterloo, Ont., 1980. 646 pp.

Bakunin, Mikhail. *The Confession of Mikhail Bakunin with Marginal Comments by Tsar Nicholas I.* Ithaca, N.Y., 1977. 200 pp.

Ballot, Charles. *L'Introduction du machinisme dans l'industrie française.* Paris, 1923. 575 pp.

Balzac, Honoré de. *La Comédie humaine.* Bibliothèque de la Pléiade, Paris, 1945–1952. 10 vols.

"Bande dessinée: Töppfer avait tout inventé," *L'Express* (Paris), 19–25 Jan. 1976, pp. 60–61.

Baratier, Edouard, ed. *Histoire de la Provence.* Toulouse, 1969. 607 pp.

Barker, Nancy Nichols. *The French Experience in Mexico, 1821–1861: A History of Constant Misunderstanding.* Chapel Hill, 1979. 264 pp.

Bart, Benjamin F. *Flaubert.* Syracuse, N.Y., 1967. 791 pp.

Baudelaire, Charles. *Salon de 1846* in *Art in Paris, 1845–1862: Salons and Other Exhibitions Reviewed by Charles Baudelaire.* Greenwich, Conn., 1965, pp. 41–120.

Baxter, James Phinney III. *The Introduction of the Ironclad Warship.* Hamden, Conn., 1968. 398 pp.

Beck, Thomas D. *French Legislators, 1800–1834: A Study in Quantitative History.* Berkeley, 1974. 202 pp.

Bédarida, François and Jean Maitron. *Christianisme et monde ouvrier.* Cahiers du mouvement social, no. 1. (Paris, 1975). 303 pp.

Beetem, Robert N. "Horace Vernet's Mural in the Palais Bourbon: Contemporary Imagery, Modern Technology, and Classical Allegory During the July Monarchy," *Art Bulletin*, LXVI (1984), pp. 254–69.

Bellanger, Claude et al., eds. *Histoire générale de la presse française.* Paris, 1969. 5 vols.

Beloff, Max, ed. *L'Europe du XIXᵉ et du XXᵉ siècle (1815–1870): Problèmes et interpretations historiques.* Milan, 1959–1967. 7 vols.

Bergeron, Louis. *Banquiers, négociants et manufacturiers parisiens du Directoire à l'Empire.* Paris. 1978. 436 pp.

Bergeron, Louis. *Les Capitalistes en France, 1780–1914.* Paris, 1978. 233 pp.

Berlin, Isaiah. *Karl Marx: His Life and Environment.* 4th ed.; Oxford, 1978. 228 pp.

Bertier de Sauvigny, G. de. *Nouvelle Histoire de Paris: La Restauration, 1815–1830.* Paris, 1977. 525 pp.

Bertier de Sauvigny, G. de. *La Restauration.* Paris, 1955. 652 pp.

Bezucha, Robert J., ed. *Modern European Social History.* Lexington, Mass., 1972. 386 pp.

Birr, M. "La Profession d'architecte à travers les âges" in Institut technique du bâtiment et des travaux publics, *Circulaire*, series A, V 1(0 Feb 1944), pp. 1–6.

Blanchard, Marcel. "La Politique ferroviaire du Second Empire," *Annales d'histoire économique et sociale*, VI (1934), pp. 529–45.

Bleaudonu, Gérard and Guy Le Gauffey. "Naissance des asiles

d'aliénés," *Annales: E.S.C.*, 30ᵉ Année (Jan.–Feb. 1975), pp. 93–121.

Bledstein, Burton J. *The Culture of Professionalism: The Middle Class and the Development of Higher Education in America*. New York, 1976. 354 pp.

Blet, Henri. *Histoire de la colonisation française*. Paris, 1946–1950. 3 vols.

Blumenkranz, Bernhard. *Histoire des juifs en France*. Toulouse, 1972. 478 pp.

Boime, Albert. "Entrepreneurial Patronage in Nineteenth-century France," in Edward C. Carter et al., eds., *Enterprise and Entrepreneurs in Nineteenth- and Twentieth-century France* (Baltimore, 1976), pp. 137–207.

Bory, Jean-Louis. *Eugène Sue: Le Roi du roman populaire*. Paris, 1962. 448 pp.

Bourgin, Hubert. *Victor Considerant, son oeuvre*. Paris, 1909. 128 pp.

Bouvier, Jean. *Un Siècle de la banque française*. Paris, 1973. 283 pp.

Bouvier, Jean et al., eds. *Conjoncture économique, structures sociales: Hommage à Ernest Labrousse*. Paris, 1974. 547 pp.

Boxer, Marilyn and Jean Quataert, eds. *Socialist Women: European Feminism in the Nineteenth and Twentieth Centuries*. New York, 1978. 260 pp.

Braudel, Fernand and Ernest Labrousse, eds. *Histoire économique et sociale de la France*, vol. III, *L'Avènement de l'ère industrielle (1789–années 1880)*. Paris, 1976, 1,071 pp.

Brooks, Peter. "A Man Named Sue," *New York Times Book Review*, 30 July 1978, pp. 3, 26–27.

Brown, Marvin L., Jr. *Louis Veuillot, French Ultramontane Catholic Journalist and Layman, 1813–1883*. Durham, N.C., 1977. 497 pp.

Bruhat, Jean. "Anticléricalisme et mouvement ouvrier en France avant 1914" in François Bédarida and Jean Maitron, eds., *Christianisme et monde ouvrier*. Cahiers du mouvement social, no. 1 (Paris, 1975), pp. 79–115.

Bruneau, Jean. *Les Débuts littéraires de Gustave Flaubert, 1831–1875.* Paris, 1962. 637 pp.

Brunet, Roger. *Les Campagnes toulousaines: Etude géographique.* Toulouse, 1965. 728 pp.

Bullen, Roger. "France and the Problem of Intervention in Spain, 1834–1836," *Historical Journal,* XX (1977), pp. 363–93.

Bullen, Roger. *Palmerston, Guizot and the Collapse of the "Entente Cordiale."* London, 1974. 352 pp.

Bulteau, Marcel-Joseph. *Description de la Cathédrale de Chartres.* Chartres, 1850. 320 pp.

Burat, Jules. *Exposition de l'industrie française, année 1844, description méthodique.* Paris, 1845. 2 vols.

Campbell, Stuart L. *The Second Empire Revisited: A Study in French Historiography.* New Brunswick, N.J., 1978. 231 pp.

Caradec, François. "La Littérature en estampes" in *Rodolphe Töppfer, M. Jabot, M. Crépin, M. Vieux Bois* . . . (Paris, 1975), pp. 5–10.

Caron, François. "Les Commandes des compagnies des chemins de fer en France, 1850–1914," *Revue d'histoire de la sidérurgie,* VI (1965), pp. 137–76.

Caron, François. "La Compagnie du Nord et ses fournisseurs (1845–1848)," *Revue du Nord,* XLV (1963), pp. 349–89.

Caron, François. *Histoire de l'exploitation d'un grand réseau français: La Compagnie d'un chemin de fer du Nord, 1846–1937.* Paris, 1973. 672 pp.

Caron, François. "Recherches sur le capital des voies de communication en France au XIXe siècle (en particulier le capital ferroviaire)" in Pierre Léon et al., eds., *L'Industrialisation en Europe au XIXe siècle* (Paris, 1972), pp. 237–66.

Carr, Edward Hallett. *The Romantic Exiles: A Nineteenth-century Portrait Gallery.* New York, 1933. 391 pp.

Chalmin, Pierre. "Quelques repères pour une histoire sociale de l'armée française au XIXe siècle," *L'Actualité de l'histoire,* XXII (Feb. 1959), pp. 18–51.

Chambre de Commerce de Paris. *Statistique de l'industrie à Paris résultant de l'enquête faite par la Chambre de Commerce pour les années 1847-1848.* Paris, 1851. 1,209 pp.

Chambre de Commerce de Paris. *Statistique de l'industrie à Paris résultant de l'enquête faite par la Chambre de Commerce pour l'année 1860.* Paris, 1864. 1,071 pp.

Charléty, Sébastien. *La Monarchie de Juillet (1830–1848).* Paris, 1921. 410 pp.

Charlton, D. G. *Positivist Thought in France During the Second Empire.* Oxford, 1959. 251 pp.

Charlton, D. G. *Secular Religions in France, 1815–1870.* Oxford, 1963. 249 pp.

Chatelain, Abel. "La Lente Progression de la Faux," *Annales: E.S.C.,* IIᵉ Année (1956), pp. 495–99.

Chatelain, Abel. *Les Migrants temporaires en France de 1800 à 1914: Histoire économique et sociale des migrants temporaires des campagnes françaises au XIXᵉ siècle et au début du XXᵉ siecle.* Lille, 1977. 2 vols.

Chevalier, Louis. *La Formation de la population parisienne au XIXᵉ siècle.* Paris, 1950. 312 pp.

Chevalier, Michel. *Isthme de Panama: Examen historique et géographique des différentes directions suivant lesquelles on pourrait le percer et des moyens d'employer.* Paris, 1844. 183 pp.

Chevalier, Michel. "Des Rapports de la France et de l'Angleterre à la fin de 1847," *Revue des deux mondes,* new series, 18ᵉ Année (1848), vol. 21, pp. 502–41.

Church, Clive. *Revolution and Red Tape: The French Ministerial Bureaucracy 1770–1850.* Oxford, 1981. 425 pp.

Clapham, John H. *The Economic History of Modern Britain.* 2d ed.; Cambridge, Eng., 1930. 3 vols.

Clark, T. J. *The Absolute Bourgeois: Artists and Politics in France, 1848–1851.* London, 1923. 224 pp.

Clark, T. J. "A Bourgeois Dance of Death: Max Bouchon on Courbet," *Burlington Magazine,* CXI (1969), pp. 208–11, 286–90.

Clark, T. J. *The Image of the People: Gustave Courbet and*

the Second French Republic, 1848–1851. Greenwich, Conn., 1973. 208 pp.

Cohen, William B. "Legacy of Empire: The Algerian Connection," *Journal of Contemporary History*, XV (1980), pp. 97–123.

Cohen, William B. *Rulers of Empire: The French Colonial Service in Africa*. Stanford, 1971. 279 pp.

Colin, A. *La Navigation commerciale au XIXᵉ siècle*. Paris, 1901. 459 pp.

Collins, E.J.T. "Labour Supply and Demand in European Agriculture, 1800–1880," in E. L. Jones and S. J. Woolf, eds., *Agrarian Change and Economic Development* (London, 1969), pp. 61–94.

Collins, Irene. *The Government and the Newspaper Press in France, 1814–1881*. London, 1959. 201 pp.

Collins, Peter. *Concrete: The Vision of a New Architecture: A Study of Auguste Perret and His Precursors*. New York, 1959. 307 pp.

Corbin, Alain. *Archaïsme et modernité en Limousin au XIXᵉ siècle, 1845–1880*. Paris, 1975. 2 vols.

Cornu, Auguste. *Karl Marx et Frédéric Engels: Leur Vie et leur oeuvre*, vol. III, *Marx à Paris*. Paris, 1962. 292 pp.

Couperie, Pierre et al. *A History of the Comic Strip*. New York, 1968. 256 pp.

Crouzet, François. "Essai de construction d'un indice de la production industrielle au XIXᵉ siècle," *Annales: E.S.C.*, 25ᵉ Année (1970), pp. 56–99.

Crouzet, François. "French Economic Growth in the Nineteenth Century Reconsidered," *History*, LIX (June 1974), pp. 167–79.

Crubellier, Maurice. *Histoire culturelle de la France, XIXᵉ–XXᵉ siècle*. Paris, 1974. 454 pp.

Daumard, Adeline. *Les Bourgeois de Paris au XIXᵉ siècle*. Paris, 1970. 382 pp.

Daumard, Adeline, ed. *Les Fortunes françaises au XIXᵉ siècle*. The Hague, 1974. 603 pp.

Daumas, Maurice, ed. *Histoire générale des techniques*. Paris, 1964–1979. 5 vols.

A Day in the Country: Impressionism and the French Landscape. Los Angeles, 1984. 375 pp.

Delavignette, R. and Charles-André Julien. *Les Constructeurs de la France d'outre mer.* Paris, 1946. 525 pp.

Delorme, Jean-Claude. *L'Ecole de Paris: 10 Architectes et leurs immeubles, 1905–1937.* Paris, 1981. 159 pp.

Devilliers, Christian, and Bernard Huet. *Le Creusot: Naissance et développement d'une ville industrielle, 1782–1914.* Seyssel, 1981. 287 pp.

Dictionnaire biographique français. Paris, 1933–1979. 14 vols.

Dommanget, Maurice. *Victor Considerant, sa vie, son oeuvre.* Paris, 1929. 231 pp.

Doukas, Kimon A. *The French Railroads and the State.* New York, 1945. 287 pp.

Droulers, Paul. "Catholicisme et mouvement ouvrier en France au XIXe siècle: L'Attitude de l'Episcopat," in François Bédarida and Jean Maitron, eds., *Christianisme et monde ouvrier.* Cahiers du mouvement social, no. 1 (Paris, 1975), pp. 37–65.

Dubuisson, M. et al. *L'Expansion du machinisme,* vol. III of Maurice Daumas, ed., *Histoire générale des techniques.* Paris, 1968. 884 pp.

Duby, Georges and Armand Wallon, eds. *Histoire de la France rurale.* Paris, 1975–1977. 4 vols.

Dunham, Arthur. "How the First French Railways Were Planned," *Journal of Economic History,* I (May 1941), pp. 12–25.

Dupeux, Georges. "La Croissance urbaine en France au XIXe siècle," *Revue d'histoire économique et sociale,* LII (1974), pp. 173–89.

Duroselle, Jean-Baptiste. *Les Débuts du Catholicisme social en France (1822–1870).* Paris, 1951. 786 pp.

Edwards, Stewart. *The Paris Commune of 1871.* London, 1971. 417 pp.

Egbert, Donald Drew. *Social Radicalism and the Arts, Western Europe: A Cultural History from the French Revolution to 1968.* New York, 1970. 821 pp.

Egret, Jean. *La Pré-Révolution française (1787–1788)*. Paris, 1962. 400 pp.

Eisenstein, Elizabeth L. *The First Professional Revolutionary: Filippo Michele Buonarroti (1761–1837): A Biographical Essay*. Cambridge, Mass., 1958. 205 pp.

Escarpet, Robert. *Sociologie de la littérature*. 5th ed., Paris, 1973. 128 pp.

Esler, Anthony. "Youth in Revolt: The French Generation of 1830" in Robert J. Bezucha, ed., *Modern European Social History* (Lexington, Mass., 1972), pp. 301–34.

Evans, David Owen. *Le Roman social sous la Monarchie de Juillet*. Paris, 1936. 168 pp.

Evans, David Owen. *Social Romanticism in France, 1830–1848*. Oxford, 1951. 149 pp.

Faucher, Léon. "Des projects de loi sur les chemins de fer," *Revue des deux mondes*, new series, 13ᵉ Année (1843), vol. 2, pp. 357–83.

Ferrier, Jean-Pierre. *La Pensée politique de Constantin Pecqueur*. Paris, 1969. 190 pp.

Festy, Octave. "Le Mouvement ouvrier à Paris en 1840," *Revue des sciences politiques*, XXX (1913), pp. 67–79, 226–40, 333–61.

Flaubert, Gustave. *The First Sentimental Education*. Berkeley, 1972. 291 pp.

Fraile, Pedro. *The Diffusion of Iron Technology in Nineteenth Century France, Spain, and Italy*. M.A. thesis, University of Texas at Austin, 1980. 112 pp.

France, Ministère de la culture at de la communication. *Hommage à Claude Monet (1840–1926)*. Paris, 1980.

France, Ministère de la culture et de l'environment. *Gustave Courbet (1819–1877)*. Paris, 1977. 272 pp.

France, Réunion des musées nationaux. *Viollet-le-Duc*. Paris, 1980. 420 pp.

Freedeman, Charles F. *Joint-stock Enterprise in France, 1807–1867: From Privileged Company to Modern Corporation*. Chapel Hill, 1979. 234 pp.

Furet, François and Jacques Ozouf. *Lire et écrire: l'Alpha-*

bétisation des français de Calvin à Jules Ferry. Paris, 1977. 2 vols.

Furet, François and Jacques Ozouf. "Trois Siècles de métissage culturel," *Annales: E.S.C.*, 32ᵉ Année (1977), pp. 488–502.

Gaillard, Jeanne. *Paris, la ville, 1852–1870: L'Urbanisme parisien à l'heure d'Haussmann; Des provinciaux aux Parisiens; La Vocation aux vocations parisiennes.* Paris, 1977. 687 pp.

Gaillard, Jeanne. "Les Usines Cail et les ouvriers métallurgistes de Grenelle," *Le Mouvement social*, XXXIII–XXXIV (1960–1961), pp. 35–53.

Garrier, Gilbert. *Paysans du Beaujolais et du Lyonnais, 1800–1970.* Grenoble, 1973. 2 vols.

Gaudry, Jules. *Note sur François Cavé, constructeur de machines.* Paris, 1975. 20 pp.

Gay, Peter. *Art and Act: On Causes in History—Manet, Gropius, Mondrian.* New York, 1976. 265 pp.

Geiger, Reed G. *The Anzin Coal Company, 1800–1833: Big Business in the Early Stages of the Industrial Revolution.* Newark, Del., 1974. 345 pp.

Gerbod, Paul. "Associations et syndicalismes universitaires de 1828 à 1928 (Dans l'enseignement secondaire public)," *Le Mouvement social*, LV (Apr.–Jun. 1966), pp. 3–45.

Gerbod, Paul. *La Condition universitaire en France au XIXᵉ siècle.* Paris, 1965. 720 pp.

Gernsheim, Helmut and Alison Gernsheim. *L.J.M. Daguerre (1787–1851), the World's First Photographer.* Cleveland, Oh., 1956. 216 pp.

Gerschenkron, Alexander. *Economic Backwardness in Historical Perspective: A Book of Essays.* Cambridge, Mass., 1966. 456 pp.

Giedion, Siegfried. *Space, Time, and Architecture: The Growth of a New Tradition.* Cambridge, Mass., 1967. 897 pp.

Gille, Bertrand. *La Banque et le crédit en France de 1815 à 1848.* Paris, 1959. 380 pp.

Gille, Bertrand. "Esquisse d'une histoire du syndicalisme patronal dans l'industrie sidérurgique française," *Revue d'histoire de la sidérurgie*, IV (1964), pp. 209–49.

Gille, Bertrand. *Histoire de la Maison Rothschild*. Geneva, 1965. 2 vols.

Gille, Bertrand. "Les Problèmes techniques de la sidérurgie française au cours du XIXᵉ siécle," *Revue d'histoire de la sidérurgie*, II (1961), pp. 15–45.

Gille, Bertrand. *Recherches sur la formation de la grande entreprise capitaliste (1815–1848)*. Paris, 1959. 164 pp.

Gille, Bertrand. *La Sidérurgie française au XIXᵉ siècle: Récherches historiques*. Geneva, 1968. 317 pp.

Gille, Bertrand. "La Sidérurgie française du XIXᵉ siècle avant l'acier," *Revue d'histoire de la sidérurgie*, VII (1966), pp. 239–75.

Gillet, Marcel. *Les Charbonnages du Nord de la France au XIXᵉ siècle*. Paris, 1973. 520 pp.

Girard, Louis. *La Garde nationale, 1814–1871*. Paris, 1964. 388 pp.

Girard, Louis, *Nouvelle Histoire de Paris: La Deuxième République et le Second Empire, 1848–1870*. Paris, 1981. 471 pp.

Girard, Louis. "Les Problèmes français" in Max Beloff et al., eds. *L'Europe du XIXᵉ et du XXᵉ siècle (1815–1870): Problèmes et interpretations historiques* (Milan, 1959–1967), I, pp. 515–43.

Gleason, John Howes. *The Genesis of Russophobia in Great Britain: A Study of the Interaction of Policy and Opinion*. Cambridge, Mass., 1950. 314 pp.

Graña, César. *Bohemian versus bourgeois: French Society and the Man of Letters in the Nineteenth Century*. New York, 1964. 220 pp.

Grandjonc, Jacques. *Marx et les communistes allemands à Paris, 1844: Contribution à l'étude du Marxisme*. Paris, 1974. 264 pp.

Grant, Elliott M. *The Career of Victor Hugo*. Cambridge, Mass., 1946. 365 pp.

Greenfield, Kent R. *Economics and Liberalism in the Risor-*

gimento: A Study in Nationalism in Lombardy, 1814–1848. Baltimore, 1934. 365 pp.

Grew, Raymond, Patrick J. Harrigan, and James B. Whitney. "The Availability of Schooling in Nineteenth-Century France," *Journal of Interdisciplinary History*," XIV (1983), pp. 25-63.

Grew, Raymond, Patrick J. Harrigan, and James B. Whitney. "La Scolarisation en France, 1829–1906," *Annales: E.S.C.*, 39e Année (1984), pp. 116-57.

Gueneau, Louis, "La Législation restrictive du travail des enfants," *Revue d'histoire économique et sociale*, XV (1927), pp. 420–503.

Guillaume, Pierre. *La Compagnie des Mines de la Loire, 1846–1854: Essai sur l'apparition de la grande industrie capitaliste en France*. Paris, 1966. 253 pp.

Guillaume, Pierre. "Grèves et organisations ouvrières chez les mineurs de la Loire au milieu du XIXe siècle," *Le Mouvement social*, XLIII (Apr.–Jun. 1963), pp. 5–18

Guizot, François. *Mémoires pour servir l'histoire de mon temps*. New ed.; Paris, 1872. 8 vols.

Hall, John Richard. *England and the Orleans Monarchy*. London, 1912. 451 pp.

Hamilton, Patrick. *A Hundred Years of Postage Stamps*. 2d ed.; London, 1940. 300 pp.

Harcourt, Bernard d'. "Négociations relatives à un projet d'établissement colonial français en 1845," *Revue d'histoire diplomatique*, I (1887), pp. 525–47.

Hardach, Gerd H. "Les Problèmes de main d'oeuvre à Decazeville," *Revue d'histoire de la sidérurgie*, VIII (1967), pp. 51–68.

Haussmann, Georges-Eugène. *Mémoires*. 4th ed.; Paris, 1890–1893. 3 vols.

Heine, Heinrich. *Lutetia*, vols. XV-XVI of *The Works of Heinrich Heine*. New York, n.d. 240 pp.

Hélias, Pierre-Jakez. *The Horse of Pride: Life in a Breton Village*. New Haven, 1978. 351 pp.

Hitchcock, Henry-Russell. *Architecuture: Nineteenth and Twentieth Centuries*. 2d ed.; Baltimore, 1963.

Hohenberg, Paul. "Migrations et fluctuations démographiques dans la France rurale, 1836–1901," *Annales: E.S.C.*, 29ᵉ Année (1974), pp. 461–97.

Howarth, T.E.B. *Citizen-king: The Life of Louis-Philippe, King of the French.* London, 1961. 358 pp.

Hungerford, Constance Cain. "Ernest Meissonier's First Military Paintings," *Arts Magazine*, LIV, no. 5 (Jan. 1980), pp. 89–107.

Isaacson, Joel. *Claude Monet.* Oxford, 1978. 240 pp.

Jardin, André and André-Jean Tudesq. *La France des notables: L'Evolution générale, 1815-1848.* Paris, 1973. 254 pp.

Jenkins, Ernest H. *A History of the French Navy from Its Beginnings to the Present Day.* London, 1973. 364 pp.

Jobard, J.B.A.M. *Industrie française: Rapport sur l'exposition française de 1839.* Brussels, 1841–1842. 2 vols.

Johnson, Christopher H. *Utopian Communism in France: Cabet and the Icarians, 1839–1851.* Ithaca, N.Y., 1974.

Johnson, Douglas. *Guizot: Aspects of French History 1787–1874.* London, 1963. 469 pp.

Johnson, Douglas, François Bédarida, and François Crouzet, eds. *Britain and France: Ten Centuries.* London, 1980. 379 pp.

Jones, E. L. and S. J. Woolf, eds. *Agrarian Change and Economic Development: The Historical Problems.* London, 1969. 172 pp.

Jones, P. M. "An Improbable Democracy: Nineteenth Century Elections in the Massif Central," *English Historical Review*, XCVI (July 1982), pp. 530–57.

Jouffroy, Louis-Maurice. *L'Ere du rail.* Paris, 1953. 224 pp.

Jouffroy, Louis-Maurice. *Une Etape de la construction des grandes lignes de chemin de fer en France: La Ligne à la frontière d'Allemagne (1825–1852).* Paris, 1932. 3 vols.

Juillard, Etienne. *La Vie rurale dans la plaine de Basse Alsace: Essai de géographie sociale.* Strasbourg, 1953. 582 pp.

Juin, Hubert. *Victor Hugo*, vol. I, *1802–1843.* Paris, 1980. 882 pp.

Julien, Charles-André. *Histoire de l'Algérie contemporaine,* vol. I, *La Conquête et les débuts de la colonisation (1827–1871)*. 8th ed.; Paris, 1964. 633 pp.

Julien, Charles-André, ed. *Les Techniciens de la colonisation (XIXᵉ–XXᵉ siècles)*. Paris, 1946. 323 pp.

Kaminski, H. E. *Bakounine: La Vie d'un révolutionnaire*. Paris, 1938. 359 pp.

Kemp, Tom. *Economic Forces in French History: An Essay in the Development of the French Economy, 1760–1914*. London, 1971. 316 pp.

Kenwood, A. G. "Railway Investment in Britain, 1825–1875," *Economica*, XXXII (1965), pp. 313–322.

Kieve, Jeffrey. *The Electrical Telegraph in the U.K.: A Social and Economic History*. New York, 1973. 310 pp.

Koepke, Robert L. "The Failure of Parliamentary Government in France, 1840–1848," *European Studies Review*, IX (1979), pp. 433–55.

Kramer, Hilton. "France's New Culture Palace," *New York Times Magazine*, 23 Jan. 1977, p. 13.

Kramer, Lloyd S. "Exile and European Thought: Heine, Marx, and Mickiewicz in July Monarchy Paris," *Historical Reflections/Réflexions historiques*, XI (1984), pp. 45–70.

Kramer, Lloyd S. *Exiles in Paris: European Intellectuals and the French Experience, 1830–1848*. Diss., Cornell Univ., Ithaca, N.Y., 1983. 436 pp.

Kriedte, Peter et al. *Industrialisierung von der Industrialisierung: Gewerbliche Warenproduktion auf dem Land in der Formationsperiode des Kapitalismus*. Göttingen, 1977. 393 pp.

Labrousse, Ernest. *Le Mouvement ouvrier et les idées sociales en France de 1815 à la fin du XIXᵉ siècle*. Paris, n.d. 3 vols.

Landes, David S. *Revolution in Time: Clocks and the Making of the Modern World*. Cambridge, Mass., 1983. 482 pp.

Landes, David S. "Vieille Banque et banque nouvelle: La Révolution financière du dix-neuvième siècle," *Revue d'histoire moderne et contemporaine*, III (1956), pp. 204–22.

Lanteri-Laura, C. "La Chronicité dans la psychiatrie moderne," *Annales: E.S.C.*, 27ᵉ Année (1972), pp. 548–68.

Latour, Amy. *Kings of Fashion*. London, 1958. 271 pp.

Lavedan, Pierre. *French Architecture*. Baltimore, 1956. 304 pp.

Lefèvre, André. *La Ligne de Strasbourg à Bâle: La Construction (1837–1846), les repercussions françaises et internationales*. Strasbourg, 1947. 144 pp.

Lehning, James R. *The Peasants of Marlhes: Economic Development and Family Organization in Nineteenth-century France*. Chapel Hill, 1980. 218 pp.

Lemoine, René. *La Loi Guizot, 28 juin 1833: Son Application dans le Département de la Somme*. Abbeville, 1933. 599 pp.

Léon, Pierre et al., eds. *L'Industrialisation en Europe au XIXe siècle*. Paris, 1972. 619 pp.

Léonard, Jacques. *La Médicine entre les pouvoirs et les savoirs*. Paris, 1981. 386 pp.

Levasseur, Emile. *Histoire des classes ouvrières et de l'industrie en France de 1789 à 1970*. 2d ed.; Paris, 1903–1904. 2 vols.

Levin, Harry. *The Gates of Horn: A Study of Five French Realists*. New York, 1963. 554 pp.

Levine, Neil. "The Book and the Building: Hugo's Theory of Architecture and Labrouste's Bibliothèque Ste-Geneviève" in Robin Middleton, ed., *The Beaux-Arts and Nineteenth-century French Architecture*, Cambridge, Mass., 1982, pp. 138–73.

Lévy-Leboyer, Maurice. *Les Banques européennes et l'industrialisation internationale dans la première moitié du XIXe siècle*. Paris, 1964. 813 pp.

Lévy-Leboyer, Maurice. "La Croissance économique en France au XIXe siècle: Resultats préliminaires," *Annales: E.S.C.*, 23e Année (1968), pp. 788–807.

Lichtheim, George. "Socialism and the Jews," *Dissent*, XV (July–Aug. 1968), pp. 314–42.

Lindsay, Jack. *Gustave Courbet: His Life and Art*. Bath, 1973. 383 pp.

Lipstadt, Hélène. "César Daly," *Macmillan Encyclopedia of Architects*, I (New York, 1982), pp. 492–93.

Lipstadt, Hélène. "César Daly: Revolutionary Architect?" *A D [Architectural Design]*, XLVIII (1978), nos. 11–12, pp. 18–29.

Locke, Robert H. "Drouillard, Benoist et Cie. (1836–1856)," *Revue d'histoire de la sidérurgie*, VIII (1962), pp. 276–99.

Louandre, Charles. "De la production intellectuelle en France depuis quinze ans," *Revue des deux mondes*, new series, 17ᵉ Année (1847), vol. 20, pp. 255–86, 416–46, 671–703.

Loubere, Leo. *Louis Blanc: His Life and His Contribution to the Rise of French Jacobin Socialism.* Evanston, Ill., 1961, 256 pp.

Loyer, François. "Art Nouveau in Architecture in France" in *Art Nouveau Belgium France* (Houston, 1976), pp. 348–403.

Macmillan Encyclopedia of Architects. New York, 1982. 4 vols.

McLellan, David. *Karl Marx: His Life and Thought.* New York, 1973. 498 pp.

McLellan, David. *The Young Hegelians and Karl Marx.* New York, 1969. 170 pp.

Maison K. E. *Honoré Daumier: Catalogue raisonné of the Paintings, Watercolours and Drawings.* London, 1968. 2 vols.

Manuel, Frank E. *The Prophets of Paris.* Cambridge, Mass., 1962. 349 pp.

Manuel, Frank E. and Fritzie P. Manuel, eds. *French Utopians: An Anthology of Ideal Societies.* New York, 1966. 426 pp.

Marczewski, Jean. *Le Produit physique de l'économie française de 1789 à 1913 (comparaison avec la Grande Bretagne)*, Cahiers de l'Institut de science économique appliquée, series AF, 4. Paris, 1965. 154 pp.

Marczewski, Jean. "Some Aspects of the Economic Growth of France, 1660–1958," *Economic Development and Cultural Change*, IX (1961), pp. 369–86.

Marczewski, Jean. "The Take-off Hypothesis and French Experience" in Walt W. Rostow, ed., *The Economics of Take-off into Sustained Growth* (New York, 1963), pp. 119–38.

Margadant, Ted W. *French Peasants in Revolt: The Insurrection of 1851*. Princeton, 1979. 379 pp.

Margadant, Ted. W. "Tradition and Modernity in Rural France during the Nineteenth Century," *Journal of Modern History*, LVI (1984), pp. 667–97.

Marillier, Jacques. "Pierre Moreau, L'Union," *L'Actualité de l'histoire*, V (Oct. 1953), pp. 5–13.

Markovitch, T.-J. *L'Industrie française de 1789 à 1964: Conclusions générales*, Cahiers de l'Institut de science économique appliquée, Series AF, 7. Paris, 1966. 324 pp.

Marriott, J.A.R. *The French Revolution of 1848 in Its Economic Aspects*, vol. I of Louis Blanc, *Organisation du travail*. Oxford, 1913. 284 pp.

Marshall, D. Bruce. *The French Colonial Myth and Constitution-making in the Fourth Republic*. New Haven, 1973. 363 pp.

Marx, Karl. *Economic and Philosophic Manuscripts of 1844*. 16th ed.; Moscow, n.d. 212 pp.

Marx, Karl. *Manuscrits de 1844, économie politique et philosophie*, vol. VII of *Oeuvres complètes de Karl Marx*. Paris, 1962. 179 pp.

Maynes, Mary Jo. "Work or School? Youth and the Family in the Midi in the Early Nineteenth Century" in Donald N. Baker and Patrick J. Harrigan, eds., *The Making of Frenchmen: Current Directions in Higher Education in France, 1679–1979* (Waterloo, Ont., 1980), pp. 115–33.

Mazoyer, Louis. "Catégories d'âge et groupes sociaux: Les Jeunes Générations françaises de 1830," *Annales d'histoire économique et sociale*, 10ᵉ Année (1938), pp. 385–423.

Mellon, Stanley. "Entente, Diplomacy, and Fantasy," *Reviews in European History*, II (Sept. 1976), pp. 373–80.

Merley, Jean. *La Haute-Loire de la fin de l'ancien régime aux débuts de la IIIᵉ République*. Le Puy, 1974. 2 vols.

Merriman, John M., ed. *1830 in France.* New York, 1975. 232 pp.

Meyer, Pierre. Review of Etienne Cabet, *Oeuvres,* vol. I, *Voyage en Icarie* in *Le Mouvement social,* IX (Jan.–Mar. 1976), pp. 117–20.

Meyers, Peter V. "Professinalization and Societal Change: Rural Teachers in Nineteenth Century France," *Journal of Social History,* IX (1976), pp. 542-58.

Meyers, Peter V. "Teachers in Revolutionary France: The *Instituteurs* in 1848," in *Consortium on Revolutionary Europe Proceedings 1977* (Athens, Ga., 1978), pp. 151–61.

Middleton, Robin D., ed. *The Beaux-arts and Nineteenth-century French Architecture.* Cambridge, Mass., 1982. 280 pp.

Middleton, Robin D. "Eugène Emmanuel Viollet-le-Duc," *Macmillan Encyclopedia of Architects* (New York, 1982), IV, pp. 324–31.

Mitzman, Arthur. "Roads, Vulgarity, Rebellion, and Pure Art: The Inner Space in Flaubert and French Culture," *Journal of Modern History,* LI (1979), pp. 504–24.

Moon, S. Joan. "Feminism and Socialism: The Utopian Synthesis of Flora Tristan" in Marilyn Boxer and Jean Quaetert, eds., *Socialist Women: European Feminism in the Nineteenth and Twentieth Centuries* (New York, 1978), pp. 19–50.

Moreau de Jonnès, Alexandre. *Statistique de l'industrie de la France.* Paris, 1856. 380 pp.

Morineau, Michel. *Les Faux-semblants d'un démarrage économique: Agriculture et démographie en France au XVIIIe siècle.* Cahiers d'Annales, no. 30 (Paris, 1971). 388 pp.

Muhlstein, Anka. *Baron James: The Rise of the French Rothschilds.* New York, 1983. 223 pp.

Neveux, Hugues. "Analyses économiques et histoire," *Revue d'histoire économique et sociale,* LII (1974), no. 1, pp. 110–14.

Nicolaevsky, Boris and Otto Maenchen-Helfen. *Karl Marx: Man and Fighter.* London, 1973. 492 pp.

Nochlin, Linda. *Gustave Courbet: A Study of Style and Society.* New York, 1976. 240 pp.

Nochlin, Linda. "The Invention of the Avant-garde: France, 1830–1880," *Art News Annual,* XXXIV (1968), pp. 10–19.

O'Brien, Patricia. *"L'Embastillement de Paris*: The Fortification of Paris During the July Monarchy," *French Historical Studies,* IX (Spring 1975), pp. 63–82.

Palmade, Guy P. *French Capitalism in the Nineteenth Century.* New York, 1972. 256 pp.

Parris, Henry. "Railway Policy in Peel's Administration," *Bulletin of the Institute of Historical Research,* XXXIII (1860), pp. 180–94.

Perroux, François. "Prises de vues sur la croissance de l'économie française, 1780–1950," *Income and Wealth,* 5th series, (1955), pp. 41–58.

Petit Laroussse. Paris, 1967. 1,797 pp.

Pevsner, Nikolaus. *Ruskin and Viollet-de-Duc: Englishness and Frenchness in the Appreciation of Gothic Architecture.* London, 1969. 48 pp.

Pevsner, Nikolaus. *The Sources of Modern Architecture and Design.* New York, 1968. 216 pp.

Peyre, Henri. "Baudelaire," *Encyclopedia Americana,* III (Danbury, Conn., 1983), pp. 367–68.

Peyre, Henri. *Connaissance de Baudelaire.* Paris, 1951.

Peyre, Henri. *The Contemporary French Novel.* New York, 1955. 363 pp.

Phillips, Charles Stanley. *The Church in France, 1789–1848: A Study in Renewal.* New York, 1966. 315 pp.

Picard, Alfred. *Les Chemins de fer français: Etude historique sur la constitution et le régime du réseau: Débuts parlementaires, actes législatifs.* . . . Paris, 1884. 6 vols.

Picard, Alfred. *Traité des chemins de fer: Economie, politique, commerce, finance.* . . . Paris, 1887. 4 vols.

Pinkney, David H. *Napoleon III and the Rebuilding of Paris.* Princeton, 1958. 245 pp.

Pinkney, David H. "The Pacification of Paris: The Military

Lesson of 1830" in John M. Merriman, ed., *France in 1830* (New York, 1975), pp. 196–98.

Ponteil, Félix. *Histoire de l'enseignement en France: Les Grandes Etapes, 1789–1964.* Paris, 1966. 454 pp.

Posener, S. *Adolphe Crémieux: A Biography.* Philadelphia, 1940. 283 pp.

Pouthas, Charles H. *Guizot pendant la Restauration: Préparation de l'homme d'état (1814–1830).* Paris, 1923. 497 pp.

Pouthas, Charles H. *La Jeunesse de Guizot (1787–1814).* Paris, 1936. 414 pp.

Pouthas, Charles H. *La Population française pendant la première moitié du XIXe siècle.* Paris, 1956. 225 pp.

Price, Roger. *The Economic Modernization of France 1730–1880.* New York, 1975. 235 pp.

Price, Roger. *The Modernization of Rural France: Communications Networks and Agricultural Market Structures in Nineteenth-century France.* London, 1983. 503 pp.

Price, Roger. "Techniques of Repression: The Control of Popular Protest in Mid-nineteenth-century France," *Historical Journal*, XXV (1982), pp. 859–87.

Prost, Antoine, *Histoire de l'enseignement en France, 1800–1967.* Paris, 1968. 524 pp.

Proudhon, Pierre-Joseph. *Carnets de P.-J. Proudhon.* 8th ed.; Paris, 1960–1968. 3 vols.

Proudhon, Pierre-Joseph. *Qu'est-ce que la propriété?* in *Oeuvres complètes* (new ed.; Paris, 1926), pp. 119–363.

Puech, Jules L. *La Vie et l'oeuvre de Flora Tristan, 1803–1844.* Paris, 1925. 515 pp.

Raimond, Michel. *Le Roman depuis la Révolution.* Paris, 1967. 387 pp.

Rancière, Jacques, *La Nuit des prolétaires.* Paris, 1981. 453 pp.

Raynaud, Ernest. *Ch. Baudelaire: Etude biographique et critique. . . .* Paris, 1922. 407 pp.

Reader, W. J. *Professional Men: The Rise of the Professional Classes in Nineteenth-century England.* London, 1966. 248 pp.

Reddy, William M. *The Rise of Market Culture: The Textile Trade and French Society, 1750–1900*. New York, 1984. 352 pp.

Reff, Theodore. *Manet and Modern Paris*. Washington, D.C., 1982. 280 pp.

Reid, Donald. *The Miners of Decazeville: A Genealogy of Deindustrialization*. Cambridge, Mass., 1985. 333 pp. 1985.

Rémusat, Charles de. *Mémoires de ma vie*. Paris, 1958–1967.

Renard, Georges. "L'Influence de l'Angleterre sur la France depuis 1830," *La Nouvelle Revue*, XXXV (July–Aug. 1885), pp. 673–715, XXXVI (Sept.–Oct. 1885), pp. 35–76.

Renouvin, Pierre. *Histoire des relations internationales*, vol. V, *Le XIXᵉ Siècle*, part I, *De 1815 à 1871*. Paris, 1954. 421 pp.

Riasanovsky, Nicholas V. *The Teaching of Charles Fourier*. Berkeley, 1969. 256 pp.

Richardson, Joanna. "Emile de Girardin, 1806–1881: The Popular Press in France," *History Today*, XXVI (1976), pp. 811–17.

Rivet, Félix. *Navigation à vapeur sur la Saône et le Rhône (1783–1863)*. Paris, 1962. 602 pp.

Rodolphe Töppfer: M. Jabot, M. Crépin, M. Vieux Bois, M. Pencil. . . . Paris, 1975, 285 pp.

Rolley, J. "La Structure de l'industrie textile en France en 1840–1841," *Histoire des entreprises*, IV (Nov. 1959), pp. 20–48.

Rolley J. "Structure de l'industrie sidérurgique en France en 1845," *Revue de l'histoire de la sidérurgie*, I (1960), pp. 33–51.

Rostow, Walt, W., ed. *The Economics of Take-off into Sustained Growth*. 2d ed.; New York, 1963. 481 pp.

Rostow, Walt W. *The Stages of Economic Growth: A Noncommunist Manifesto*. 2d ed.; Cambridge, Eng., 1971. 253 pp.

Rousseau, Pierre. *Histoire des techniques*. Paris, 1956. 526 pp.

Roy, Joseph Antoine. *Histoire de la famille Schneider et du Creusot*. Paris, 1962. 156 pp.

Rubin, James Henry. *Realism and Social Vision in Courbet and Proudhon*. Princeton, 1980. 177 pp.

Saint-Chamas, Roger de. *L'Architecte*. Paris, 1957. 171 pp.

Sanson, Rosamonde. *Les 14 Juillet (1789–1975): Fête et conscience nationale*. Paris, 1975. 221 pp.

Sartre, Jean-Paul. *L'Idiot de la famille: Gustave Flaubert de 1821 à 1857*. Paris, 1971. 3 vols.

Schapiro, Meyer. "Courbet and Popular Imagery: An Essay on Realism and Naïveté," *Journal of the Warburg and Courtauld Institutes*, IV (1940–1941), pp. 164–91.

Scharf, Aaron. *Art and Photography*. Baltimore, 1974. 397 pp.

Schefer, Christian. *L'Algérie et l'évolution de la colonisation française*. 8th ed.; Paris, 1928. 542 pp.

Schnapper, Bernard. "La Politique des 'points d'appui' et la fondation des comptoirs fortifiés dans le Golfe de Guinée, 1837–1843," *Revue historique*, 85ᵉ Année, vol. CCXXV (Jan. 1961), pp. 99–120.

Schneider, Pierre. "Viollet-le-Prophète," *L'Express* (Paris), 22 Mar. 1980, pp. 12–14.

Sée, Henri. *Histoire économique de la France*. Paris, 1939–1951. 2 vols.

Seitz, William C. *Claude Monet*. New York, n.d. 159 pp.

Selections from the Armand Hammer Daumier Collection. Los Angeles, 1976. n.p.

Sewell, William H., Jr. *Work and Revolution in France: The Language of Labor from the Old Regime to 1848*. Cambridge, Eng., 1980. 340 pp.

Shinn, Terry. "Des Corps de l'Etat au secteur industriel: Genèse de la profession d'ingénieur, 1750–1920," *Revue française de sociologie*, XIX (1978), pp. 39–71.

Silly, Jean-Bernard. "La Disparition de la petite métallurgie rurale," *Revue d'histoire de la sidérurgie*, II (1961), pp. 47–61.

Silly, Jean-Bernard. "Les Plus Grands Sociétés métallurgiques et 1881," *Revue d'histoire de la sidérurgie*, VI (1965), pp. 255–72.

Silly, Jean-Bernard. "La Reprise du Creusot, 1836–1848," *Revue d'histoire des mines et de la métallurgie*, I (1969), pp. 233–78.

Simpson, F. A. *The Rise of Louis Napoleon*. 3d ed.; London, 1950. 400 pp.

Singer, Charles et al., eds. *A History of Technology*, vol. IV, *The Industrial Revolution, 1750–1850*. Oxford, 1958. 728 pp.

Société centrale des architectes. *Observations presentées par la Société sur la necessité d'un diplôme d'architecte*. 8th ed.; Paris, 1847. 23 pp.

Société des gens de lettres. *Au Service des écrivains de notre temps*. Paris, 1971. 12 pp.

Société des ingénieurs civils de France. *Soixantenaire, 1848–1908*. Paris, 1908. 100 pp.

Sorlin, Pierre. *La Société française, 1840–1914*. Paris, 1969–1971. 2 vols.

Starkie, Enid. *Baudelaire*. New York, 1933. 511 pp.

Stearns, Peter N. *Paths to Authority: The Middle Classes and the Industrial Labor Force in France, 1820–1848*. Urbana, Ill., 1973. 222 pp.

Stearns, Peter N. "Patterns of Industrial Strike Activity in France During the July Monarchy," *American Historical Review*, LXX (1965), pp. 371–94.

Steegmuller, Francis, ed. *The Letters of Gustave Flaubert, 1830–1857*. Cambridge, Mass., 1980. 2 vols.

Stendhal. *Travels in the South of France*, Elisabeth Abbott, trans. New York, 1970. 276 pp.

Stendhal. *Vie de Henry Brulard*, Henri Martineau, ed. Paris, 1949. 2 vols.

Strumingher, Laura S. *What Were Little Girls and Boys Made Of? Primary Education in Rural France*. Albany, N.Y., 1983. 209 pp.

Sullivan, Anthony Thrall. *Thomas-Robert Bugeaud: France and Algeria, 1784–1849: Politics, Power, and the Good Society*. Hamden, Conn., 1983. 216 pp.

Summerson, Sir John, ed. *Eugène Emmanuel Viollet-le-Duc.* London, 1980. 96 pp.

Sussman, George D. "The Glut of Doctors in Mid-nineteenth-century France," *Comparative Studies in Society and History,* XIX (1977), pp. 287–94.

Szajkowski, Zosa S. "The Jewish Saint-Simonians and Socialist Anti-Semites in France," *Jewish Social Studies,* IX (1947), pp. 33–60.

Talin d'Eyzac, E.-F. *Histoire du chemin de fer et de la Compagnie d'Orléans.* Paris, 1854. 158 pp.

Tanaka, Toshihiro. "Note on the Relationship Between the English Interests and the French Interests in French Railway Companies of the 1840s," *Journal of Economics of Fukuoka University,* XXVII (1982), pp. 281–316.

Tannenbaum, Edward R. "The Beginnings of Bleeding Heart Liberalism: Eugene Sue's *Les Mystères de Paris,*" *Comparative Studies in Society and History,* XXIII (1981), pp. 491–507.

Tarlé, Eugène. "La Grande Coalition des mineurs de Rive-de-Gier en 1844," *Revue historique,* CLXXVII (1936), pp. 249–78.

Tavard, G. H. "Assumptionists," *New Catholic Encyclopedia* (New York, 1967), I, pp. 975–76.

Thabault, Roger. *Mon Village, ses hommes, ses routes, son école.* Paris, 1945. 250 pp.

Théophraste (pseudonym of Louis Clot). *J. F. Cail.* Paris, 1856. 23 pp.

Thuillier, André. *Economie et société nivernaises au début du XIXe siècle.* Paris, 1974. 484 pp.

Thuillier, Guy. *Aspects de l'économie nivernaise au XIXe siècle.* Paris, 1966. 553 pp.

Thuillier, Guy. *Bureaucratie et bureaucrats en France au XIXe siècle.* Geneva, 1980. 672 pp.

Thuillier, Guy. *Georges Dufaud et les débuts du grand capitalisme dans la métallurgie en Nivernais au XIXe siècle.* Paris, 1959. 254 pp.

Thuillier, Guy. *La Promotion sociale.* 2d ed.; Paris, 1969. 128 pp.

Thureau-Dangin, Paul. *Histoire de la Monarchie de Juillet*. 2d ed.; Paris, 1884–1892. 7 vols.

Tilly, Charles. "The Changing Place of Collective Violence" in Melvin Richter, ed., *Essays in Theory and History: An Approach to the Social Sciences* (Cambridge, Eng., 1970), pp. 139–64.

Tilly, Charles. "How Protest Modernized in France" in William O. Aydelotte et al., eds., *The Dimensions of Quantitative Research in History* (Princeton, 1972), pp. 192–255.

Tilly, Charles and Lynn Lees. "Le Peuple de juin 1848," *Annales: E.S.C.*, 29ᵉ Année (1974), pp. 1061–91.

Tilly, Charles, Louise Tilly, and Richard Tilly. *The Rebellious Century, 1830–1930*. Cambridge, Mass., 1975. 354 pp.

Toussenel, Alphonse. *Les Juifs, rois de l'époque: Histoire de la féodalité financière*. Paris, 1845. 342 pp.

Toutain, J.-C. *La Consommation alimentaire en France de 1789 à 1964, Economies et sociétés*, Cahiers de l'Institut de science économique appliquée, V, no. 11. Geneva, 1971. 141 pp.

Toutain, J.-C. *La Population de la France de 1700 à 1959*, Cahiers de l'Institut de science économique appliquée, Series AF, 3. Paris, 1963. 254 pp.

Toutain, J.-C. *Le Produit de l'agriculture française de 1700 à 1958*, vol II, *La Croissance*, Cahiers de l'Institut de science économique appliquée, Series AF, 2. Paris, 1961. 285 pp.

Toutain, J.-C. *Les Transports en France de 1830 à 1965*, Cahiers de l'Institut de science économique appliquée, Series AF, 9. Paris, 1967. 306 pp.

Trenard, Louis. "Les Etudes médicales sous Louis-Philippe" in *Actes du 91ᵉ Congrès des Sociétés savantes* (Rennes, 1966), Section d'Histoire moderne et contemporaine, vol. III, *De la Restauration à la Deuxième Guerre mondiale* (Paris, 1969), pp. 167–214.

Trenard, Louis, *Salvandy et son temps, 1795–1856*. Lille, 1968. 944 pp.

Tresse, R. "Le Développement de la fabrication des faux en

France de 1785 à 1827 et ses conséquences sur la pratique des moissons," *Annales: E.S.C.*, 10ᵉ Année (1955), pp. 341–58.

Tristan, Flora. *The Worker's Union*, Beverly Livingston. ed. and trans. Urbana, Ill., 1983. 159 pp.

Tudesq, André-Jean. "Les Chefs de cabinet sous la Monarchie de Juillet: L'Exemple d'Alphonse Génie" in Michel Antoine et al., *Origines et histoire des cabinets des ministres*, (Geneva, 1975), p. 39–53.

Tudesq, André-Jean. *Les Conseillers-généraux en France au temps de Guizot, 1840–1848*. Paris, 1967. 292 pp.

Tudesq, André-Jean. *Les Grands Notables en France (1840–1849): Etude historique d'une psychologie sociale*. Paris, 1964. 2 vols.

Tudesq, André-Jean. "Les Pairs de France au temps de Guizot," *Revue d'histoire moderne contemporaine*, III (1956), pp. 262–83.

Tudesq, André-Jean. "Les Structures sociales du régime censitaire" in Jean Bouvier et al., eds., *Conjoncture économique, structures sociales: Hommage à Ernest Labrousse* (Paris, 1974), pp. 477–90.

Van Zanten, Ann Lorenz. "Form and Society: César Daly and the *Revue générale de l'architecture*," *Oppositions*, VIII (Spring 1977), pp. 137–45.

Van Zanten, David T. "Henri Labrouste," *Macmillan Encyclopedia of Architects*, II (New York, 1982), p. 594.

Vial, Jean. *L'Industrialisation de la sidérurgie française, 1814–1864*. Paris, 1967. 473 pp.; Annexe, 110 pp.

Vidalenc, Jean. "La Province et les journées de juin," *Etudes d'histoire moderne et contemporaine*, II (1948), pp. 83–144.

Vidler, A. R. *A Century of Social Catholicism, 1820–1920*. London, 1964. 171 pp.

Vidler, Anthony "The Dream of a New Architecture," *Oppositions*, VIII (1977), p. 135.

Vigier, Philippe. *La Monarchie de Juillet*. 5th ed.; Paris, 1976. 127 pp.

Vigier, Philippe. *La Vie quotidienne en province et à Paris pendant les journées de 1848, 1847–1851.* Paris, 1982. 443 pp.

Vigny, Alfred de. "La Maison de Berger," *Revue des deux mondes*, new series, 14ᵉ Année (1844), vol. 14, pp. 302–13.

Vigny, Alfred de. *Oeuvres complètes*, vol. I. Bibliothèque de la Pléiade, Paris, 1964. 982 pp.

Vincent, Howard P. *Daumier and His World.* Evanston, Ill., 1968. 267 pp.

Watelet, Jacques Grégoire. "Art Nouveau and the Applied Arts in Belgium" in *Art Nouveau Belgium France* (Houston, 1976), pp. 120–24.

Weber, Eugen. "Comment la politique vint aux paysans: A Second Look at Peasant Politization," *American Historical Review*, LXXXVII (1982), pp. 357–89.

Weiss, John Hubbel. *The Making of Technological Man: The Social Origins of French Engineering Education.* Cambridge, Mass., 1982. 177 pp.

Weisz, George. "The Politics of Medical Professionalization in France 1845–1848," *Journal of Social History*, XII (1978), pp. 3–30.

White, Ruth L. *"L'Avenir" de La Mennais: Son Rôle dans la presse de son temps.* Paris, 1974. 239 pp.

Wiebe, Robert H. *The Search for Order, 1870–1920.* New York, 1967. 333 pp.

Williams, Roger L. *The Horror of Life.* Chicago, 1980. 381 pp.

Wright, Gordon. *France in Modern Times: From the Enlightenment to the Present.* 3d ed.; New York, 1981. 516 pp.

Wright, Vincent. "L'Ecole nationale d'administration de 1848–1849: Un Echec révélateur," *Revue historique*, CCLV (1976), pp. 21–42.

Wylie, Lawrence, ed. *Chanzeaux: A Village in Anjou.* Cambridge, Mass., 1966. 383 pp.

Young, Arthur. *Travels in France and Italy During the Years 1787, 1788 and 1789.* London, n.d. 373 pp.

Zeldin, Theodore. *France, 1848–1945.* Oxford, 1973–1977. 2 vols.

· INDEX ·

LIBRARY OF CONGRESS CATALOGING-IN-PUBLICATION DATA

Pinkney, David H.
Decisive years in France, 1840-1847.

Bibliography: p.   Includes index.
1. France—History—Louis Philip, 1830-1848.
I. Title.
DC266.P56 1985   944.06′3   85-43304
ISBN 0-691-05467-3 (alk. paper)